REANIMATOR

Joe Rybandt, Executive Editor • Matt Idelson, Senior Editor • Rachel Pinnelas, Associate Editor • Anthony Marques, Assistant Editor • Kevin Ketner, Editorial Assistant

Jason Ullmeyer, Art Director • Geoff Harkins, Senior Graphic Designer • Cathleen Heard, Graphic Designer • Alexis Persson, Production Artist

Nick Barrucci, CEO / Publisher • Juan Collado, President / COO

Brandon Dante Primavera, V.P. of IT and Operations • Chris Caniano, Digital Associate • Rachel Kilbury, Digital Assistant

Alan Payne, V.P. of Sales and Marketing • Keith Davidsen, Marketing Director • Pat O'Connell, Sales Manager

Rich Young, Director of Business Development

DYNAMITE. f O t y You Tube

ISBN: 978-1-5241-0044-5

Online at www.DYNAMITE.com
On Instagram @Dynamitecomics
On Twitter @Dynamitecomics

On Facebook /Dynamitecomics
On Tumblr dynamitecomics.tumblr.com
On YouTube /Dynamitecomics

First Printing
10 9 8 7 6 5 4 3 2 1
Printed in China

WRITTEN BY KEITH DAVIDSEN

COLORS BY JORGE SUTIL

COLLECTION COVER BY FRANCESCO FRANCAVILLA

BOOK DESIGN BY JASON ULLMEYER

DEDICATED TO BRYAN CHAPMAN

ART BY RANDY VALIENTE

LETTERS BY MARSHALL DILLON

THIS VOLUME COLLECTS ISSUES ONE THROUGH FOUR OF THE DYNAMITE ENTERTAINMENT SERIES.

THE HISTORY OF DYNAMITE'S
HERBERT WEST,
THE REANIMATOR

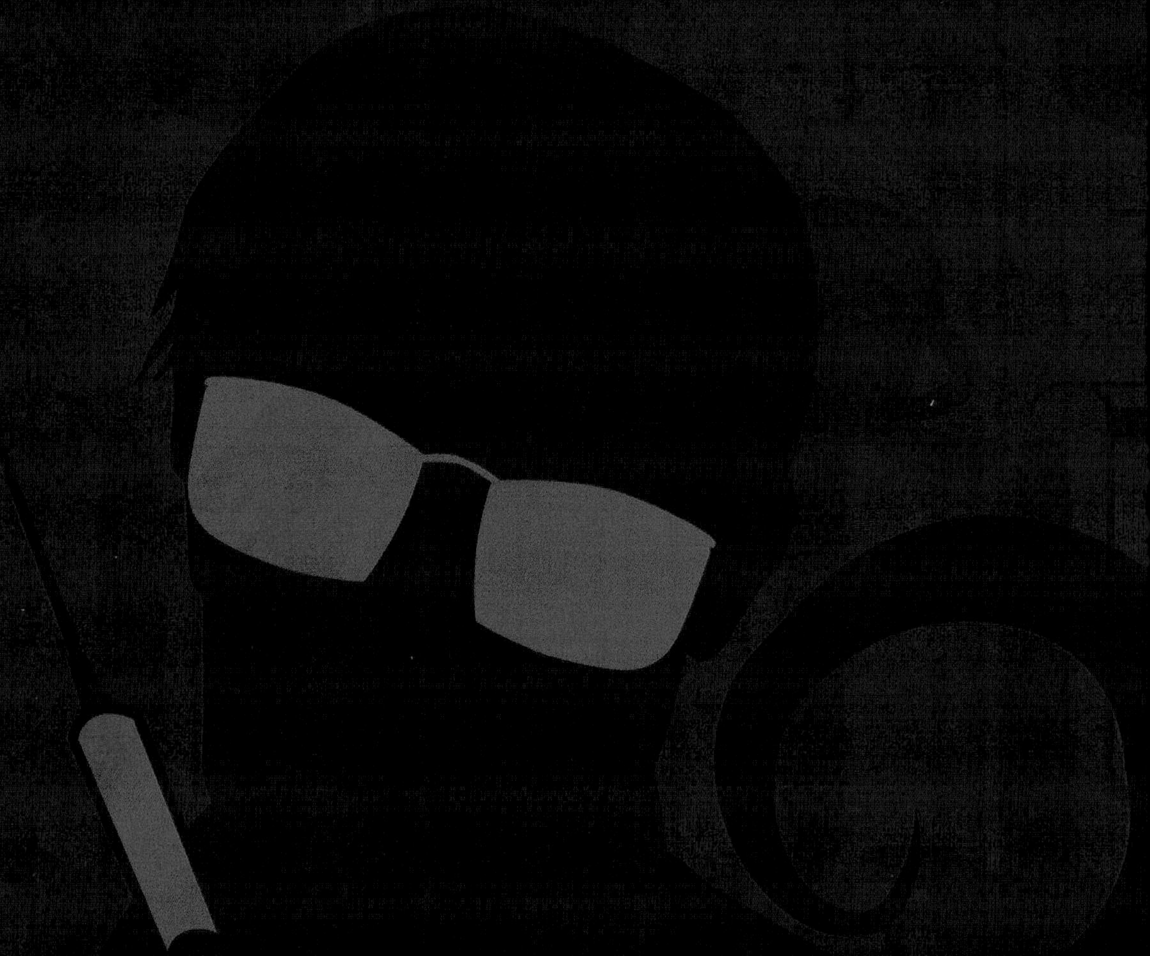

Herbert West was, only recently, an ambitious medical student at Miskatonic University. His singular focus in life was to conquer death by purely scientific means. He conducted unorthodox experiments on animal subjects, and his most profound creation – a yellow-colored reanimation formula – could revive a deceased subject for a time before its life functions would end in a violent explosion. Convinced of the grandeur of his research, West chafed under authority and railed against skeptics. Still, he maintained some measure of sound moral judgment. When the chance to underhandedly remove Dean Halsey – his main detractor – as a threat to his work, he chose the more virtuous path… at a terrible price.

University chairman Dr. Whately, who also served as head of the nearby Arkham mental institution, was a devotee of an ancient, all-powerful Outer God known as Yog-Sothoth. The elderly schemer recognized a potential ally in Herbert West, but not until the young man's conscience could be removed… literally. Turning to the Necronomicon, an unholy book littered with demon resurrection passages, Whately spoke an incantation that tore West mentally and physically asunder. His lower body first transformed into a heap of writhing tentacles, and the skin of his chest was shredded apart, as an exact body duplicate burst forward. As the sinister doppelgänger stepped out, the dead husk that was once Herbert West's body collapsed to the floor, dead.

And yet, West survived… in a fashion. Whately had aimed to raise an evil army in Yog-Sothoth's name, and only Herbert West's brilliant scientific mind – unimpeded by ethics – could accomplish the task. To serve that end, Whately's spell confined the young student's conscience (what one might call his very soul) into the Mirror Prison, a dimension of exile where reside demonic Deadites and beings of far greater malevolence. The doppelgänger that then stood by Whately's side was possessed by a Deadite spirit, a creature without moral compunctions… but retaining all of his ambition and knowledge.

The West doppelgänger took employment at Arkham, and made several breakthroughs in reanimation by experimenting on mental patients and university students. His subjects no longer suffered catastrophic tissue rejection, as did his earlier experiments on animals, but a complete return to higher brain function yet eluded him. Still, in his quest to become a self-styled god of flesh – a true Reanimator – the duplicate West had succeeded in building an obedient army of mindless slaves, the hybridization of mortal remains and otherworldly creatures (so frequently comprised of arachnid legs and tentacles),

and the reanimation of human tissue (like eyes and digestive organs) independent of the body.

Meanwhile, Dr. Whately's machinations were coming to a head. A man named Ashley J. Williams had been apprehended by the police under suspicion of mass murder. Williams, whose fate was tragically intertwined with the evil of the Necronomicon, was needed as part of Whately's ritual for returning lost Yog-Sothoth to Earth. The asylum head arranged for Williams to be remanded into his custody, but the unlikely Chosen One broke free and instigated a full-fledged riot.

Amid the turmoil, the West doppelgänger proved to be a slave to his template's scientific passions. When Dr. Whately ordered him to forego his continuing experiment and focus on Yog-Sothoth's resurrection, the dark duplicate refused. Whately then ripped West's head from its shoulders. The doppelgänger survived, its body capable of existing independently of (but still controlled by) its head, while the head sprouted tentacles for mobility. Shortly after the two parts reconstituted themselves, the soul of Herbert West made its escape from the Mirror Prison, leaping back into his mortal form and driving the possessing spirit out. His conscience returned and free of demonic influence, Herbert West survived the fall of Arkham, as Ash Williams defeated Dr. Whately and destroyed the entire facility, undead legions and all.

In the wake of Arkham's destruction, West was a wanted man. With hundreds of patients, students, and personnel dead, the authorities needed someone to take the blame. Although no one could ever piece together the particulars of what happened that night, evidence was discovered of bizarre experiments, the patchwork grafting of organs and limbs into unnatural combinations. A surviving medical student, known for his radical theories and brazen disregard of authority, made for convenient scapegoat.

In the days leading up to his capture, West turned his attention away from science. While the medical victory over death was still his life's work, he turned instead to the study of arcane texts, most notably Dr. Whately's copy of the Necronomicon. Its existence had brought him to death and to life, had cleaved his soul and his mind. He sought to better understand what had been done to him… and in the process, stumbled upon a doomsday prophecy – the same world-ending event during the year 2012 that was predicted by the ancient Mayans.

Arrested and institutionalized at Miskatonic Asylum in Essex, Massachusetts, West pleaded to be set free. Knowing the prophecy as he did, he felt compelled to play a part in Earth's survival. His captors dismissed his fears as lunatic ramblings. Without other options, West affected his own escape and headed to Yucatan, former seat of the Mayan people.

In the shadow of a jungle pyramid, Herbert West joined with an assemblage of unlikely heroes, many attuned to the mystical upheaval: blood-drinking detective Vampirella, Egyptian goddess and shape-shifter Pantha, monster-hunting Eva, Greek warrior goddess Athena, time-lost swordswoman Red Sonja, and the vampire lord Dracula. Together, they determined that a time-travelling sorcerer named Kulan Gath would facilitate the end of the planet, thereby accruing infinite power.

West would take an active role in the conflict against Gath's intended apocalypse. With his understanding of the Necronomicon, he cast the spell that sent each of his allies to a different continent, locations where they might face the sorcerer's Mayan avatars of destruction. When assaulted by the storm god Chaac, West also used the Book of the Dead offensively, conjuring a spout of fire at his enemy... only moments before an unaffected god skewered him with a sword.

For a second time, Herbert West was dead. And yet, fate would once again place Ash Williams by the young scientist's side. Perhaps mere coincidence led the Chosen One to vacation at this scene of conflict, or fate had once again placed him in the vicinity of the Necronomicon. Regardless, Williams was there at just the right moment. He held no ill will towards West, having realized in those last chaotic moments at Arkham that the young scientist was a pawn in Dr. Whately's schemes, and so retrieved a syringe of reanimation formula from West's satchel. In seconds, he was revived, hale and hearty.

Together, Herbert West and Ash Williams helped turn the tide and save the world. When next they would meet, however, circumstances would once again set them at odds.

Shortly after the Mayan prophecy affair, West again took up the Book of the Dead, an undertaking that would not only unhinge him from the normal progression of time, but also his mind from sanity. He was hurled backwards to the year 1906. Between memory loss from the experience, and with the absence of his copy of the Necronomicon, he had neither the inclination nor means to return to the modern era. Perhaps with such a familiar setting as Miskatonic University nearby, and the presence of a Dr. Halsey on the faculty (presumably an ancestor of his own academic rival), his fractured mind took easily to the notion that he belonged in the time and place. As a result, he enrolled in the school and took up his scientific pursuits anew... although by comparison to his successes in the 21st century, he had taken a huge step back in his own development.

During his years at Miskatonic, West was unable to perfect his reanimation solution. The skeptical Dr. Halsey of that era was a hindrance to the young scientist's progress, limiting him to animal subjects only. It was only after Halsey died -- of exposure to typhus while heroically treating an epidemic -- that a recently deceased body became available for experimentation. West injected the corpse with an early version of his solution, and although Halsey rose, his mental faculty had degraded. Indeed, the undead monstrosity escaped and rampaged through the region, cannibalizing victims before his capture and incarceration at an asylum in nearby Sefton. West concluded that the failure of his compound resulted from the lack of freshness in Halsey's body.

If West claimed to be a doctor prior to his exile in the early 20th century, then he officially earned the title as a Miskatonic graduate. Perhaps as a symbol of his station, the newly minted Dr. Herbert West began to share his unorthodox work with trusted and enraptured assistants. His first was a schoolmate during his time at Miskatonic, one whom Ash Williams would later suspect had died as a test subject of the unhinged doctor.

The second confederate in West's unending experiment was Major Sir Eric Moreland Clapham-Lee, a medic and commanding officer in the first World War. West had joined the war effort on its western front, predominantly for the easy access to fresh corpses. He discovered that he could reanimate limbs independent of the whole, which was of interest to Clapham-Lee. Fate, however, would give the Major first-hand knowledge of the procedure: when his plane went down, his body was donated to unconventional science. West reanimated the Major's head and body as two separate living entities. While the body was destroyed in a German bombardment, West brought the head back to the United States, where it languished in his laboratory for several years... with little to do but wish for West's death. The head was eventually disposed of by incineration.

In 1922, Dr. Herbert West was once again reunited with Ash Williams. Thrown through time, Williams had landed in the very cemetery that the doctor frequented for materials. Between the effects of time travel, a head injury, and perhaps his own self-involvement, the Chosen One did not recognize his enemy-turned-ally, although he had a faint feeling of familiarity. West's own time-traveling trauma, coupled with the continuing turn of his obsession to borderline lunacy, made him every bit the amnesiac as Williams.

Upon his arrival in the early 20th century, Williams was unconscious for two weeks, during which the doctor repaired his damaged right arm by attaching a replacement human hand. Once he woke, he discovered that West had hidden the Necronomicon; without the book of spells, Williams could not return to his proper timeline. Blackmailed, he reluctantly agreed to work as the doctor's assistant in exchange for the book's return.

Their forced partnership was the beginning of the end for Herbert West's experiments in the early 20th century. First, the reanimated hand that was grafted to Ash Williams' arm had murderous impulses of its own – not only did it ruin experiments, but it attempted to strangle the doctor before the Chosen One sawed it off. Shortly after, West's obsession with the reanimation process caused him to turn once again to mystic means of revival, and so he spoke an incantation… and awoke every experiment he'd ever performed and buried after its failure. The vengeful corpses assaulted West and Williams, and the familiar scene of carnage shook both men from their amnesiac states. In the final moments of the conflict, as the tomb legion tore West to pieces, they recognized each other.

Herbert West was last seen dragged away by reanimated corpses in multiple pieces, with his head carefully placed inside a box. But for a man who had survived death twice before, and whose life's work was conquering mortality, would that truly be the end for the Reanimator? ■

Read the full stories in Dynamite's
• Army of Darkness Omnibus Volume 1 Trade Paperback
• Prophecy Trade Paperback
• Army of Darkness / Reanimator one-shot

THE WONDER AND DIABOLISM

ONE

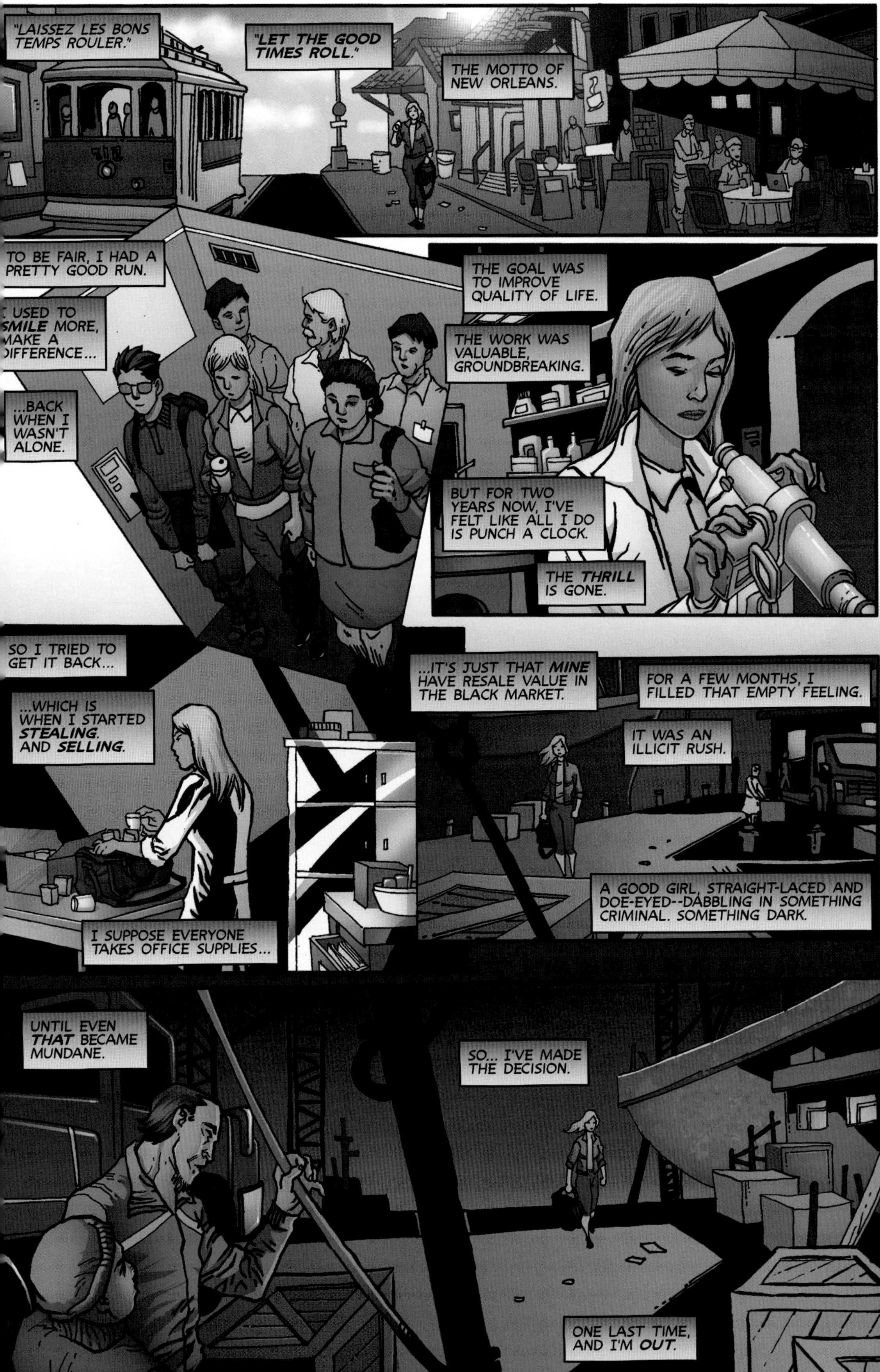
"LAISSEZ LES BONS TEMPS ROULER."
"LET THE GOOD TIMES ROLL."
THE MOTTO OF NEW ORLEANS.
TO BE FAIR, I HAD A PRETTY GOOD RUN.
I USED TO SMILE MORE, MAKE A DIFFERENCE...
...BACK WHEN I WASN'T ALONE.
THE GOAL WAS TO IMPROVE QUALITY OF LIFE.
THE WORK WAS VALUABLE, GROUNDBREAKING.
BUT FOR TWO YEARS NOW, I'VE FELT LIKE ALL I DO IS PUNCH A CLOCK.
THE THRILL IS GONE.
SO I TRIED TO GET IT BACK...
...WHICH IS WHEN I STARTED STEALING. AND SELLING.
I SUPPOSE EVERYONE TAKES OFFICE SUPPLIES...
...IT'S JUST THAT MINE HAVE RESALE VALUE IN THE BLACK MARKET.
FOR A FEW MONTHS, I FILLED THAT EMPTY FEELING.
IT WAS AN ILLICIT RUSH.
A GOOD GIRL, STRAIGHT-LACED AND DOE-EYED--DABBLING IN SOMETHING CRIMINAL. SOMETHING DARK.
UNTIL EVEN THAT BECAME MUNDANE.
SO... I'VE MADE THE DECISION.
ONE LAST TIME, AND I'M OUT.

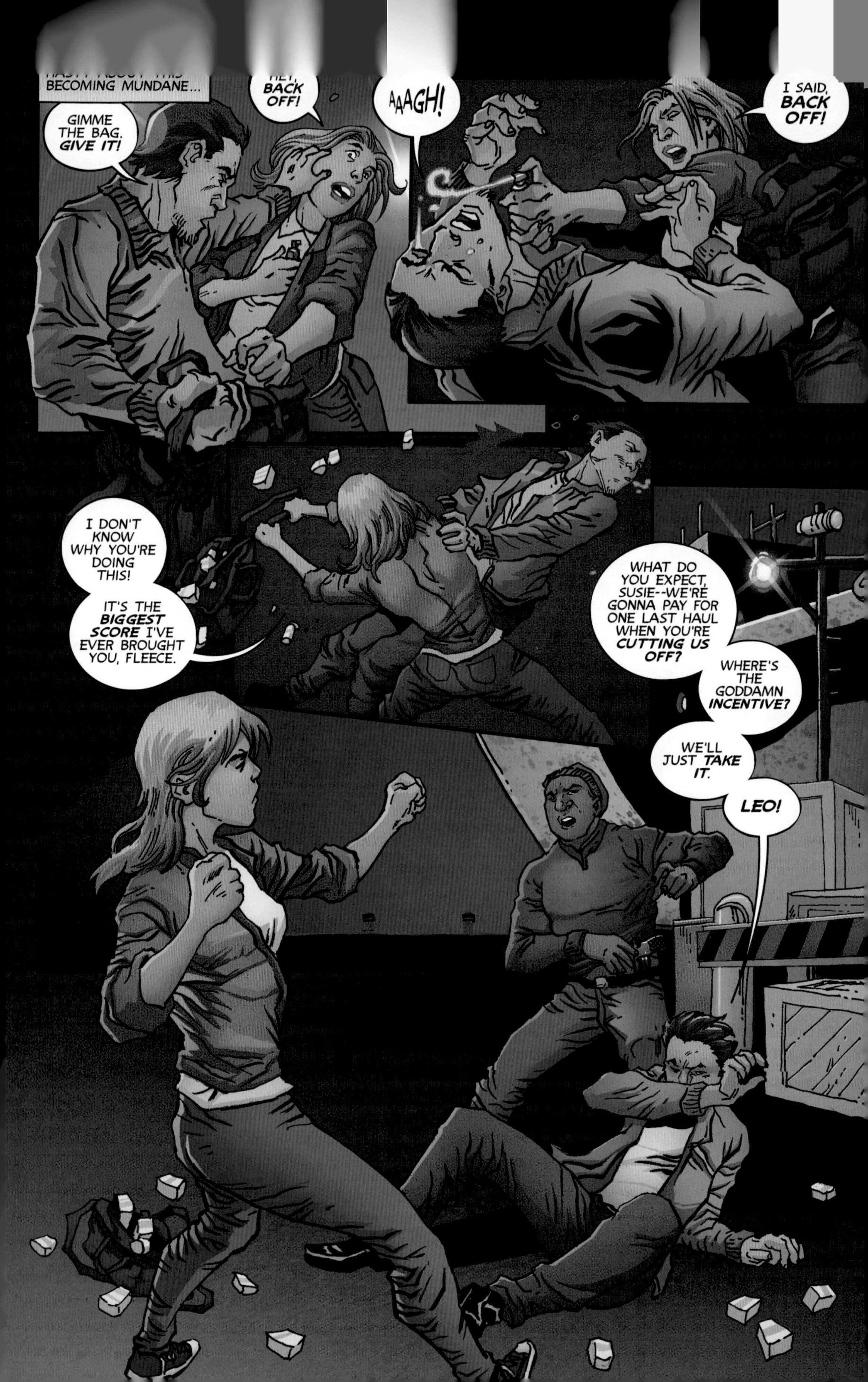

BECOMING MUNDANE...
GIMME THE BAG. GIVE IT!
HEY, BACK OFF!
AAAGH!
I SAID, BACK OFF!
I DON'T KNOW WHY YOU'RE DOING THIS!
IT'S THE BIGGEST SCORE I'VE EVER BROUGHT YOU, FLEECE.
WHAT DO YOU EXPECT, SUSIE--WE'RE GONNA PAY FOR ONE LAST HAUL WHEN YOU'RE CUTTING US OFF?
WHERE'S THE GODDAMN INCENTIVE?
WE'LL JUST TAKE IT.
LEO!

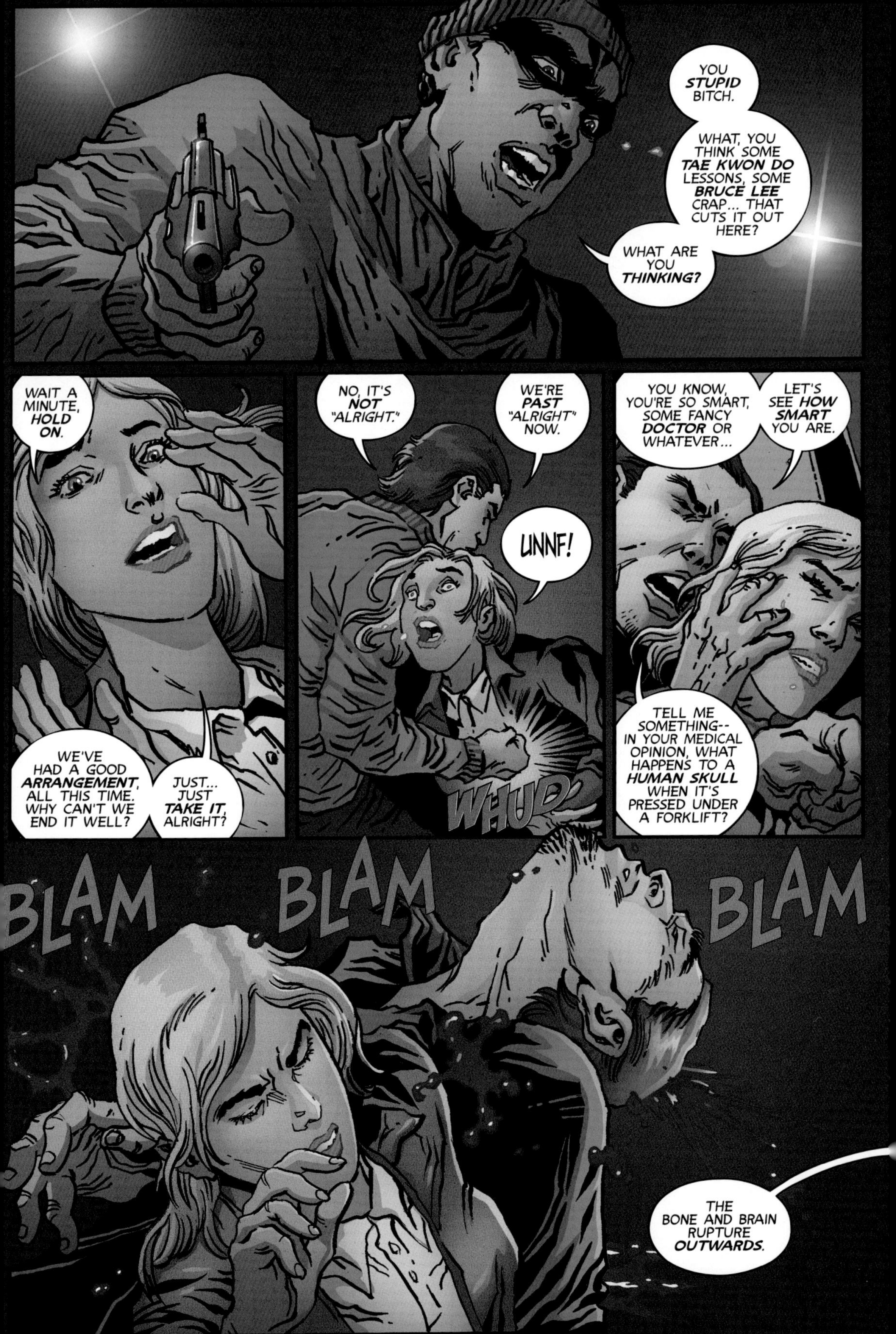
YOU STUPID BITCH.
WHAT, YOU THINK SOME TAE KWON DO LESSONS, SOME BRUCE LEE CRAP... THAT CUTS IT OUT HERE?
WHAT ARE YOU THINKING?
WAIT A MINUTE, HOLD ON.
WE'VE HAD A GOOD ARRANGEMENT, ALL THIS TIME. WHY CAN'T WE END IT WELL?
JUST... JUST TAKE IT, ALRIGHT?
NO, IT'S NOT "ALRIGHT."
WE'RE PAST "ALRIGHT" NOW.
UNNF!
WHUD
YOU KNOW, YOU'RE SO SMART, SOME FANCY DOCTOR OR WHATEVER...
LET'S SEE HOW SMART YOU ARE.
TELL ME SOMETHING-- IN YOUR MEDICAL OPINION, WHAT HAPPENS TO A HUMAN SKULL WHEN IT'S PRESSED UNDER A FORKLIFT?
BLAM
BLAM
BLAM
THE BONE AND BRAIN RUPTURE OUTWARDS.

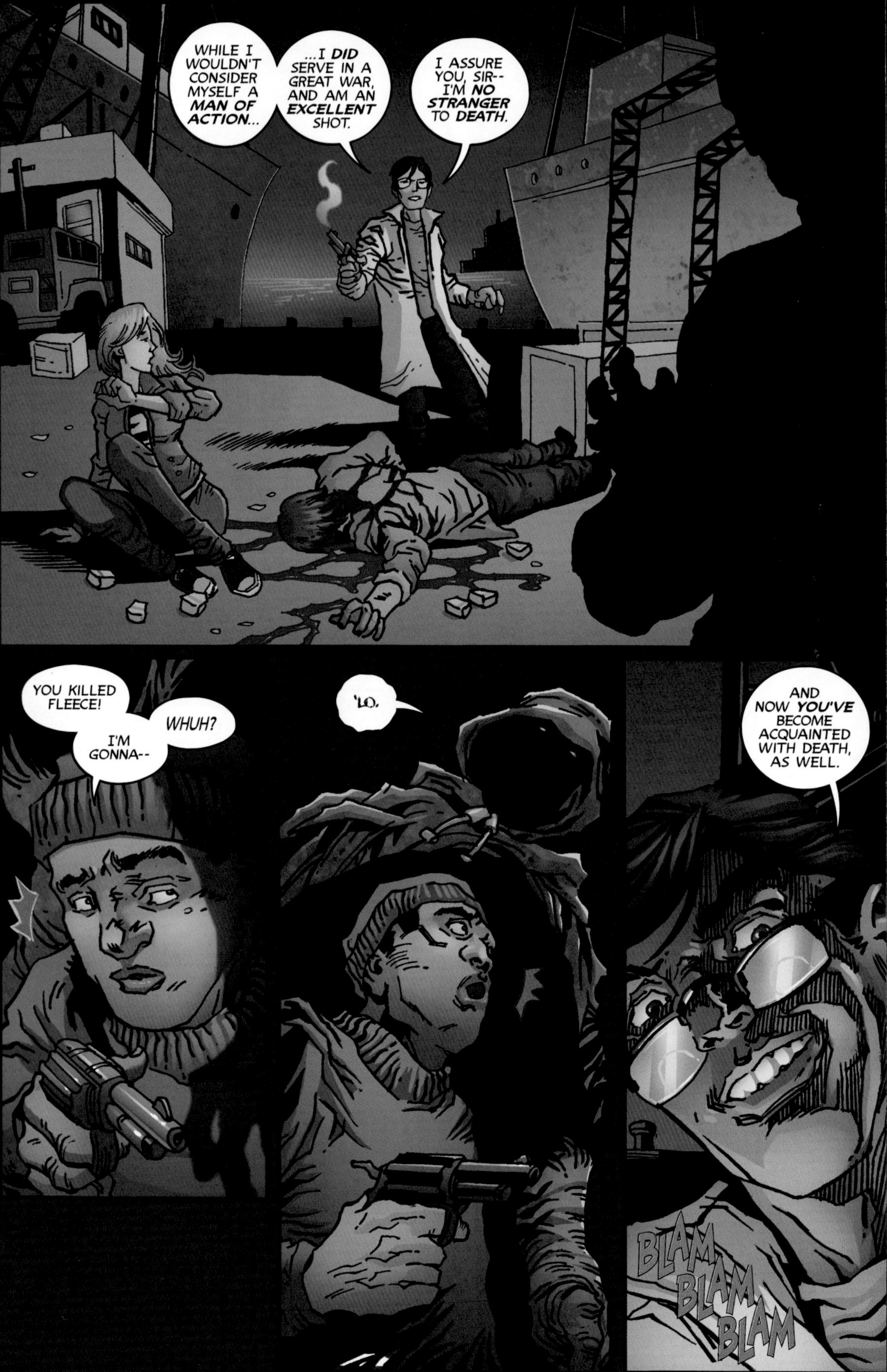
WHILE I WOULDN'T CONSIDER MYSELF A MAN OF ACTION...
...I DID SERVE IN A GREAT WAR, AND AM AN EXCELLENT SHOT.
I ASSURE YOU, SIR-- I'M NO STRANGER TO DEATH.
YOU KILLED FLEECE!
I'M GONNA--
WHUH?
'LO.
AND NOW YOU'VE BECOME ACQUAINTED WITH DEATH, AS WELL.
BLAM BLAM BLAM

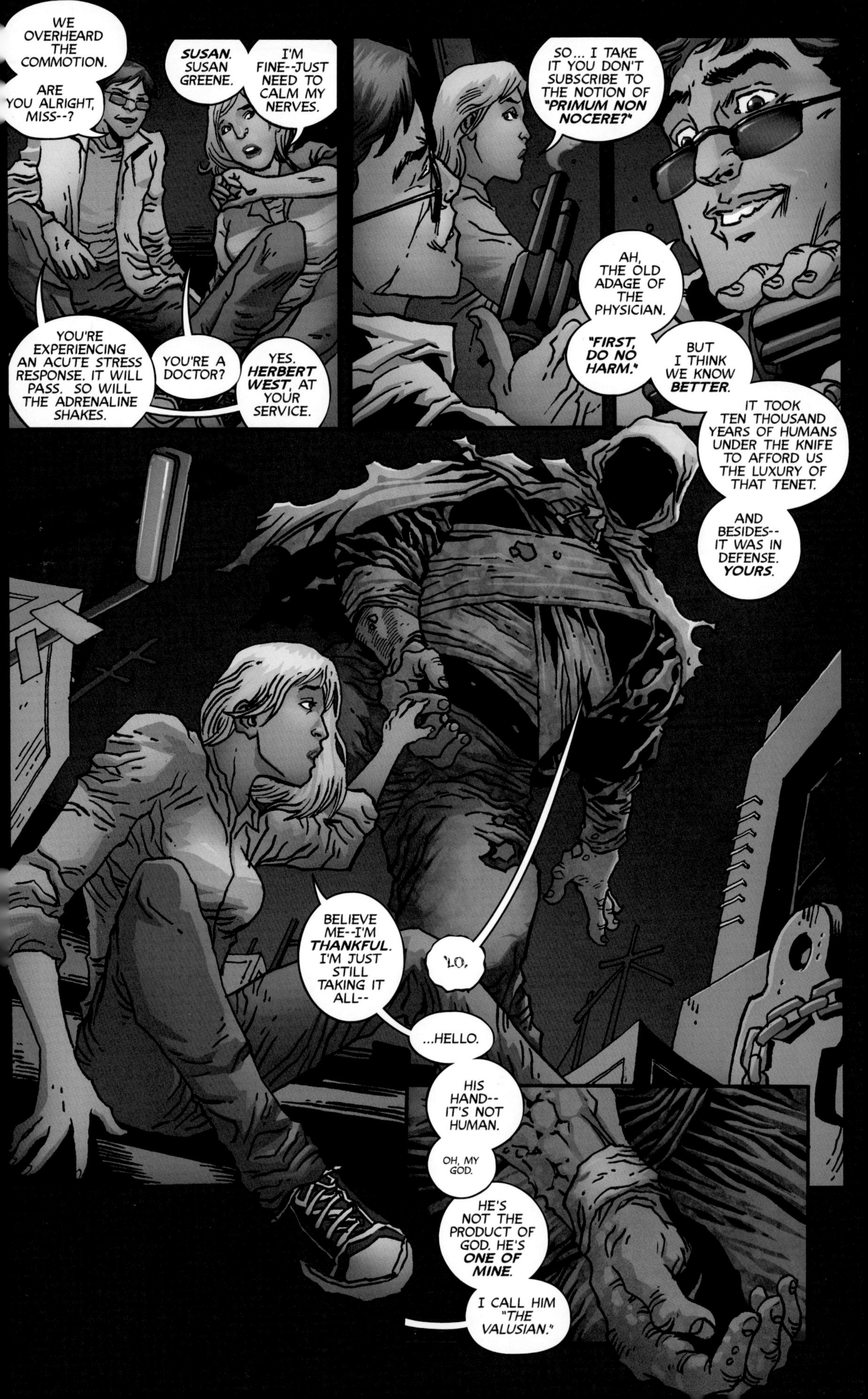
WE OVERHEARD THE COMMOTION.
ARE YOU ALRIGHT, MISS--?
SUSAN. SUSAN GREENE.
I'M FINE--JUST NEED TO CALM MY NERVES.
YOU'RE EXPERIENCING AN ACUTE STRESS RESPONSE. IT WILL PASS. SO WILL THE ADRENALINE SHAKES.
YOU'RE A DOCTOR?
YES. HERBERT WEST, AT YOUR SERVICE.
SO... I TAKE IT YOU DON'T SUBSCRIBE TO THE NOTION OF "PRIMUM NON NOCERE?"
AH, THE OLD ADAGE OF THE PHYSICIAN.
"FIRST, DO NO HARM."
BUT I THINK WE KNOW BETTER.
IT TOOK TEN THOUSAND YEARS OF HUMANS UNDER THE KNIFE TO AFFORD US THE LUXURY OF THAT TENET.
AND BESIDES-- IT WAS IN DEFENSE. YOURS.
BELIEVE ME--I'M THANKFUL. I'M JUST STILL TAKING IT ALL--
'LO,
...HELLO.
HIS HAND-- IT'S NOT HUMAN.
OH, MY GOD.
HE'S NOT THE PRODUCT OF GOD. HE'S ONE OF MINE.
I CALL HIM "THE VALUSIAN."

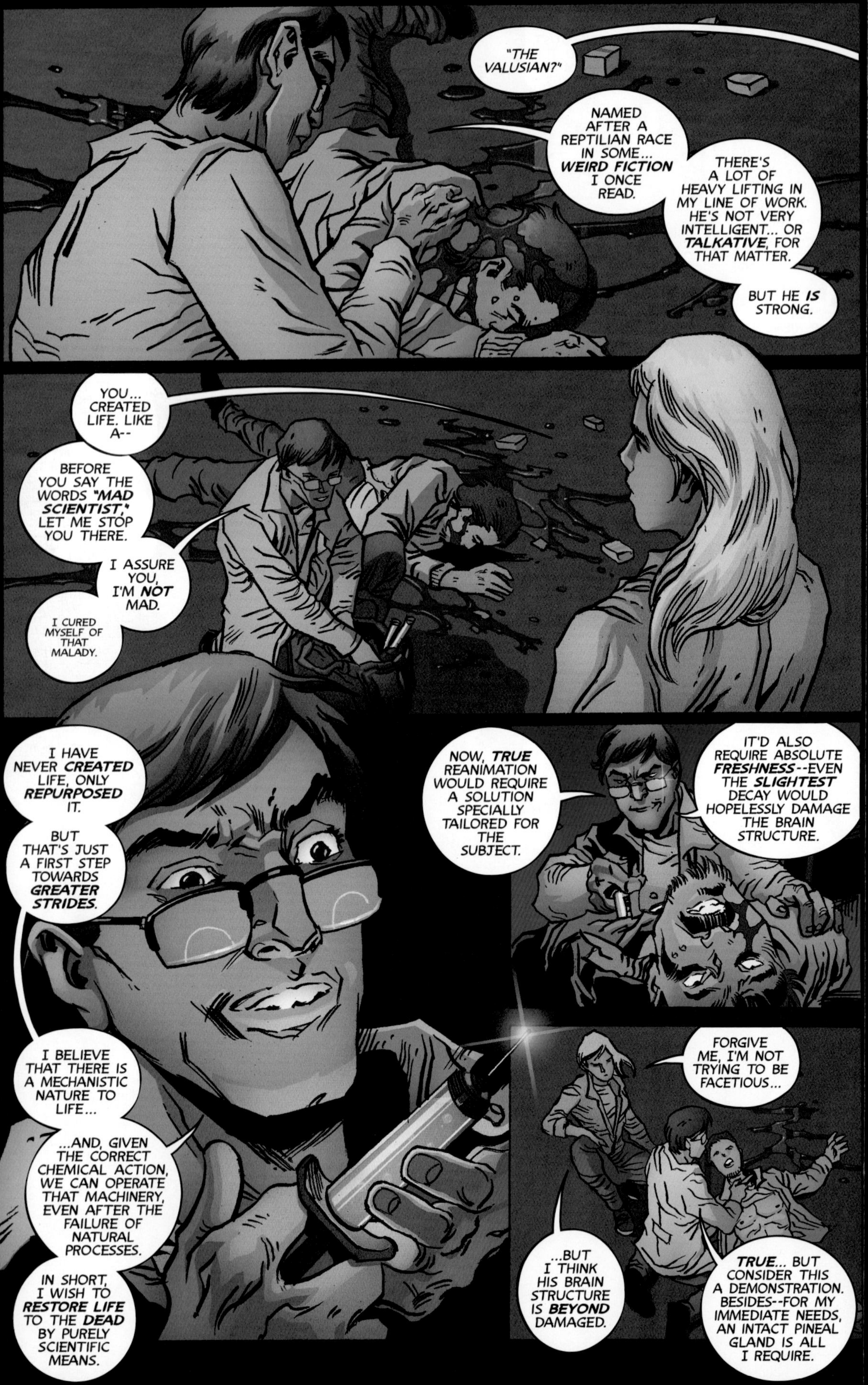
"THE VALUSIAN?"
NAMED AFTER A REPTILIAN RACE IN SOME... WEIRD FICTION I ONCE READ.
THERE'S A LOT OF HEAVY LIFTING IN MY LINE OF WORK. HE'S NOT VERY INTELLIGENT... OR TALKATIVE, FOR THAT MATTER.
BUT HE IS STRONG.
YOU... CREATED LIFE. LIKE A--
BEFORE YOU SAY THE WORDS "MAD SCIENTIST," LET ME STOP YOU THERE.
I ASSURE YOU, I'M NOT MAD.
I CURED MYSELF OF THAT MALADY.
I HAVE NEVER CREATED LIFE, ONLY REPURPOSED IT.
BUT THAT'S JUST A FIRST STEP TOWARDS GREATER STRIDES.
I BELIEVE THAT THERE IS A MECHANISTIC NATURE TO LIFE...
...AND, GIVEN THE CORRECT CHEMICAL ACTION, WE CAN OPERATE THAT MACHINERY, EVEN AFTER THE FAILURE OF NATURAL PROCESSES.
IN SHORT, I WISH TO RESTORE LIFE TO THE DEAD BY PURELY SCIENTIFIC MEANS.
NOW, TRUE REANIMATION WOULD REQUIRE A SOLUTION SPECIALLY TAILORED FOR THE SUBJECT.
IT'D ALSO REQUIRE ABSOLUTE FRESHNESS--EVEN THE SLIGHTEST DECAY WOULD HOPELESSLY DAMAGE THE BRAIN STRUCTURE.
FORGIVE ME, I'M NOT TRYING TO BE FACETIOUS...
...BUT I THINK HIS BRAIN STRUCTURE IS BEYOND DAMAGED.
TRUE... BUT CONSIDER THIS A DEMONSTRATION. BESIDES--FOR MY IMMEDIATE NEEDS, AN INTACT PINEAL GLAND IS ALL I REQUIRE.

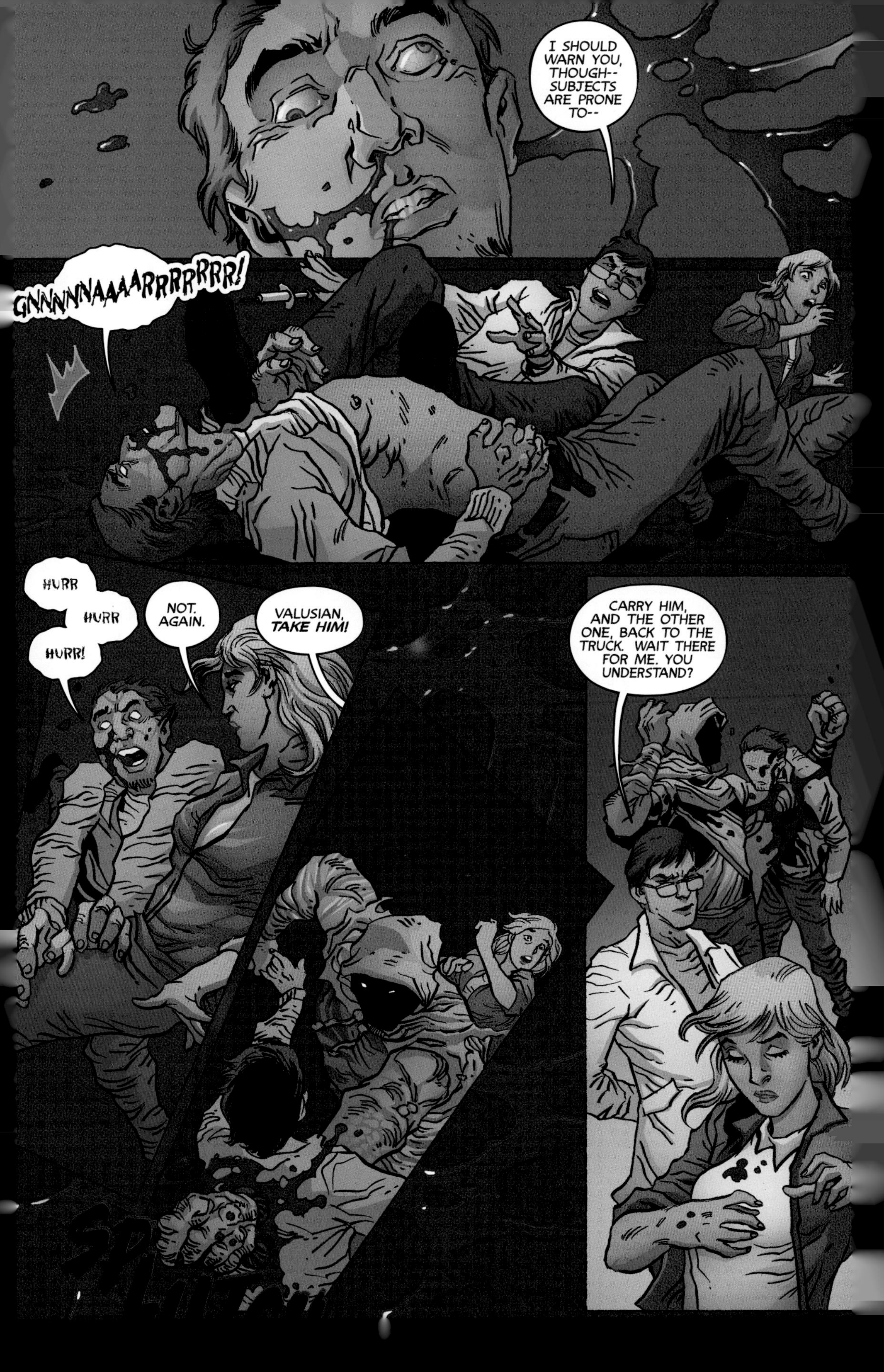
I SHOULD WARN YOU, THOUGH-- SUBJECTS ARE PRONE TO--
GNNNNNAAAARRRRRRR!
HURR
HURR
HURR!
NOT. AGAIN.
VALUSIAN, TAKE HIM!
CARRY HIM, AND THE OTHER ONE, BACK TO THE TRUCK. WAIT THERE FOR ME. YOU UNDERSTAND?

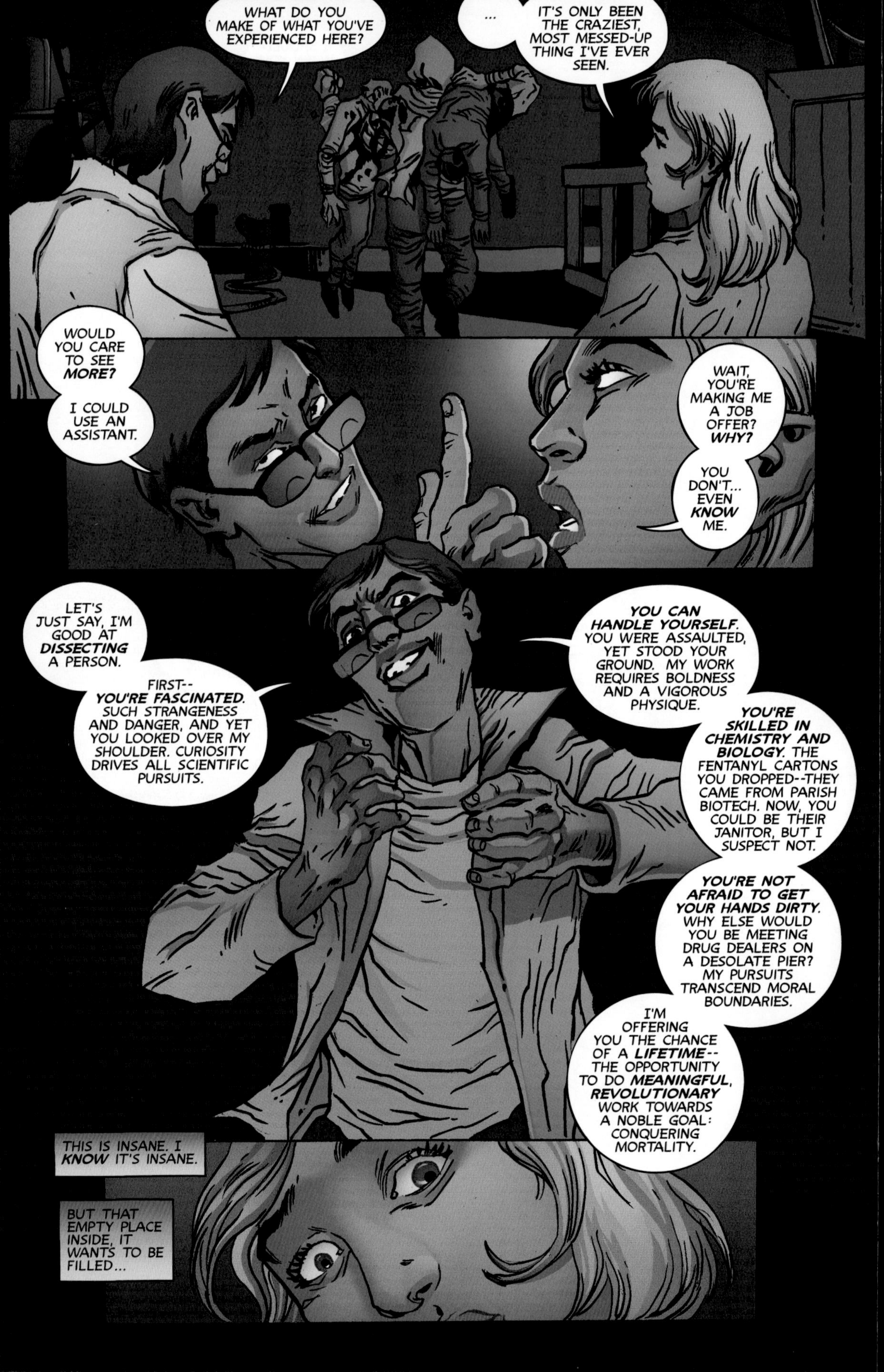
WHAT DO YOU MAKE OF WHAT YOU'VE EXPERIENCED HERE?
...
IT'S ONLY BEEN THE CRAZIEST, MOST MESSED-UP THING I'VE EVER SEEN.
WOULD YOU CARE TO SEE ***MORE?***
I COULD USE AN ASSISTANT.
WAIT, YOU'RE MAKING ME A JOB OFFER? ***WHY?***
YOU DON'T... EVEN ***KNOW*** ME.
LET'S JUST SAY, I'M GOOD AT ***DISSECTING*** A PERSON.
FIRST-- ***YOU'RE FASCINATED.*** SUCH STRANGENESS AND DANGER, AND YET YOU LOOKED OVER MY SHOULDER. CURIOSITY DRIVES ALL SCIENTIFIC PURSUITS.
YOU CAN HANDLE YOURSELF. YOU WERE ASSAULTED, YET STOOD YOUR GROUND. MY WORK REQUIRES BOLDNESS AND A VIGOROUS PHYSIQUE.
YOU'RE SKILLED IN CHEMISTRY AND BIOLOGY. THE FENTANYL CARTONS YOU DROPPED--THEY CAME FROM PARISH BIOTECH. NOW, YOU COULD BE THEIR JANITOR, BUT I SUSPECT NOT.
YOU'RE NOT AFRAID TO GET YOUR HANDS DIRTY. WHY ELSE WOULD YOU BE MEETING DRUG DEALERS ON A DESOLATE PIER? MY PURSUITS TRANSCEND MORAL BOUNDARIES.
I'M OFFERING YOU THE CHANCE OF A ***LIFETIME***-- THE OPPORTUNITY TO DO ***MEANINGFUL, REVOLUTIONARY*** WORK TOWARDS A NOBLE GOAL: CONQUERING MORTALITY.
THIS IS INSANE. I ***KNOW*** IT'S INSANE.
BUT THAT EMPTY PLACE INSIDE, IT WANTS TO BE FILLED...

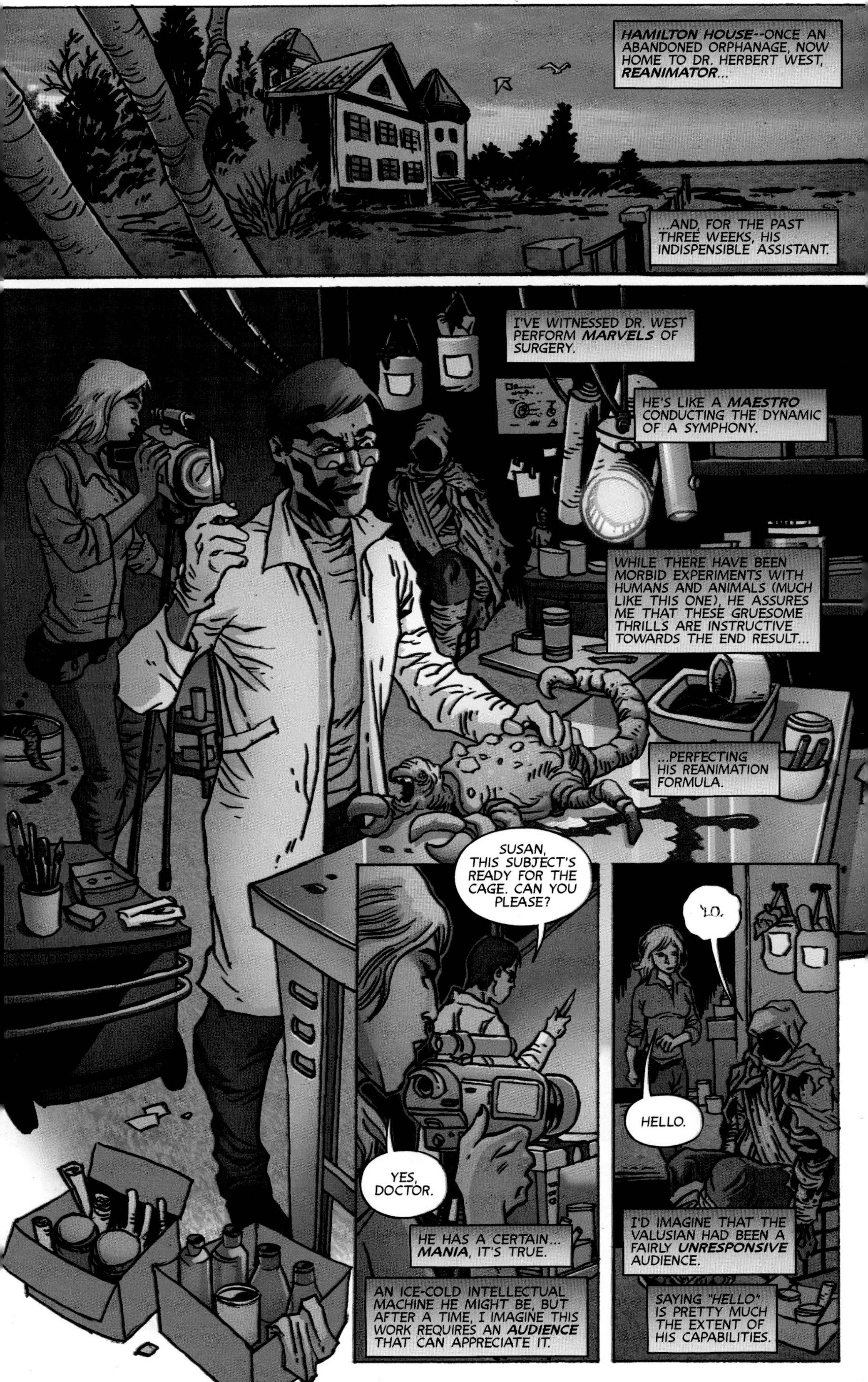
HAMILTON HOUSE--ONCE AN ABANDONED ORPHANAGE, NOW HOME TO DR. HERBERT WEST, REANIMATOR...
...AND, FOR THE PAST THREE WEEKS, HIS INDISPENSIBLE ASSISTANT.
I'VE WITNESSED DR. WEST PERFORM MARVELS OF SURGERY.
HE'S LIKE A MAESTRO CONDUCTING THE DYNAMIC OF A SYMPHONY.
WHILE THERE HAVE BEEN MORBID EXPERIMENTS WITH HUMANS AND ANIMALS (MUCH LIKE THIS ONE), HE ASSURES ME THAT THESE GRUESOME THRILLS ARE INSTRUCTIVE TOWARDS THE END RESULT...
...PERFECTING HIS REANIMATION FORMULA.
SUSAN, THIS SUBJECT'S READY FOR THE CAGE. CAN YOU PLEASE?
YES, DOCTOR.
HE HAS A CERTAIN... MANIA, IT'S TRUE.
AN ICE-COLD INTELLECTUAL MACHINE HE MIGHT BE, BUT AFTER A TIME, I IMAGINE THIS WORK REQUIRES AN AUDIENCE THAT CAN APPRECIATE IT.
'LO.
HELLO.
I'D IMAGINE THAT THE VALUSIAN HAD BEEN A FAIRLY UNRESPONSIVE AUDIENCE.
SAYING "HELLO" IS PRETTY MUCH THE EXTENT OF HIS CAPABILITIES.

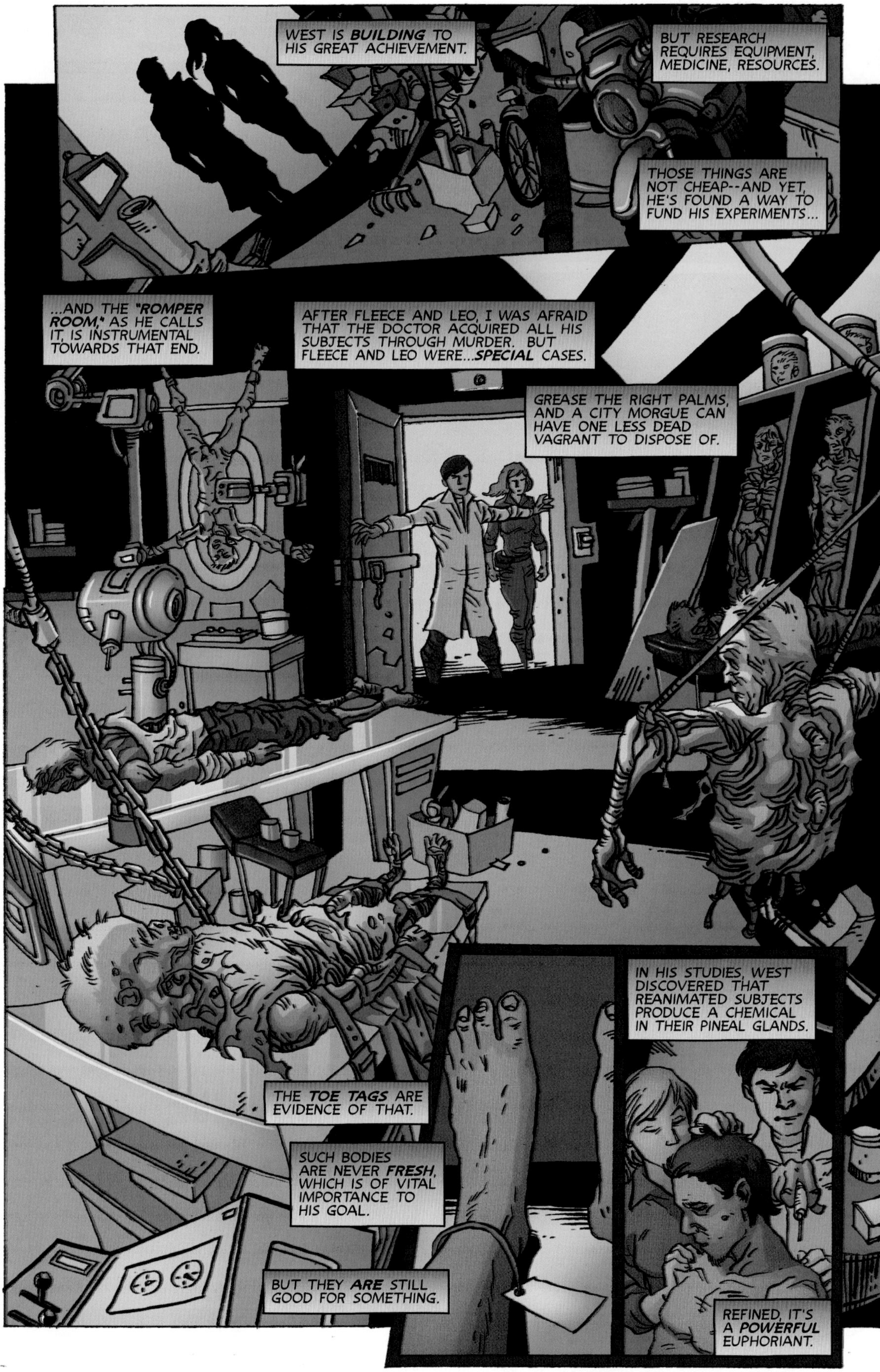
WEST IS BUILDING TO HIS GREAT ACHIEVEMENT.
BUT RESEARCH REQUIRES EQUIPMENT, MEDICINE, RESOURCES.
THOSE THINGS ARE NOT CHEAP--AND YET, HE'S FOUND A WAY TO FUND HIS EXPERIMENTS...
...AND THE "ROMPER ROOM," AS HE CALLS IT, IS INSTRUMENTAL TOWARDS THAT END.
AFTER FLEECE AND LEO, I WAS AFRAID THAT THE DOCTOR ACQUIRED ALL HIS SUBJECTS THROUGH MURDER. BUT FLEECE AND LEO WERE...SPECIAL CASES.
GREASE THE RIGHT PALMS, AND A CITY MORGUE CAN HAVE ONE LESS DEAD VAGRANT TO DISPOSE OF.
THE TOE TAGS ARE EVIDENCE OF THAT.
SUCH BODIES ARE NEVER FRESH, WHICH IS OF VITAL IMPORTANCE TO HIS GOAL.
BUT THEY ARE STILL GOOD FOR SOMETHING.
IN HIS STUDIES, WEST DISCOVERED THAT REANIMATED SUBJECTS PRODUCE A CHEMICAL IN THEIR PINEAL GLANDS.
REFINED, IT'S A POWERFUL EUPHORIANT.

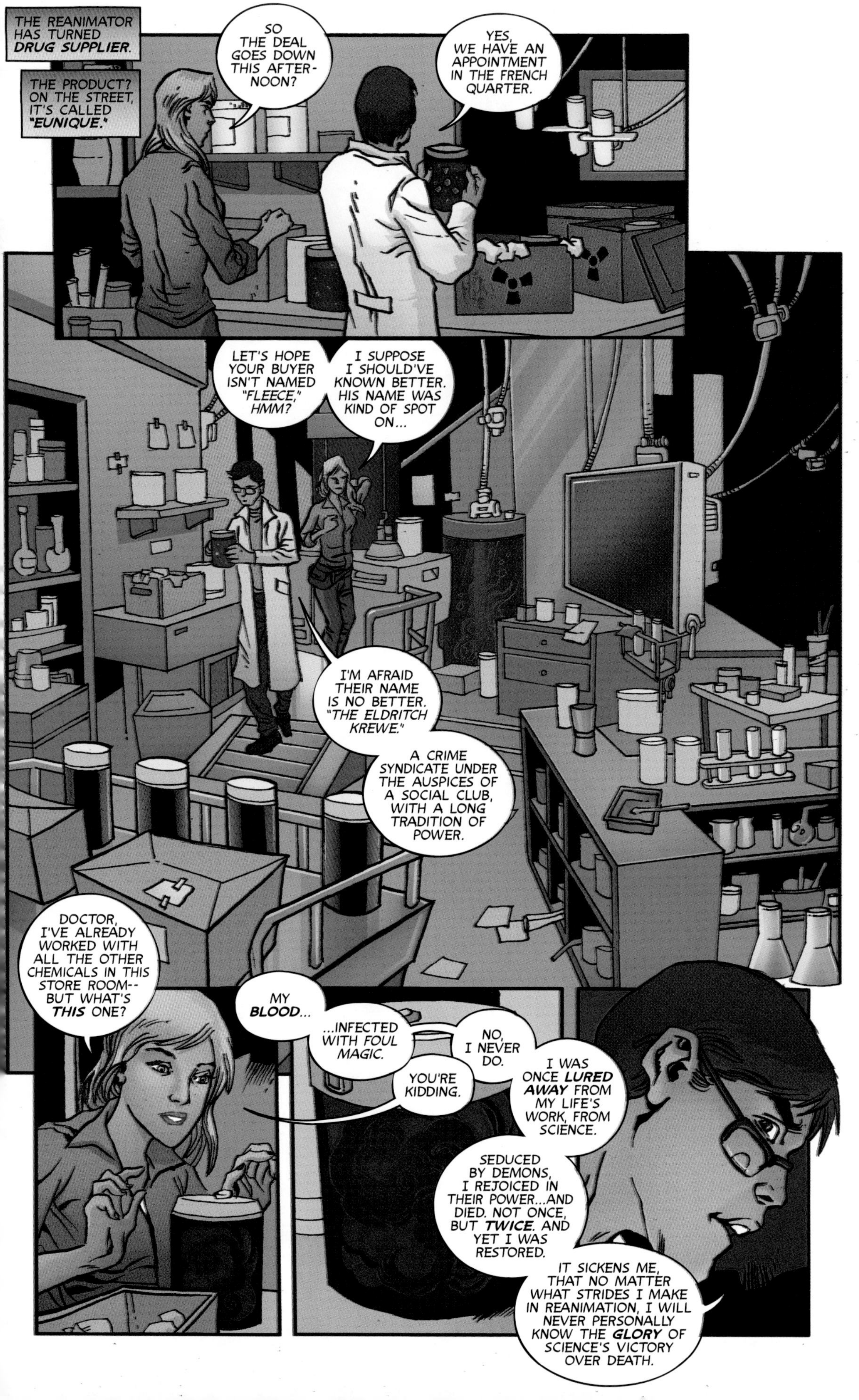
THE REANIMATOR HAS TURNED DRUG SUPPLIER.
THE PRODUCT? ON THE STREET, IT'S CALLED "EUNIQUE."
SO THE DEAL GOES DOWN THIS AFTER-NOON?
YES, WE HAVE AN APPOINTMENT IN THE FRENCH QUARTER.
LET'S HOPE YOUR BUYER ISN'T NAMED "FLEECE," HMM?
I SUPPOSE I SHOULD'VE KNOWN BETTER. HIS NAME WAS KIND OF SPOT ON...
I'M AFRAID THEIR NAME IS NO BETTER. "THE ELDRITCH KREWE."
A CRIME SYNDICATE UNDER THE AUSPICES OF A SOCIAL CLUB, WITH A LONG TRADITION OF POWER.
DOCTOR, I'VE ALREADY WORKED WITH ALL THE OTHER CHEMICALS IN THIS STORE ROOM-- BUT WHAT'S THIS ONE?
MY BLOOD...
...INFECTED WITH FOUL MAGIC.
YOU'RE KIDDING.
NO, I NEVER DO.
I WAS ONCE LURED AWAY FROM MY LIFE'S WORK, FROM SCIENCE.
SEDUCED BY DEMONS, I REJOICED IN THEIR POWER...AND DIED. NOT ONCE, BUT TWICE. AND YET I WAS RESTORED.
IT SICKENS ME, THAT NO MATTER WHAT STRIDES I MAKE IN REANIMATION, I WILL NEVER PERSONALLY KNOW THE GLORY OF SCIENCE'S VICTORY OVER DEATH.

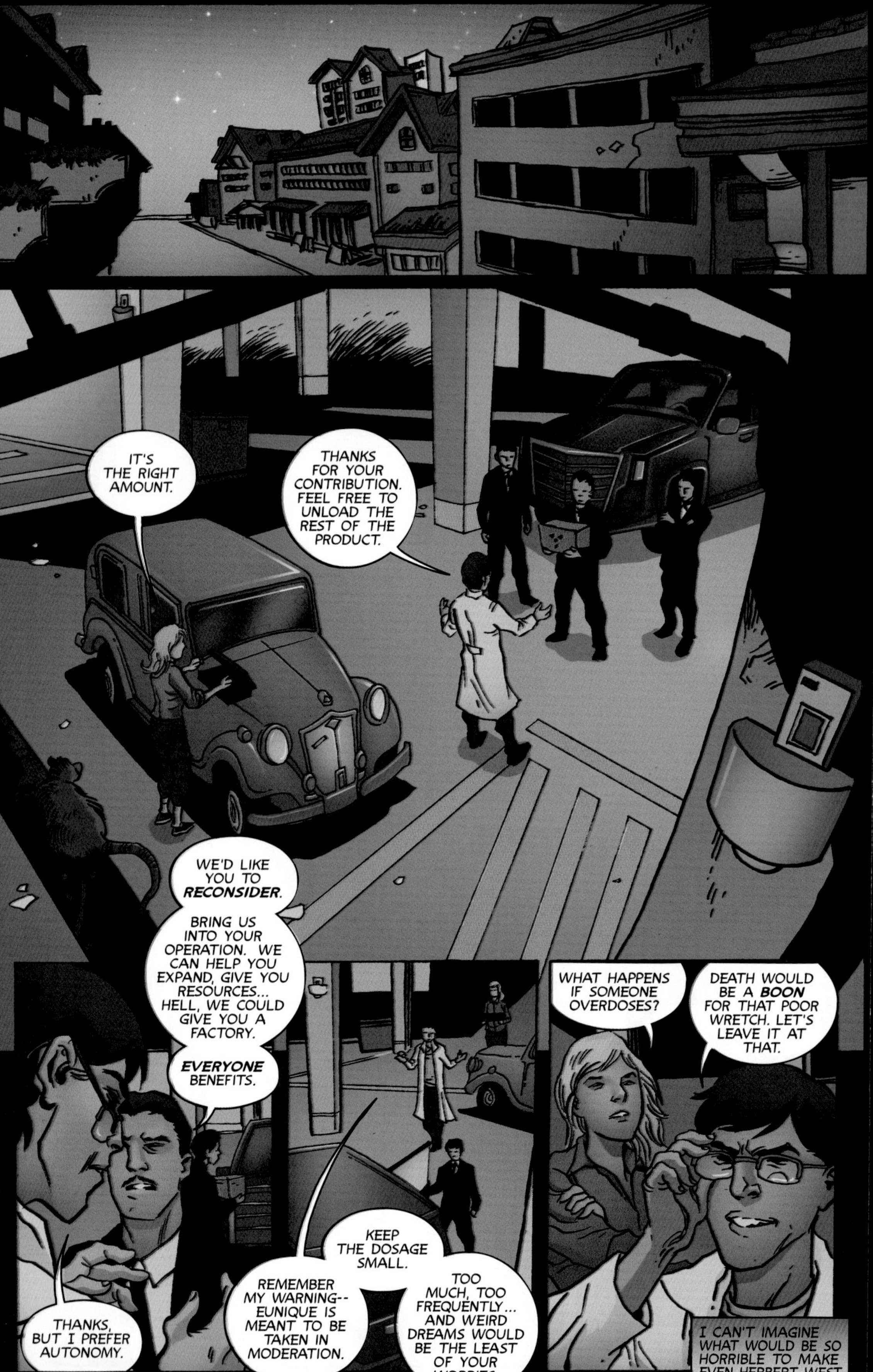
IT'S THE RIGHT AMOUNT.
THANKS FOR YOUR CONTRIBUTION. FEEL FREE TO UNLOAD THE REST OF THE PRODUCT.
WE'D LIKE YOU TO ***RECONSIDER***.
BRING US INTO YOUR OPERATION. WE CAN HELP YOU EXPAND, GIVE YOU RESOURCES... HELL, WE COULD GIVE YOU A FACTORY.
EVERYONE BENEFITS.
THANKS, BUT I PREFER AUTONOMY.
KEEP THE DOSAGE SMALL.
REMEMBER MY WARNING-- EUNIQUE IS MEANT TO BE TAKEN IN MODERATION.
TOO MUCH, TOO FREQUENTLY... AND WEIRD DREAMS WOULD BE THE LEAST OF YOUR WORRIES.
WHAT HAPPENS IF SOMEONE OVERDOSES?
DEATH WOULD BE A ***BOON*** FOR THAT POOR WRETCH. LET'S LEAVE IT AT THAT.
I CAN'T IMAGINE WHAT WOULD BE SO HORRIBLE TO MAKE EVEN HERBERT WEST SHUDDER.

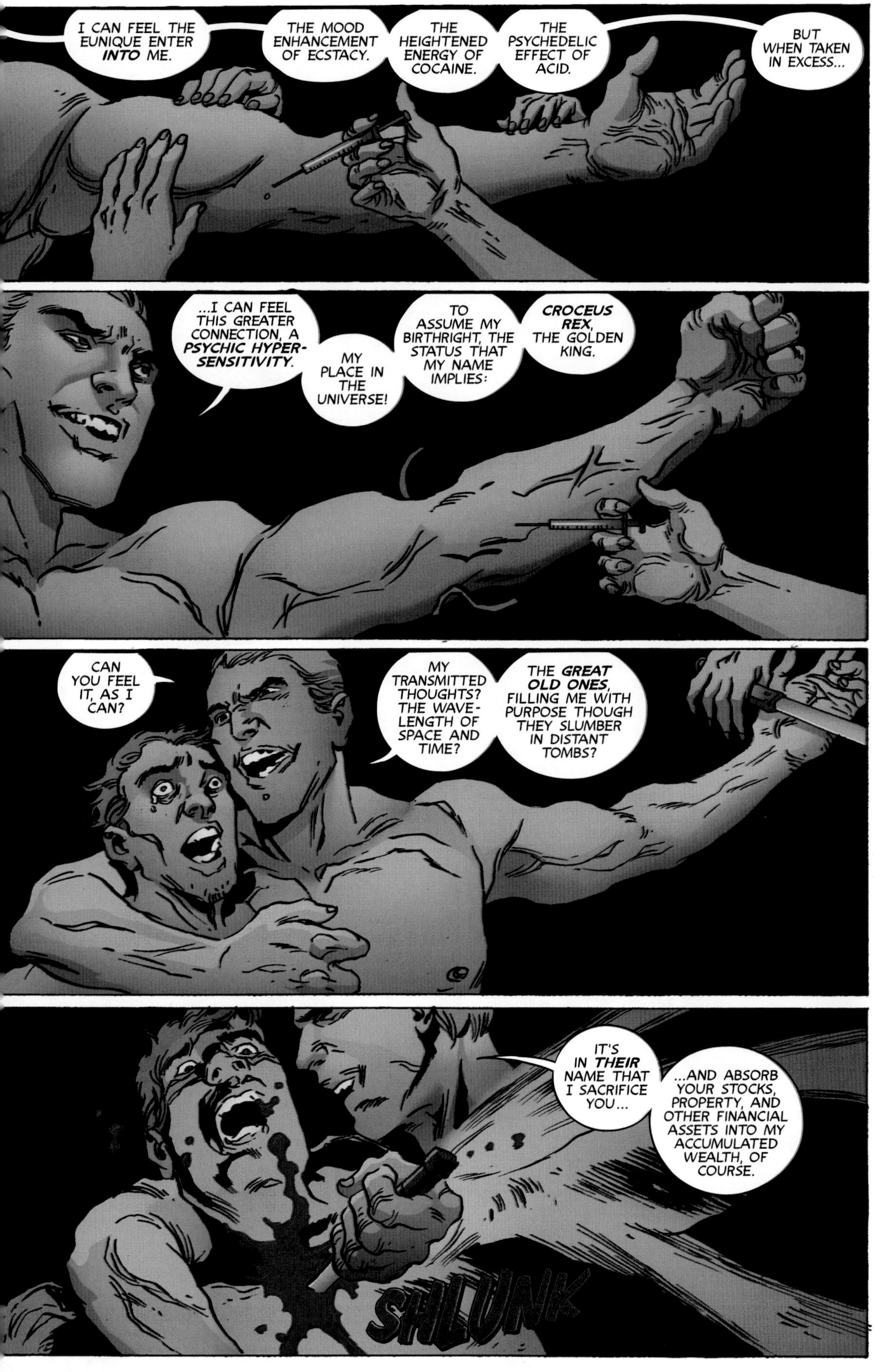
I CAN FEEL THE EUNIQUE ENTER **INTO** ME.
THE MOOD ENHANCEMENT OF ECSTACY.
THE HEIGHTENED ENERGY OF COCAINE.
THE PSYCHEDELIC EFFECT OF ACID.
BUT WHEN TAKEN IN EXCESS...
...I CAN FEEL THIS GREATER CONNECTION, A ***PSYCHIC HYPER-SENSITIVITY***.
MY PLACE IN THE UNIVERSE!
TO ASSUME MY BIRTHRIGHT, THE STATUS THAT MY NAME IMPLIES:
CROCEUS REX, THE GOLDEN KING.
CAN YOU FEEL IT, AS I CAN?
MY TRANSMITTED THOUGHTS? THE WAVE-LENGTH OF SPACE AND TIME?
THE ***GREAT OLD ONES***, FILLING ME WITH PURPOSE THOUGH THEY SLUMBER IN DISTANT TOMBS?
IT'S IN ***THEIR*** NAME THAT I SACRIFICE YOU...
...AND ABSORB YOUR STOCKS, PROPERTY, AND OTHER FINANCIAL ASSETS INTO MY ACCUMULATED WEALTH, OF COURSE.
SHLUNK

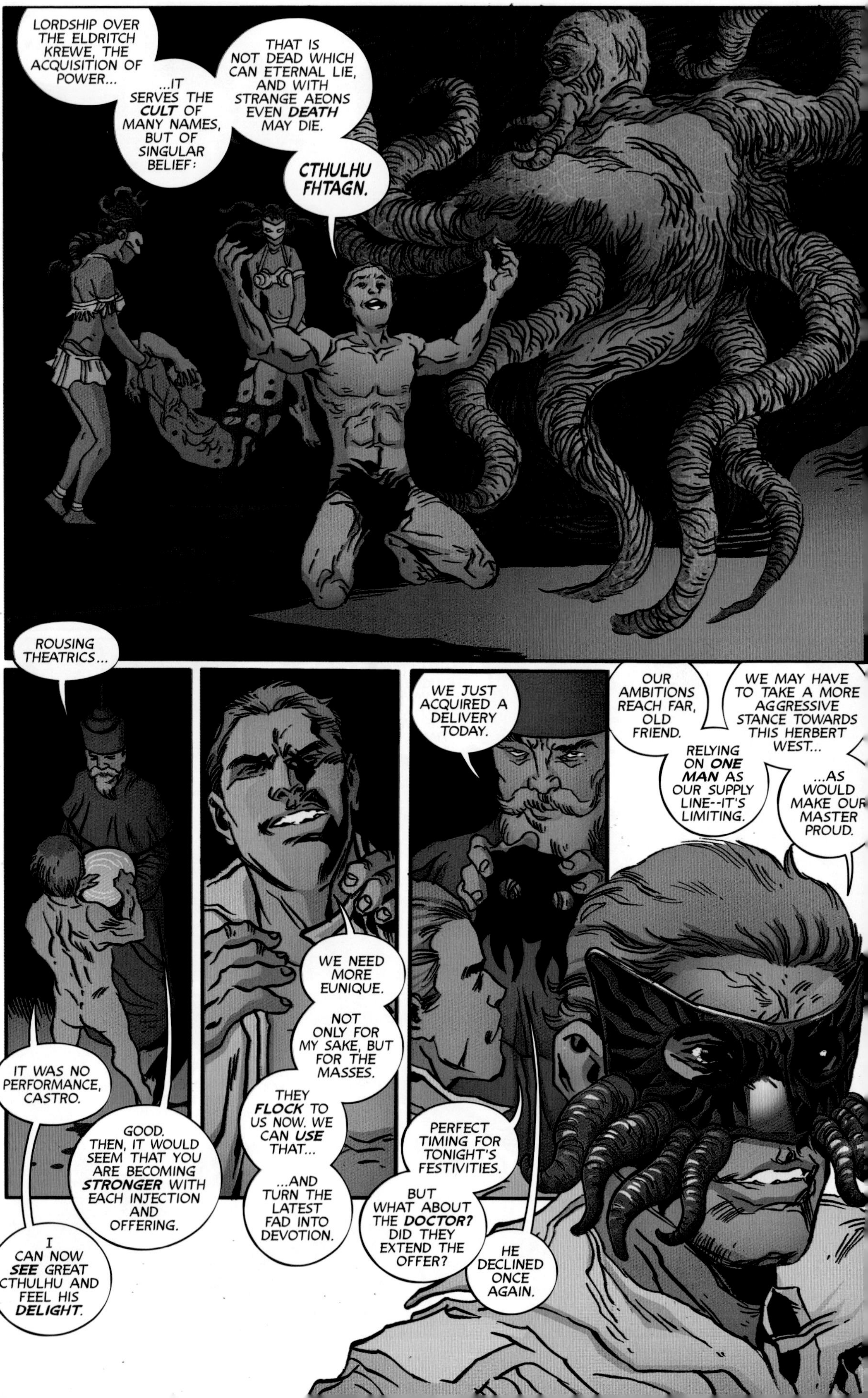
LORDSHIP OVER THE ELDRITCH KREWE, THE ACQUISITION OF POWER...
...IT SERVES THE CULT OF MANY NAMES, BUT OF SINGULAR BELIEF:
THAT IS NOT DEAD WHICH CAN ETERNAL LIE, AND WITH STRANGE AEONS EVEN DEATH MAY DIE.
CTHULHU FHTAGN.
ROUSING THEATRICS...
IT WAS NO PERFORMANCE, CASTRO.
GOOD. THEN, IT WOULD SEEM THAT YOU ARE BECOMING STRONGER WITH EACH INJECTION AND OFFERING.
I CAN NOW SEE GREAT CTHULHU AND FEEL HIS DELIGHT.
WE NEED MORE EUNIQUE.
NOT ONLY FOR MY SAKE, BUT FOR THE MASSES.
THEY FLOCK TO US NOW. WE CAN USE THAT...
...AND TURN THE LATEST FAD INTO DEVOTION.
WE JUST ACQUIRED A DELIVERY TODAY.
PERFECT TIMING FOR TONIGHT'S FESTIVITIES.
BUT WHAT ABOUT THE DOCTOR? DID THEY EXTEND THE OFFER?
HE DECLINED ONCE AGAIN.
OUR AMBITIONS REACH FAR, OLD FRIEND.
RELYING ON ONE MAN AS OUR SUPPLY LINE--IT'S LIMITING.
WE MAY HAVE TO TAKE A MORE AGGRESSIVE STANCE TOWARDS THIS HERBERT WEST...
...AS WOULD MAKE OUR MASTER PROUD.

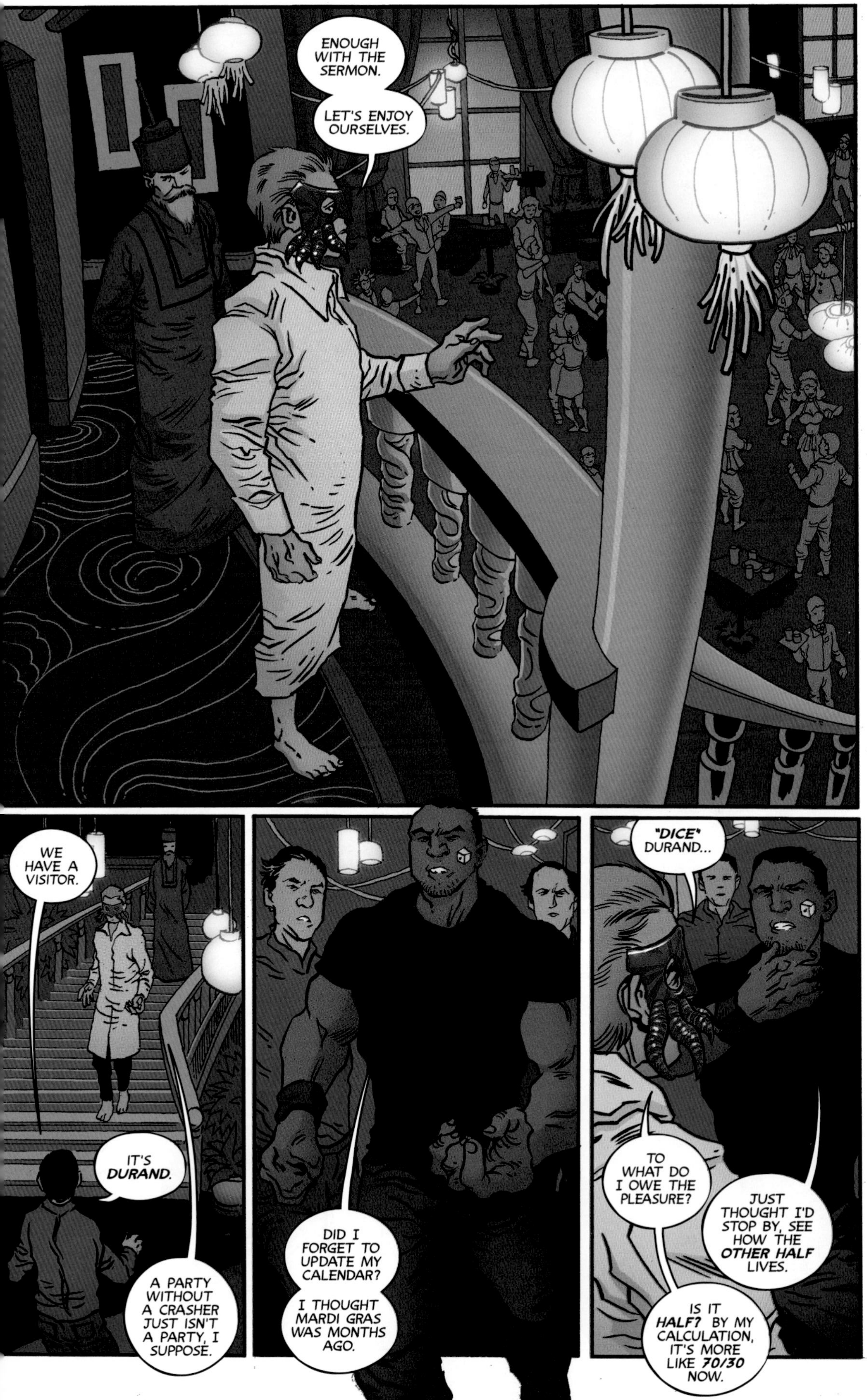
ENOUGH WITH THE SERMON.
LET'S ENJOY OURSELVES.
WE HAVE A VISITOR.
IT'S DURAND.
A PARTY WITHOUT A CRASHER JUST ISN'T A PARTY, I SUPPOSE.
DID I FORGET TO UPDATE MY CALENDAR?
I THOUGHT MARDI GRAS WAS MONTHS AGO.
"DICE" DURAND...
TO WHAT DO I OWE THE PLEASURE?
JUST THOUGHT I'D STOP BY, SEE HOW THE OTHER HALF LIVES.
IS IT HALF? BY MY CALCULATION, IT'S MORE LIKE 70/30 NOW.

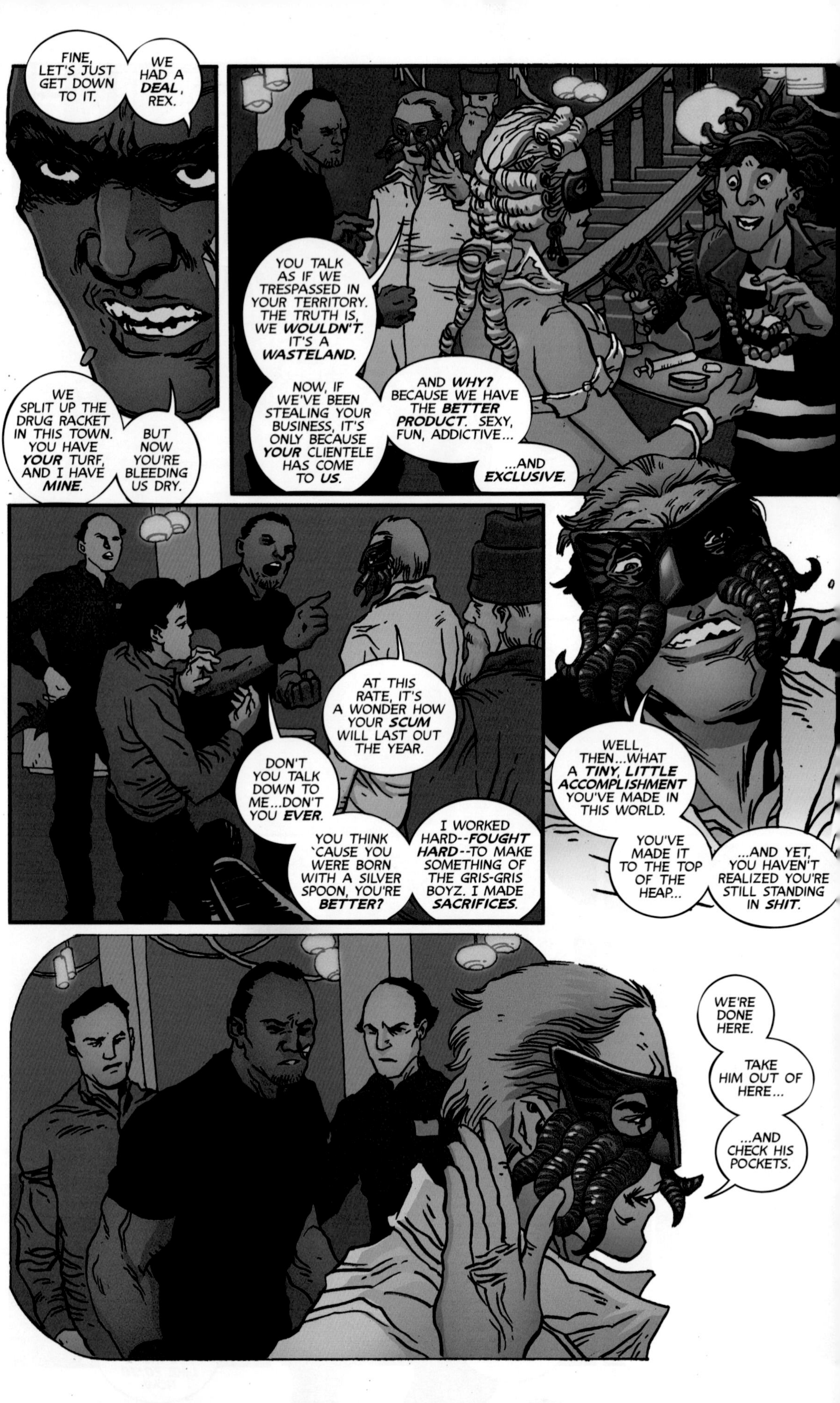
FINE, LET'S JUST GET DOWN TO IT.
WE HAD A DEAL, REX.
WE SPLIT UP THE DRUG RACKET IN THIS TOWN. YOU HAVE YOUR TURF, AND I HAVE MINE.
BUT NOW YOU'RE BLEEDING US DRY.
YOU TALK AS IF WE TRESPASSED IN YOUR TERRITORY. THE TRUTH IS, WE WOULDN'T. IT'S A WASTELAND.
NOW, IF WE'VE BEEN STEALING YOUR BUSINESS, IT'S ONLY BECAUSE YOUR CLIENTELE HAS COME TO US.
AND WHY? BECAUSE WE HAVE THE BETTER PRODUCT. SEXY, FUN, ADDICTIVE...
...AND EXCLUSIVE.
AT THIS RATE, IT'S A WONDER HOW YOUR SCUM WILL LAST OUT THE YEAR.
DON'T YOU TALK DOWN TO ME...DON'T YOU EVER.
YOU THINK `CAUSE YOU WERE BORN WITH A SILVER SPOON, YOU'RE BETTER?
I WORKED HARD--FOUGHT HARD--TO MAKE SOMETHING OF THE GRIS-GRIS BOYZ. I MADE SACRIFICES.
WELL, THEN...WHAT A TINY, LITTLE ACCOMPLISHMENT YOU'VE MADE IN THIS WORLD.
YOU'VE MADE IT TO THE TOP OF THE HEAP...
...AND YET, YOU HAVEN'T REALIZED YOU'RE STILL STANDING IN SHIT.
WE'RE DONE HERE.
TAKE HIM OUT OF HERE...
...AND CHECK HIS POCKETS.

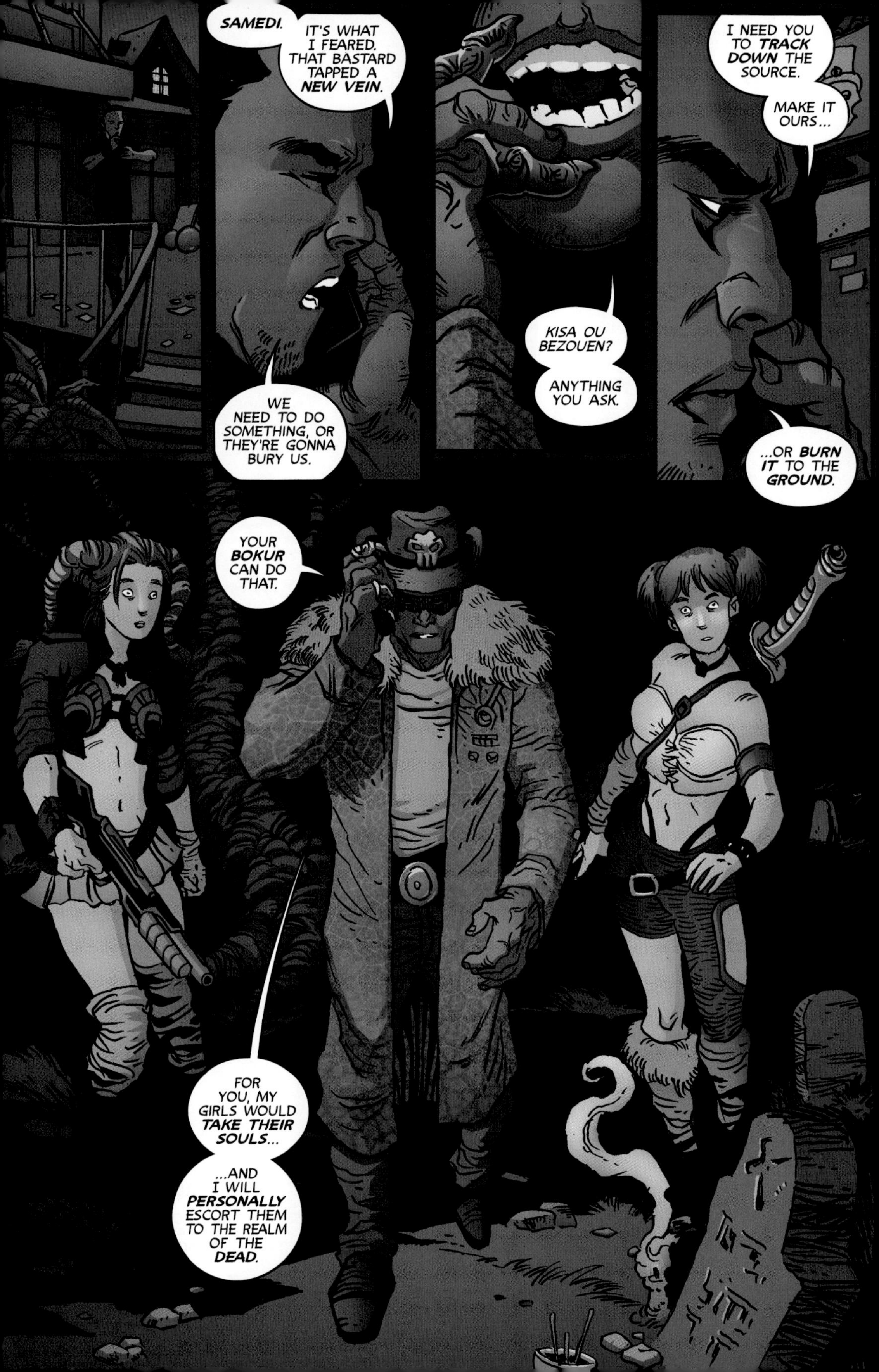
SAMEDI.
IT'S WHAT I FEARED. THAT BASTARD TAPPED A NEW VEIN.
WE NEED TO DO SOMETHING, OR THEY'RE GONNA BURY US.
KISA OU BEZOUEN?
ANYTHING YOU ASK.
I NEED YOU TO TRACK DOWN THE SOURCE.
MAKE IT OURS...
...OR BURN IT TO THE GROUND.
YOUR BOKUR CAN DO THAT.
FOR YOU, MY GIRLS WOULD TAKE THEIR SOULS...
...AND I WILL PERSONALLY ESCORT THEM TO THE REALM OF THE DEAD.

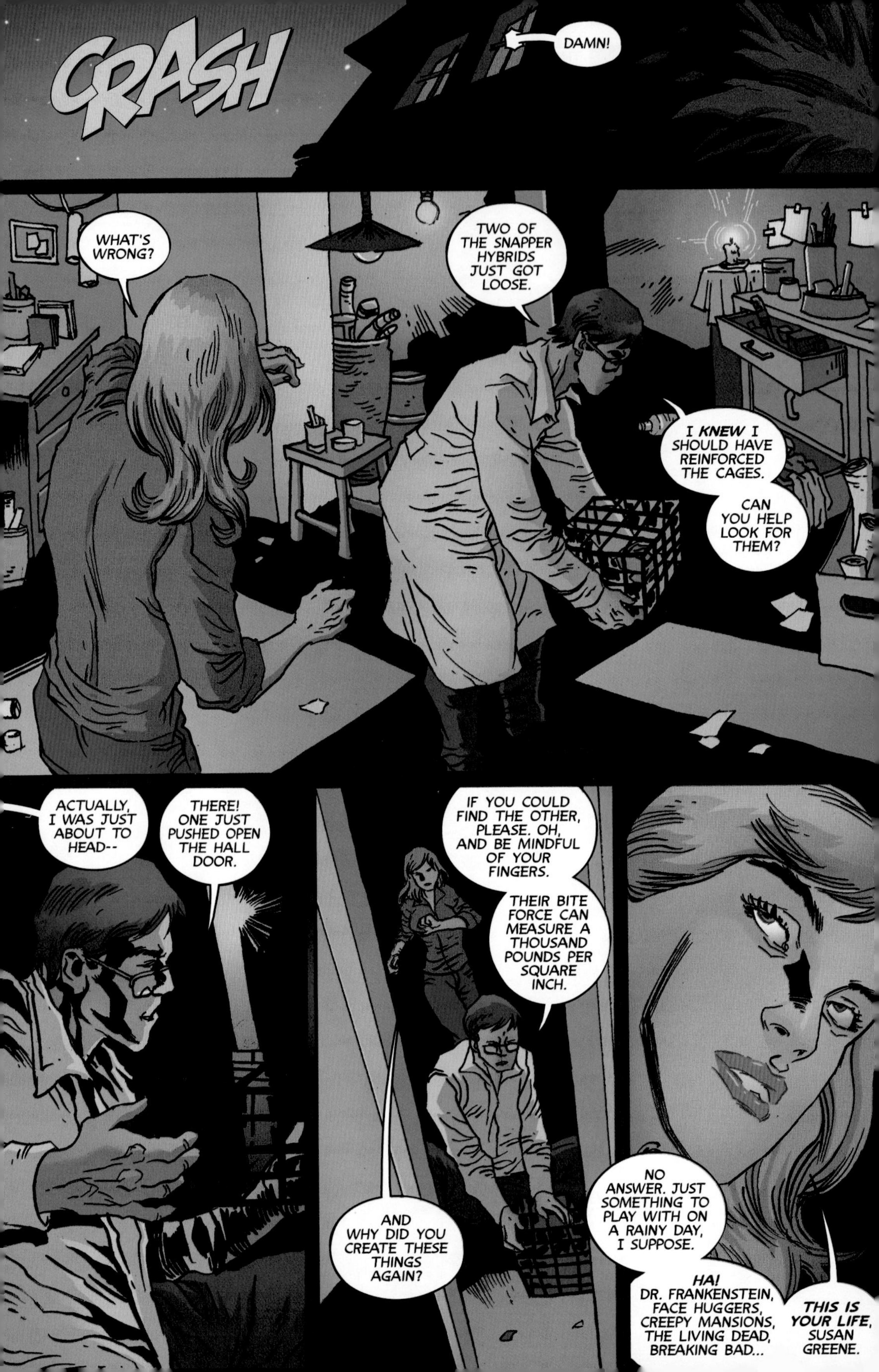
CRASH
DAMN!
WHAT'S WRONG?
TWO OF THE SNAPPER HYBRIDS JUST GOT LOOSE.
I KNEW I SHOULD HAVE REINFORCED THE CAGES.
CAN YOU HELP LOOK FOR THEM?
ACTUALLY, I WAS JUST ABOUT TO HEAD--
THERE! ONE JUST PUSHED OPEN THE HALL DOOR.
IF YOU COULD FIND THE OTHER, PLEASE. OH, AND BE MINDFUL OF YOUR FINGERS.
THEIR BITE FORCE CAN MEASURE A THOUSAND POUNDS PER SQUARE INCH.
AND WHY DID YOU CREATE THESE THINGS AGAIN?
NO ANSWER. JUST SOMETHING TO PLAY WITH ON A RAINY DAY, I SUPPOSE.
HA! DR. FRANKENSTEIN, FACE HUGGERS, CREEPY MANSIONS, THE LIVING DEAD, BREAKING BAD...
THIS IS YOUR LIFE, SUSAN GREENE.

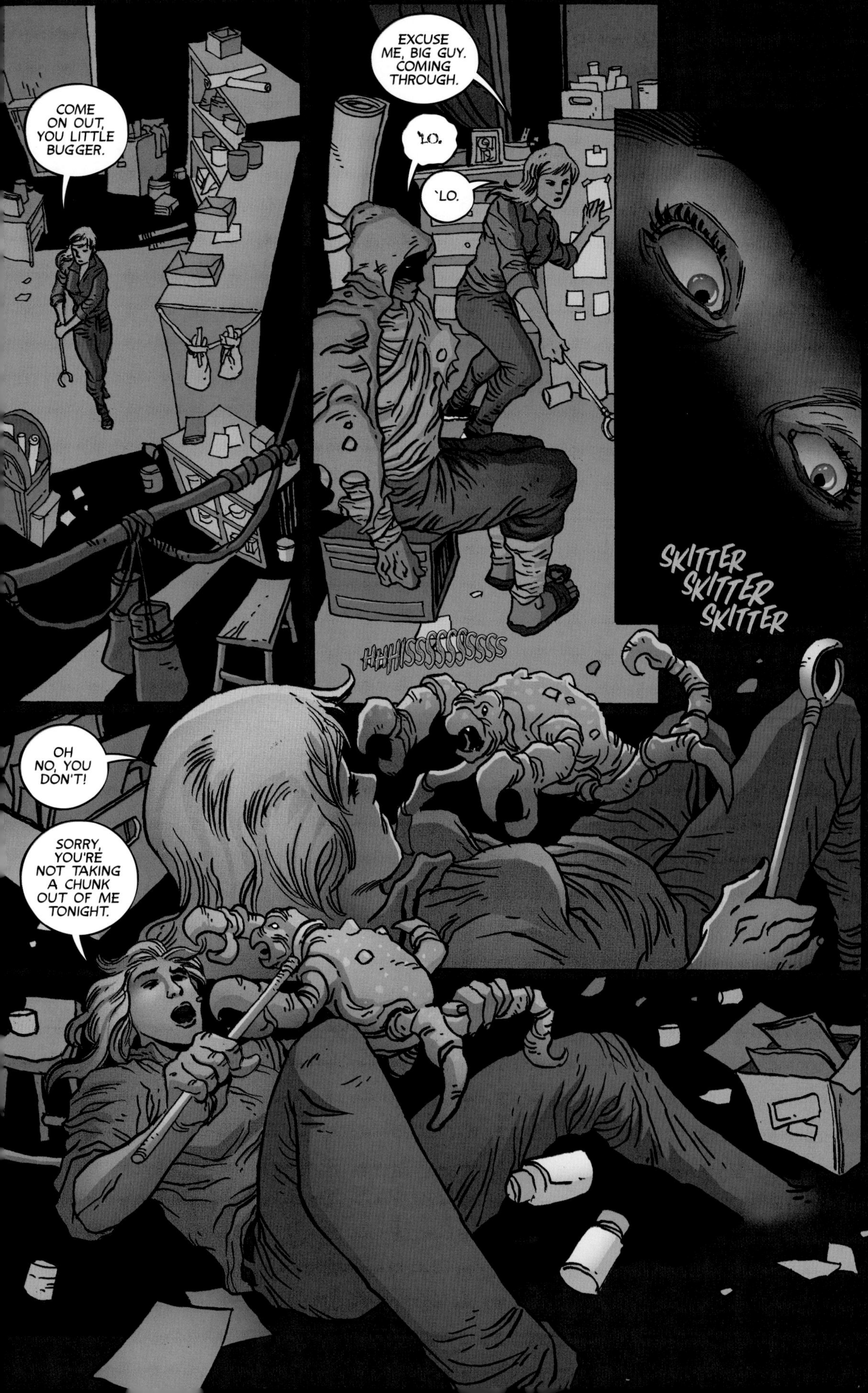
COME ON OUT, YOU LITTLE BUGGER.
EXCUSE ME, BIG GUY. COMING THROUGH.
'LO.
`LO.
SKITTER SKITTER SKITTER
HHHISSSSSSSSSS
OH NO, YOU DON'T!
SORRY, YOU'RE NOT TAKING A CHUNK OUT OF ME TONIGHT.

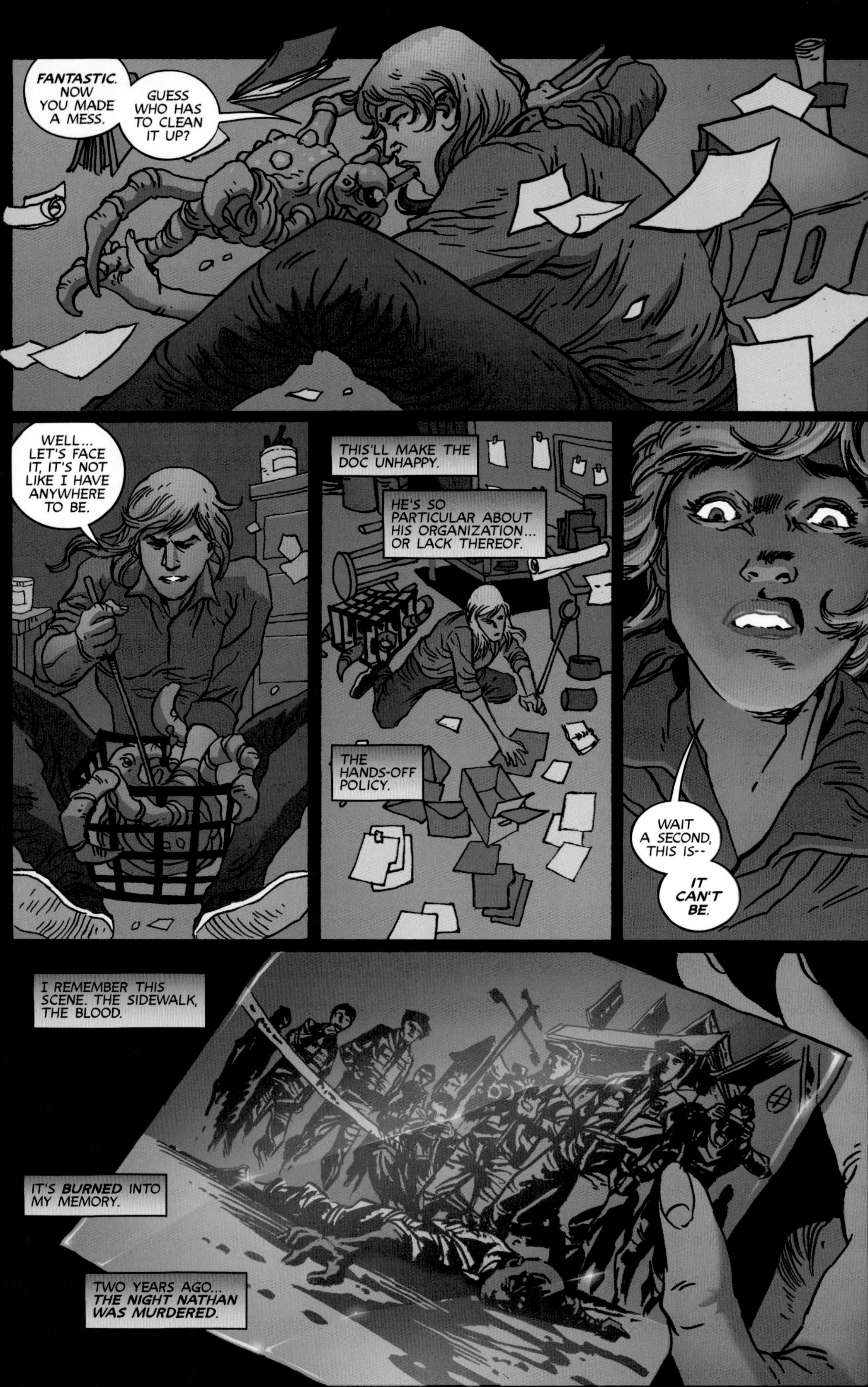
FANTASTIC. NOW YOU MADE A MESS.
GUESS WHO HAS TO CLEAN IT UP?
WELL... LET'S FACE IT, IT'S NOT LIKE I HAVE ANYWHERE TO BE.
THIS'LL MAKE THE DOC UNHAPPY.
HE'S SO PARTICULAR ABOUT HIS ORGANIZATION... OR LACK THEREOF.
THE HANDS-OFF POLICY.
WAIT A SECOND, THIS IS--
IT CAN'T BE.
I REMEMBER THIS SCENE. THE SIDEWALK, THE BLOOD.
IT'S BURNED INTO MY MEMORY.
TWO YEARS AGO... THE NIGHT NATHAN WAS MURDERED.

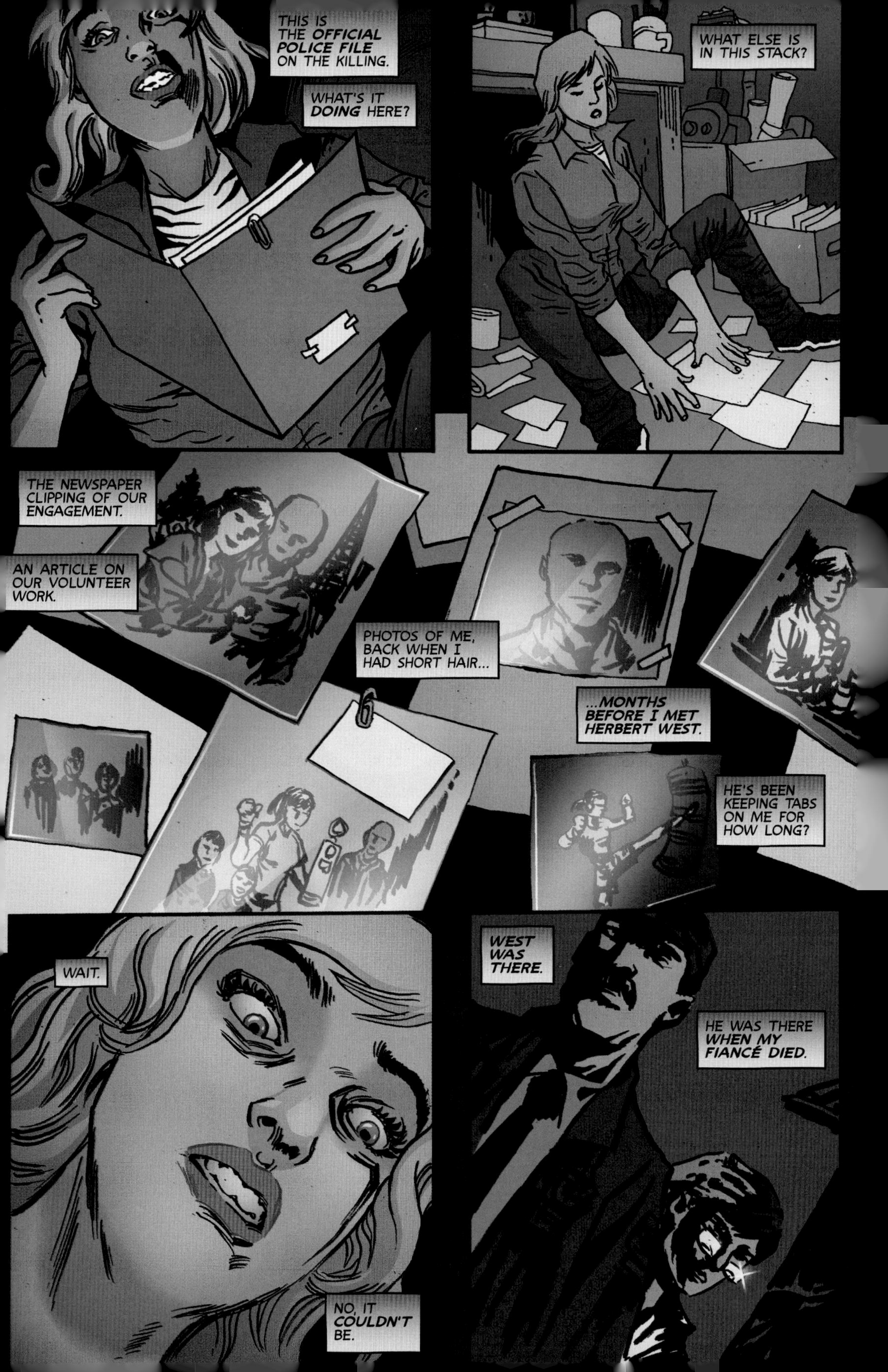
THIS IS THE OFFICIAL POLICE FILE ON THE KILLING.
WHAT'S IT DOING HERE?
WHAT ELSE IS IN THIS STACK?
THE NEWSPAPER CLIPPING OF OUR ENGAGEMENT.
AN ARTICLE ON OUR VOLUNTEER WORK.
PHOTOS OF ME, BACK WHEN I HAD SHORT HAIR...
...MONTHS BEFORE I MET HERBERT WEST.
HE'S BEEN KEEPING TABS ON ME FOR HOW LONG?
WAIT.
NO, IT COULDN'T BE.
WEST WAS THERE.
HE WAS THERE WHEN MY FIANCÉ DIED.

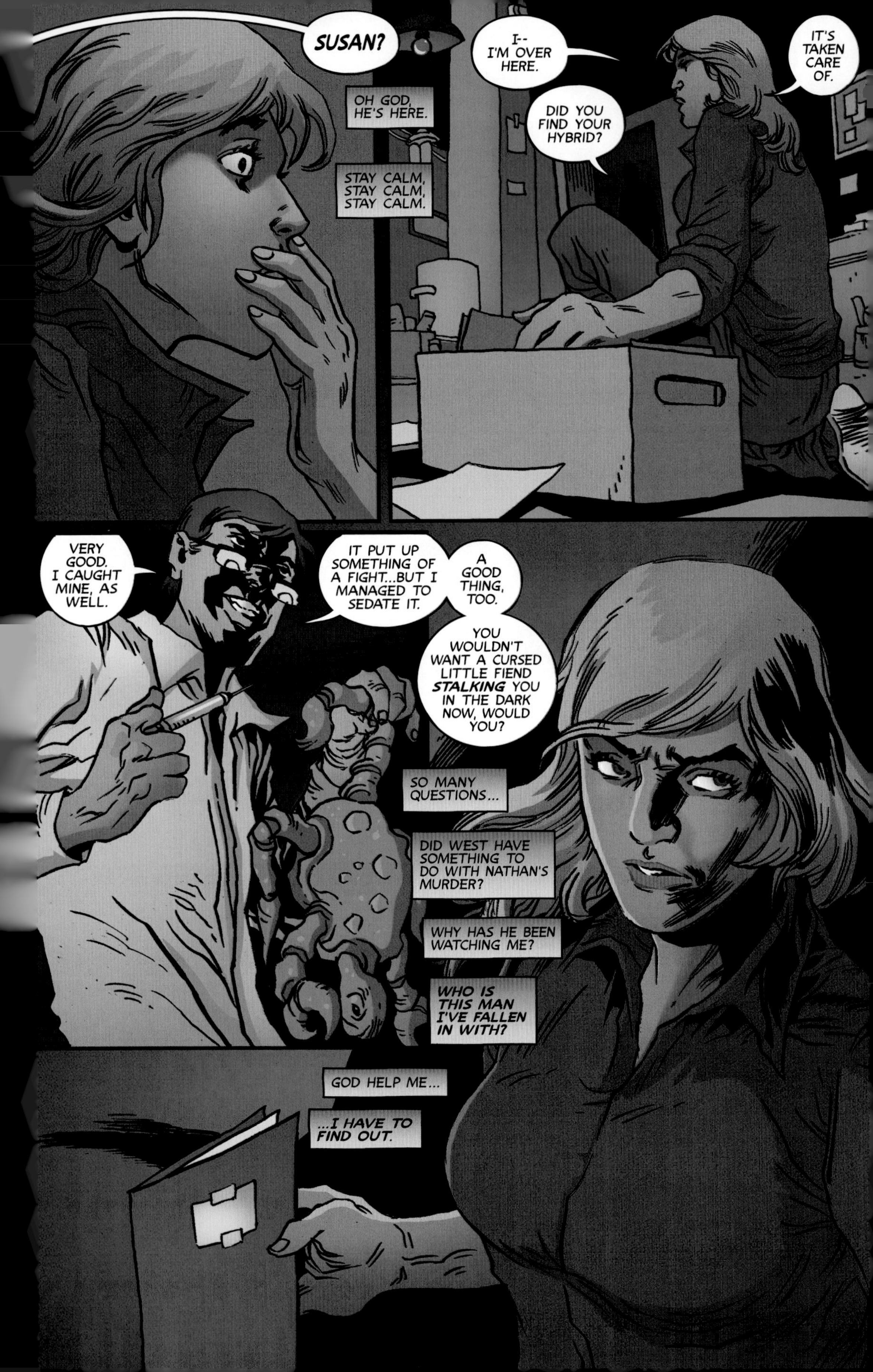

SUSAN?
OH GOD, HE'S HERE.
STAY CALM, STAY CALM, STAY CALM.
I-- I'M OVER HERE.
IT'S TAKEN CARE OF.
DID YOU FIND YOUR HYBRID?
VERY GOOD. I CAUGHT MINE, AS WELL.
IT PUT UP SOMETHING OF A FIGHT...BUT I MANAGED TO SEDATE IT.
A GOOD THING, TOO.
YOU WOULDN'T WANT A CURSED LITTLE FIEND STALKING YOU IN THE DARK NOW, WOULD YOU?
SO MANY QUESTIONS...
DID WEST HAVE SOMETHING TO DO WITH NATHAN'S MURDER?
WHY HAS HE BEEN WATCHING ME?
WHO IS THIS MAN I'VE FALLEN IN WITH?
GOD HELP ME...
...I HAVE TO FIND OUT.

MAKING MAD

TWO

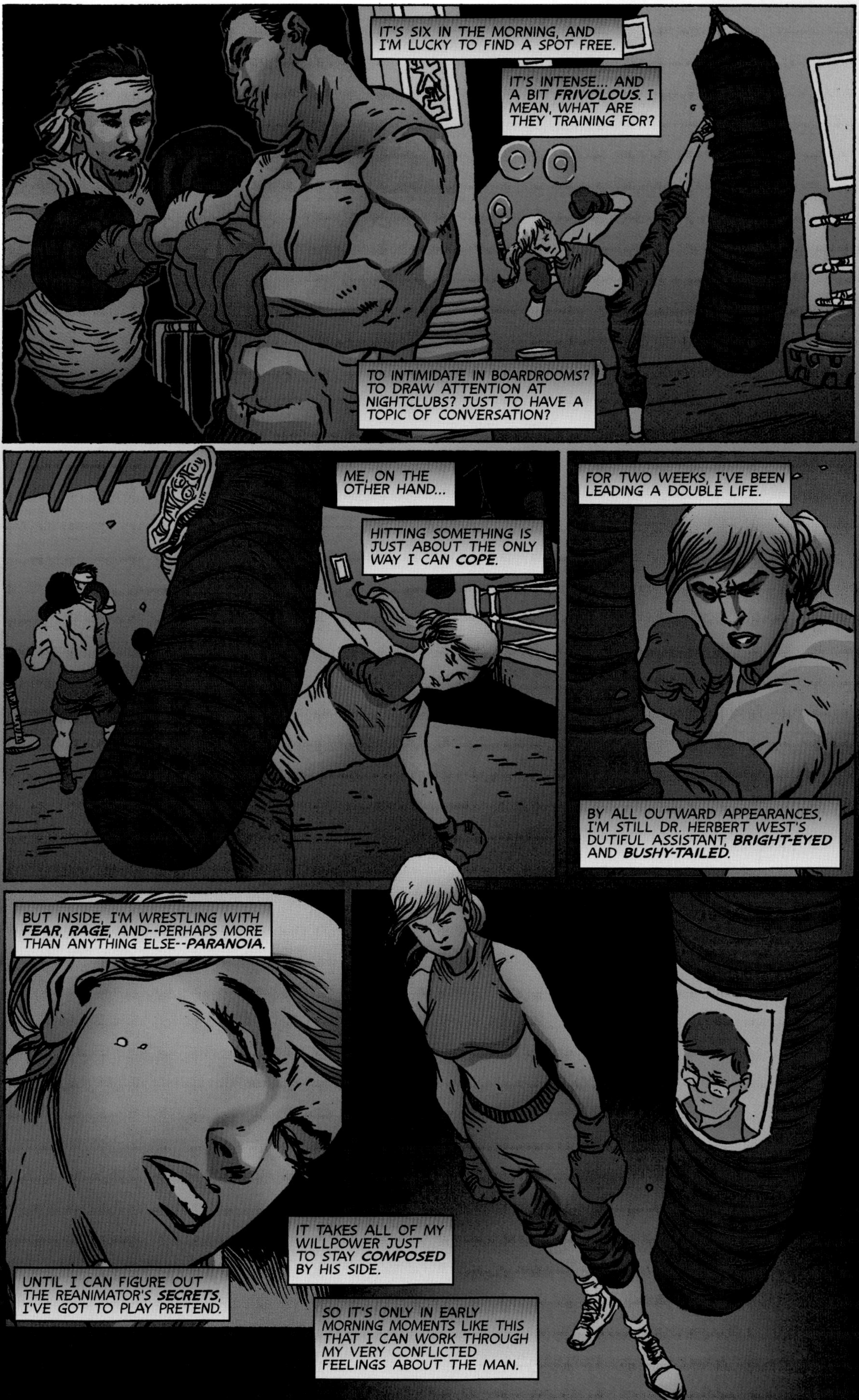
IT'S SIX IN THE MORNING, AND I'M LUCKY TO FIND A SPOT FREE.
IT'S INTENSE... AND A BIT FRIVOLOUS. I MEAN, WHAT ARE THEY TRAINING FOR?
TO INTIMIDATE IN BOARDROOMS? TO DRAW ATTENTION AT NIGHTCLUBS? JUST TO HAVE A TOPIC OF CONVERSATION?
ME, ON THE OTHER HAND...
HITTING SOMETHING IS JUST ABOUT THE ONLY WAY I CAN COPE.
FOR TWO WEEKS, I'VE BEEN LEADING A DOUBLE LIFE.
BY ALL OUTWARD APPEARANCES, I'M STILL DR. HERBERT WEST'S DUTIFUL ASSISTANT, BRIGHT-EYED AND BUSHY-TAILED.
BUT INSIDE, I'M WRESTLING WITH FEAR, RAGE, AND--PERHAPS MORE THAN ANYTHING ELSE--PARANOIA.
UNTIL I CAN FIGURE OUT THE REANIMATOR'S SECRETS, I'VE GOT TO PLAY PRETEND.
IT TAKES ALL OF MY WILLPOWER JUST TO STAY COMPOSED BY HIS SIDE.
SO IT'S ONLY IN EARLY MORNING MOMENTS LIKE THIS THAT I CAN WORK THROUGH MY VERY CONFLICTED FEELINGS ABOUT THE MAN.

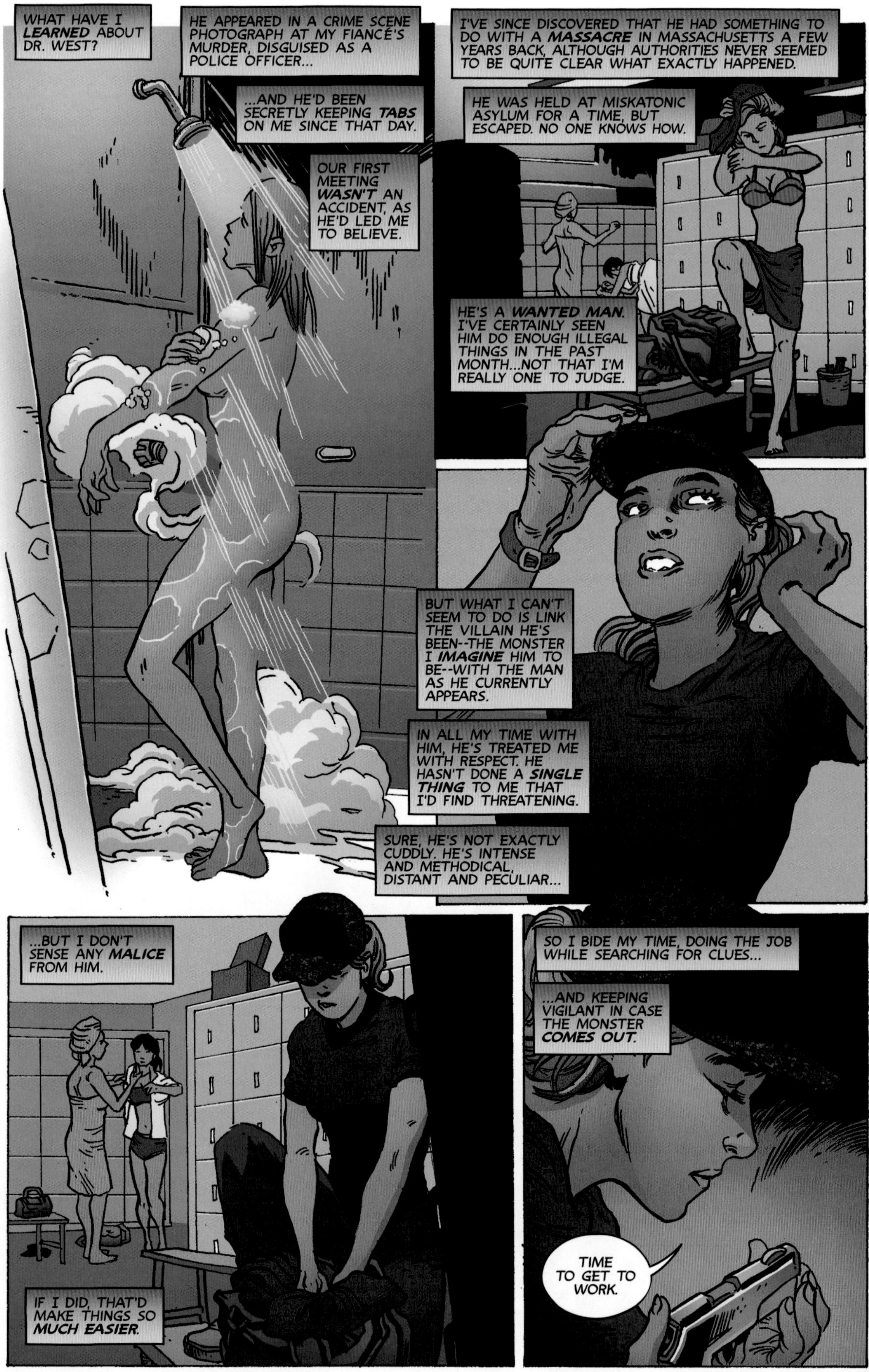
WHAT HAVE I LEARNED ABOUT DR. WEST?
HE APPEARED IN A CRIME SCENE PHOTOGRAPH AT MY FIANCÉ'S MURDER, DISGUISED AS A POLICE OFFICER...
...AND HE'D BEEN SECRETLY KEEPING TABS ON ME SINCE THAT DAY.
OUR FIRST MEETING WASN'T AN ACCIDENT, AS HE'D LED ME TO BELIEVE.
I'VE SINCE DISCOVERED THAT HE HAD SOMETHING TO DO WITH A MASSACRE IN MASSACHUSETTS A FEW YEARS BACK, ALTHOUGH AUTHORITIES NEVER SEEMED TO BE QUITE CLEAR WHAT EXACTLY HAPPENED.
HE WAS HELD AT MISKATONIC ASYLUM FOR A TIME, BUT ESCAPED. NO ONE KNOWS HOW.
HE'S A WANTED MAN. I'VE CERTAINLY SEEN HIM DO ENOUGH ILLEGAL THINGS IN THE PAST MONTH...NOT THAT I'M REALLY ONE TO JUDGE.
BUT WHAT I CAN'T SEEM TO DO IS LINK THE VILLAIN HE'S BEEN--THE MONSTER I IMAGINE HIM TO BE--WITH THE MAN AS HE CURRENTLY APPEARS.
IN ALL MY TIME WITH HIM, HE'S TREATED ME WITH RESPECT. HE HASN'T DONE A SINGLE THING TO ME THAT I'D FIND THREATENING.
SURE, HE'S NOT EXACTLY CUDDLY. HE'S INTENSE AND METHODICAL, DISTANT AND PECULIAR...
...BUT I DON'T SENSE ANY MALICE FROM HIM.
IF I DID, THAT'D MAKE THINGS SO MUCH EASIER.
SO I BIDE MY TIME, DOING THE JOB WHILE SEARCHING FOR CLUES...
...AND KEEPING VIGILANT IN CASE THE MONSTER COMES OUT.
TIME TO GET TO WORK.

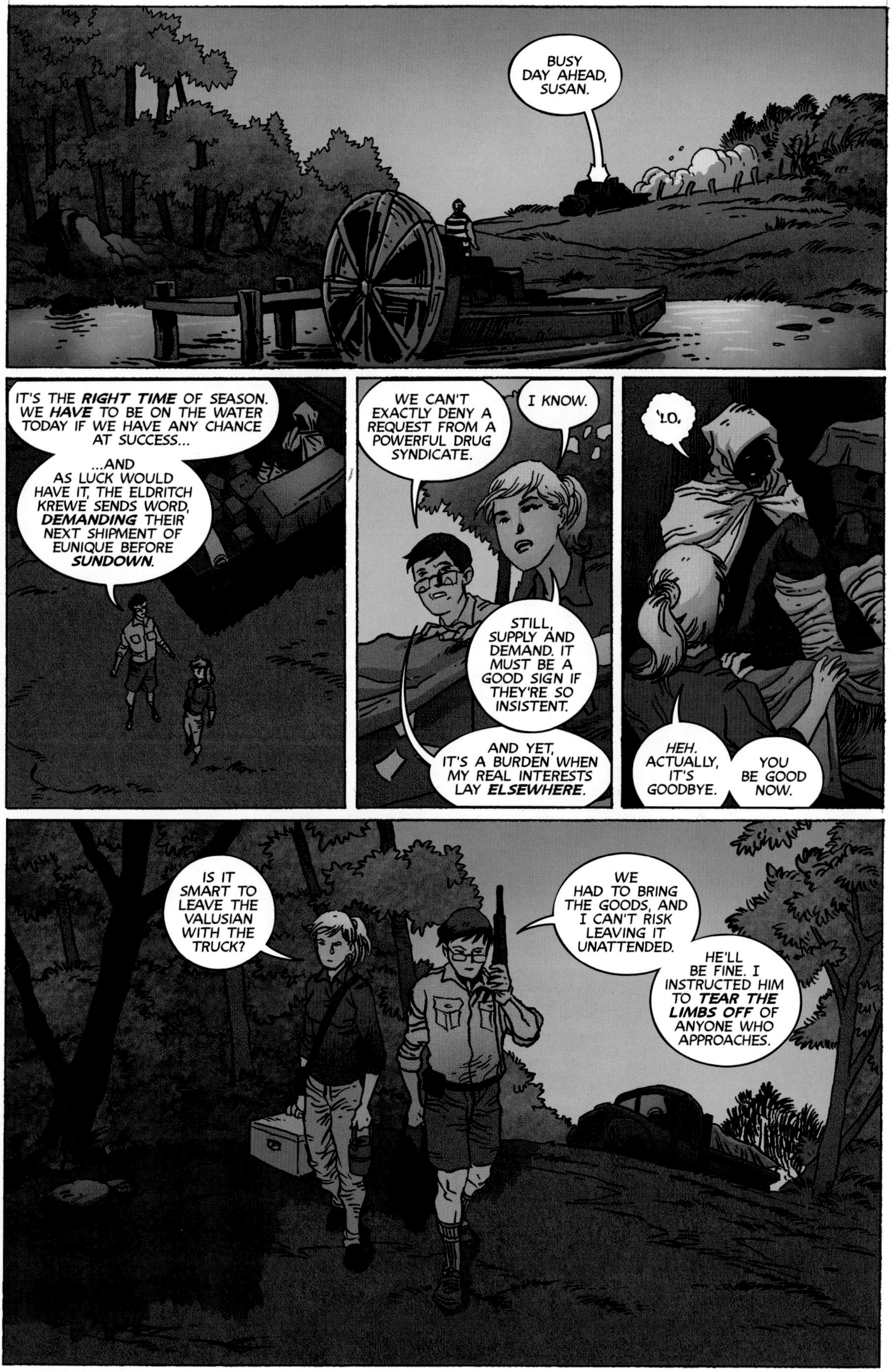
BUSY DAY AHEAD, SUSAN.
IT'S THE RIGHT TIME OF SEASON. WE HAVE TO BE ON THE WATER TODAY IF WE HAVE ANY CHANCE AT SUCCESS...
...AND AS LUCK WOULD HAVE IT, THE ELDRITCH KREWE SENDS WORD, DEMANDING THEIR NEXT SHIPMENT OF EUNIQUE BEFORE SUNDOWN.
WE CAN'T EXACTLY DENY A REQUEST FROM A POWERFUL DRUG SYNDICATE.
I KNOW.
STILL, SUPPLY AND DEMAND. IT MUST BE A GOOD SIGN IF THEY'RE SO INSISTENT.
AND YET, IT'S A BURDEN WHEN MY REAL INTERESTS LAY ELSEWHERE.
'LO.
HEH. ACTUALLY, IT'S GOODBYE.
YOU BE GOOD NOW.
IS IT SMART TO LEAVE THE VALUSIAN WITH THE TRUCK?
WE HAD TO BRING THE GOODS, AND I CAN'T RISK LEAVING IT UNATTENDED.
HE'LL BE FINE. I INSTRUCTED HIM TO TEAR THE LIMBS OFF OF ANYONE WHO APPROACHES.

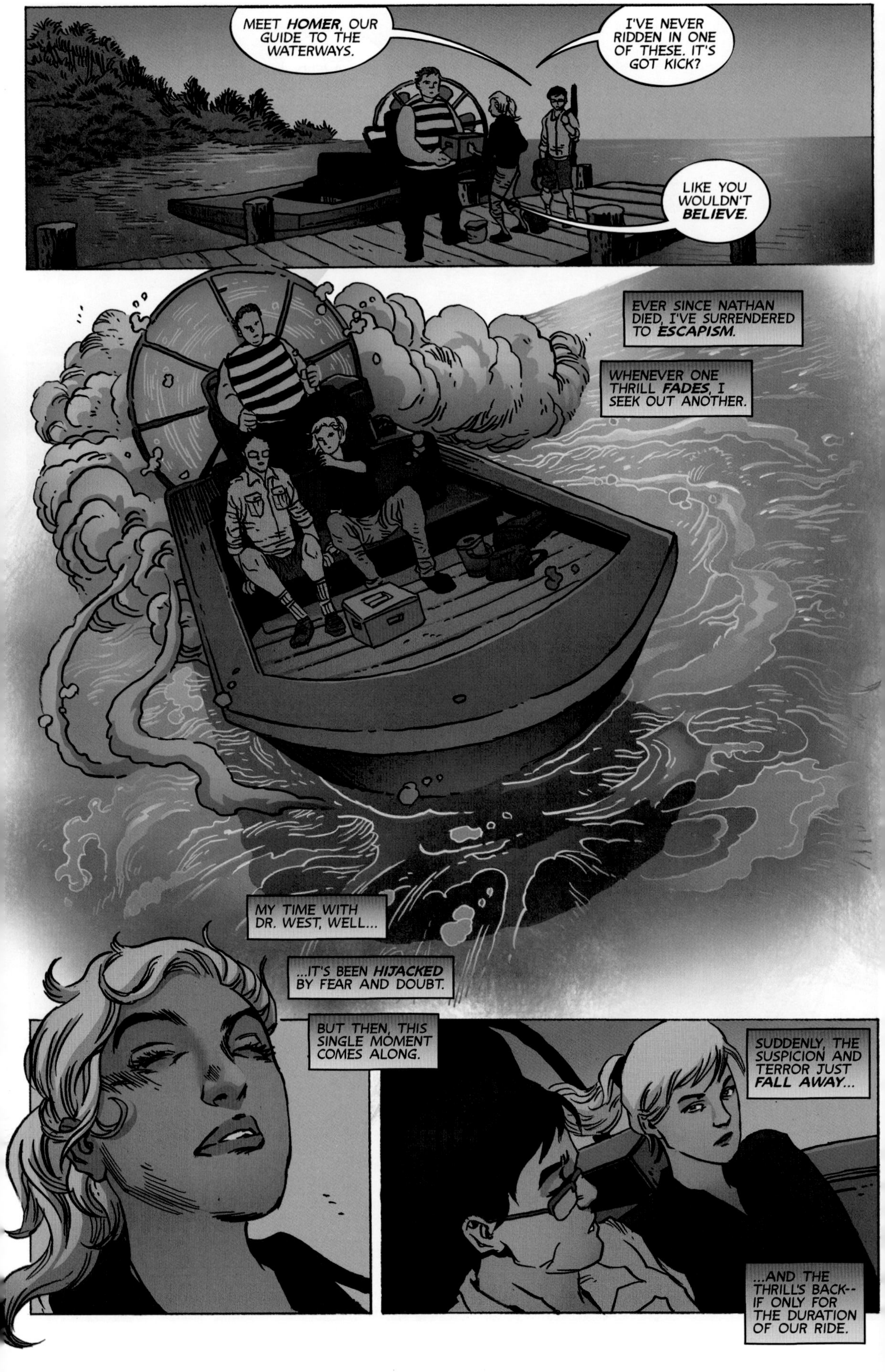
MEET HOMER, OUR GUIDE TO THE WATERWAYS.
I'VE NEVER RIDDEN IN ONE OF THESE. IT'S GOT KICK?
LIKE YOU WOULDN'T BELIEVE.
EVER SINCE NATHAN DIED, I'VE SURRENDERED TO ESCAPISM.
WHENEVER ONE THRILL FADES, I SEEK OUT ANOTHER.
MY TIME WITH DR. WEST, WELL...
...IT'S BEEN HIJACKED BY FEAR AND DOUBT.
BUT THEN, THIS SINGLE MOMENT COMES ALONG.
SUDDENLY, THE SUSPICION AND TERROR JUST FALL AWAY...
...AND THE THRILL'S BACK-- IF ONLY FOR THE DURATION OF OUR RIDE.

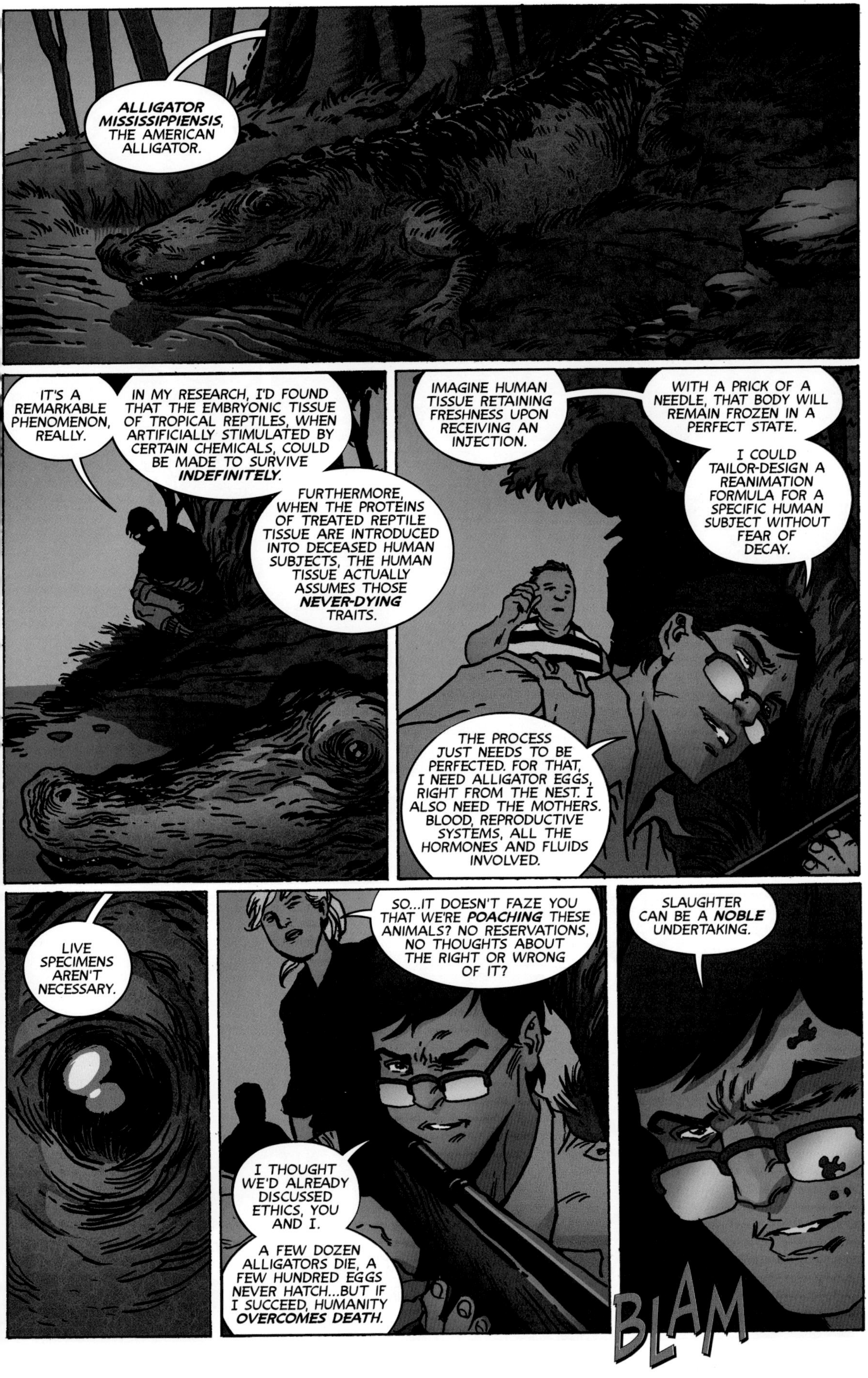
ALLIGATOR MISSISSIPPIENSIS, THE AMERICAN ALLIGATOR.
IT'S A REMARKABLE PHENOMENON, REALLY.
IN MY RESEARCH, I'D FOUND THAT THE EMBRYONIC TISSUE OF TROPICAL REPTILES, WHEN ARTIFICIALLY STIMULATED BY CERTAIN CHEMICALS, COULD BE MADE TO SURVIVE INDEFINITELY.
FURTHERMORE, WHEN THE PROTEINS OF TREATED REPTILE TISSUE ARE INTRODUCED INTO DECEASED HUMAN SUBJECTS, THE HUMAN TISSUE ACTUALLY ASSUMES THOSE NEVER-DYING TRAITS.
IMAGINE HUMAN TISSUE RETAINING FRESHNESS UPON RECEIVING AN INJECTION.
WITH A PRICK OF A NEEDLE, THAT BODY WILL REMAIN FROZEN IN A PERFECT STATE.
I COULD TAILOR-DESIGN A REANIMATION FORMULA FOR A SPECIFIC HUMAN SUBJECT WITHOUT FEAR OF DECAY.
THE PROCESS JUST NEEDS TO BE PERFECTED. FOR THAT, I NEED ALLIGATOR EGGS, RIGHT FROM THE NEST. I ALSO NEED THE MOTHERS. BLOOD, REPRODUCTIVE SYSTEMS, ALL THE HORMONES AND FLUIDS INVOLVED.
LIVE SPECIMENS AREN'T NECESSARY.
SO...IT DOESN'T FAZE YOU THAT WE'RE POACHING THESE ANIMALS? NO RESERVATIONS, NO THOUGHTS ABOUT THE RIGHT OR WRONG OF IT?
I THOUGHT WE'D ALREADY DISCUSSED ETHICS, YOU AND I.
A FEW DOZEN ALLIGATORS DIE, A FEW HUNDRED EGGS NEVER HATCH...BUT IF I SUCCEED, HUMANITY OVERCOMES DEATH.
SLAUGHTER CAN BE A NOBLE UNDERTAKING.
BLAM

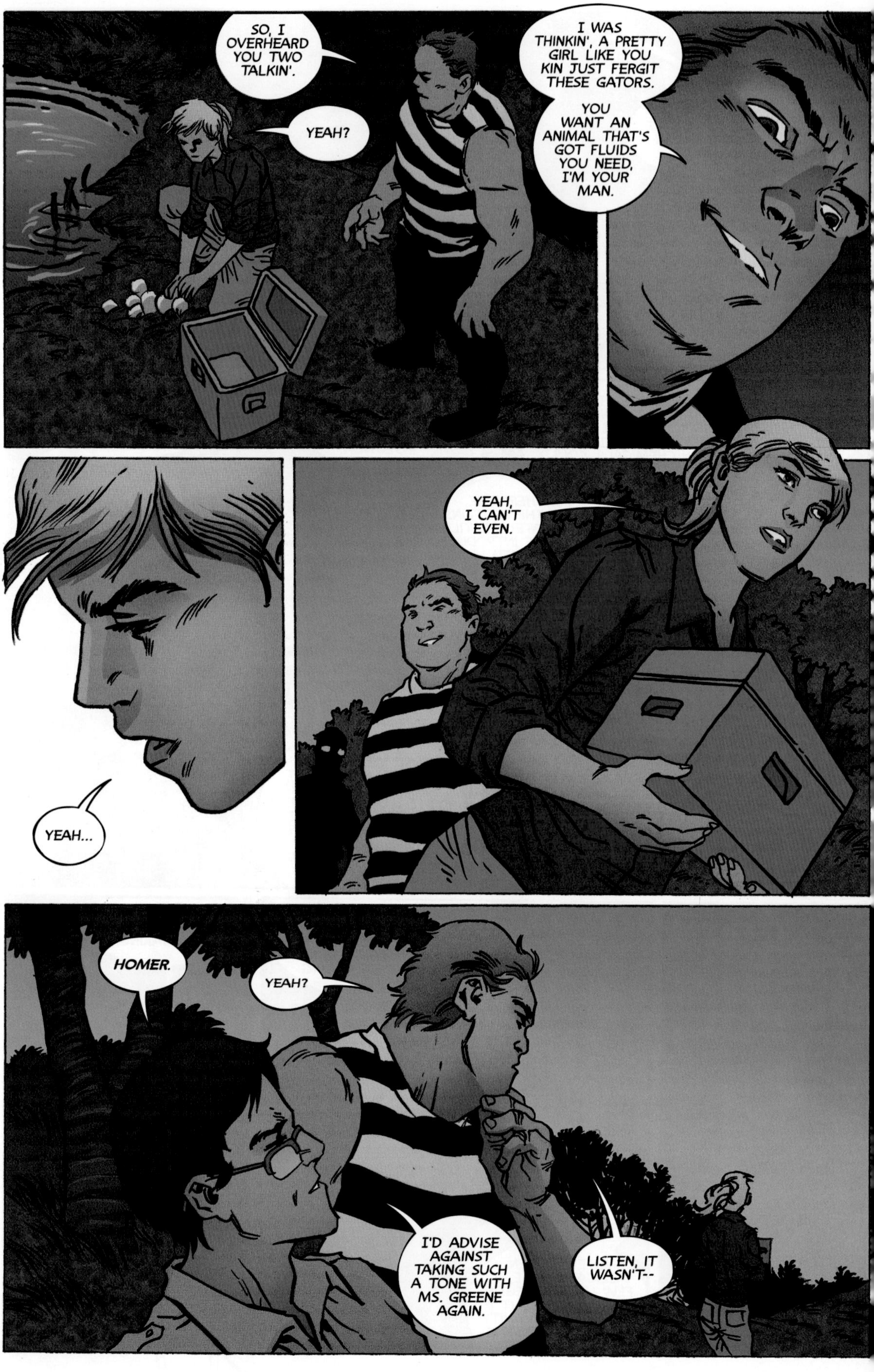
SO, I OVERHEARD YOU TWO TALKIN'.
YEAH?
I WAS THINKIN', A PRETTY GIRL LIKE YOU KIN JUST FERGIT THESE GATORS.
YOU WANT AN ANIMAL THAT'S GOT FLUIDS YOU NEED, I'M YOUR MAN.
YEAH, I CAN'T EVEN.
YEAH...
HOMER.
YEAH?
I'D ADVISE AGAINST TAKING SUCH A TONE WITH MS. GREENE AGAIN.
LISTEN, IT WASN'T--

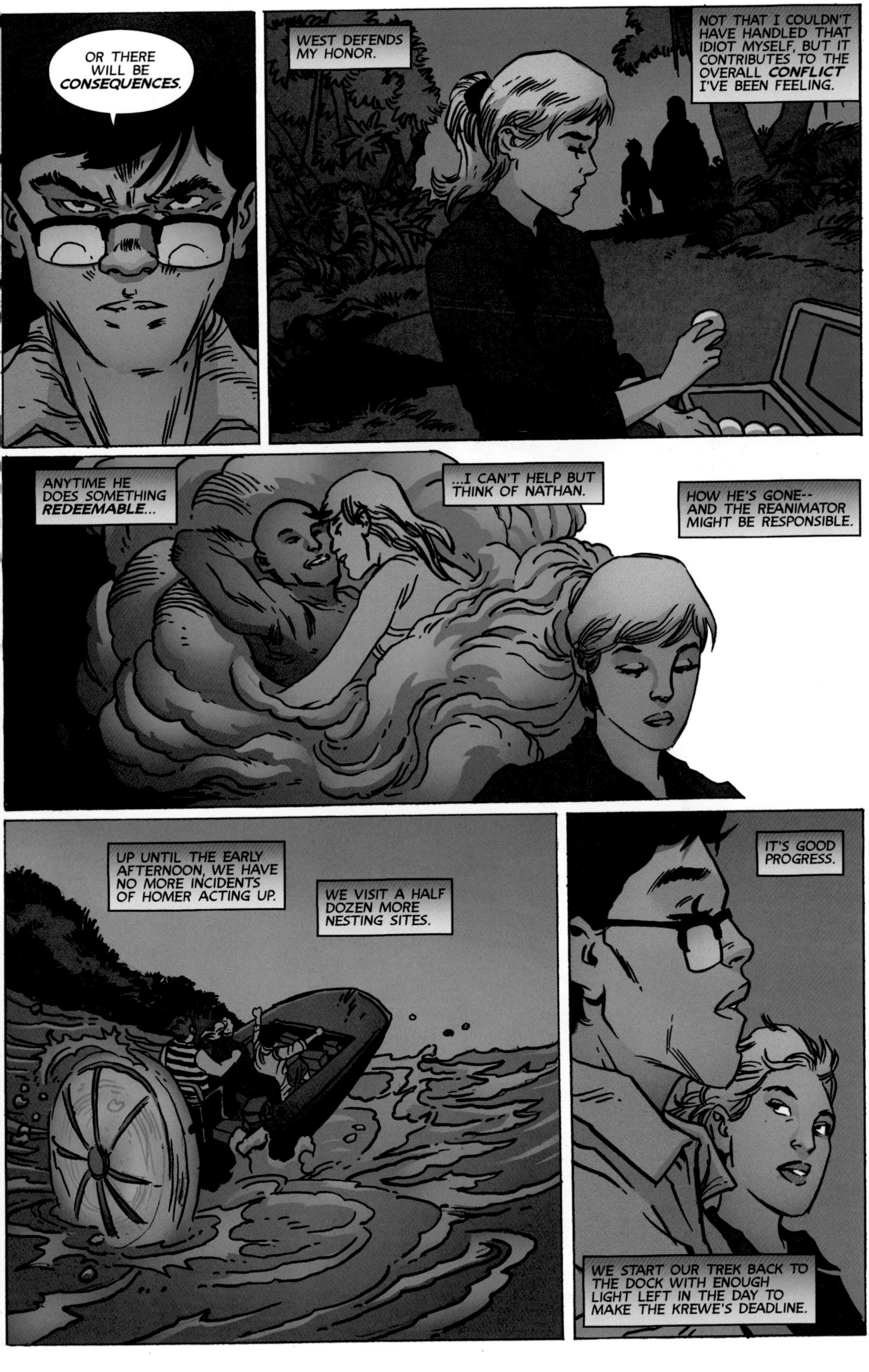
OR THERE WILL BE CONSEQUENCES.
WEST DEFENDS MY HONOR.
NOT THAT I COULDN'T HAVE HANDLED THAT IDIOT MYSELF, BUT IT CONTRIBUTES TO THE OVERALL CONFLICT I'VE BEEN FEELING.
ANYTIME HE DOES SOMETHING REDEEMABLE...
...I CAN'T HELP BUT THINK OF NATHAN.
HOW HE'S GONE-- AND THE REANIMATOR MIGHT BE RESPONSIBLE.
UP UNTIL THE EARLY AFTERNOON, WE HAVE NO MORE INCIDENTS OF HOMER ACTING UP.
WE VISIT A HALF DOZEN MORE NESTING SITES.
IT'S GOOD PROGRESS.
WE START OUR TREK BACK TO THE DOCK WITH ENOUGH LIGHT LEFT IN THE DAY TO MAKE THE KREWE'S DEADLINE.

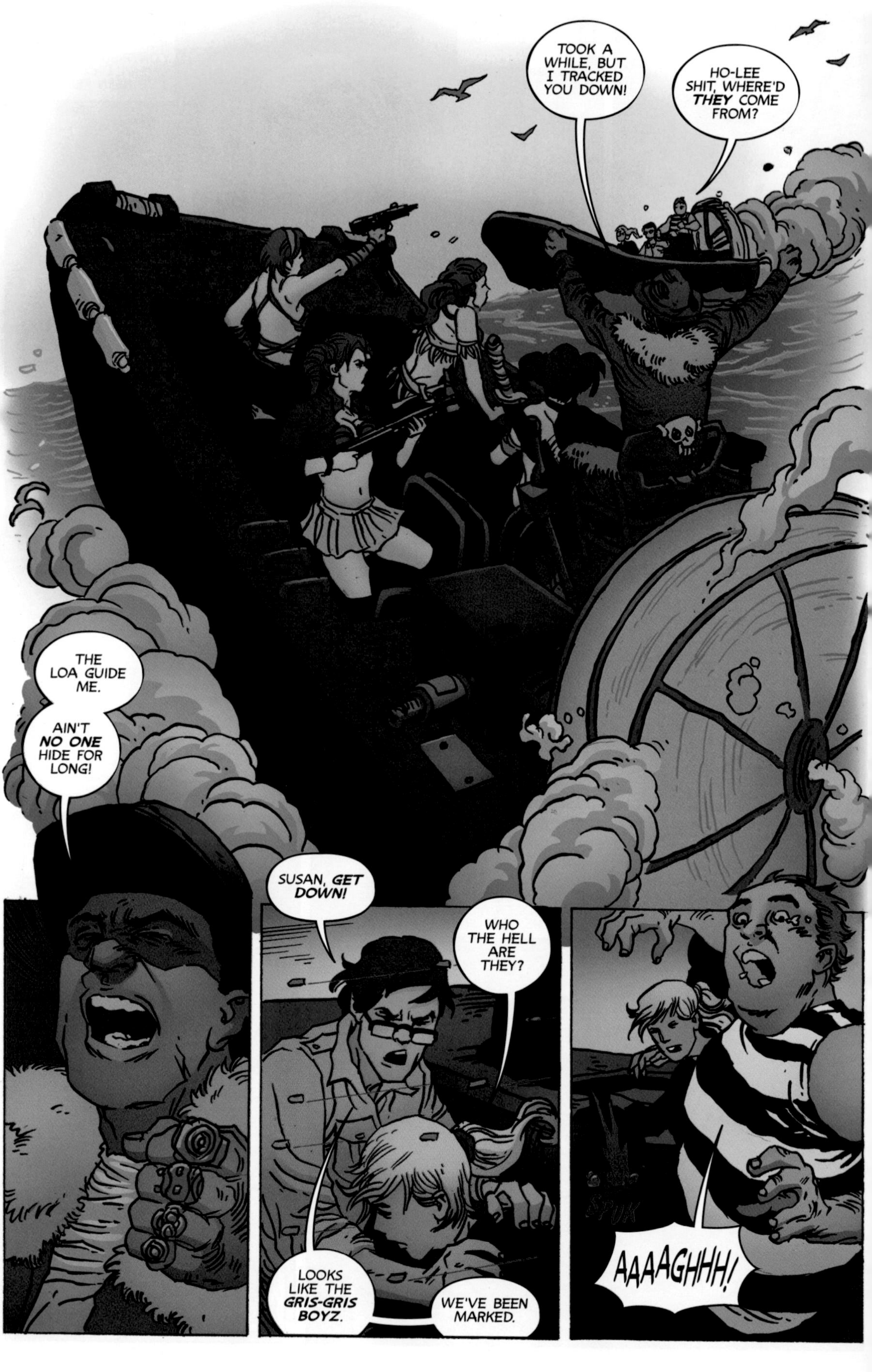
TOOK A WHILE, BUT I TRACKED YOU DOWN!
HO-LEE SHIT, WHERE'D *THEY* COME FROM?
THE LOA GUIDE ME.
AIN'T *NO ONE* HIDE FOR LONG!
SUSAN, *GET DOWN!*
WHO THE HELL ARE THEY?
LOOKS LIKE THE *GRIS-GRIS* BOYZ.
WE'VE BEEN MARKED.
AAAAGHHH!

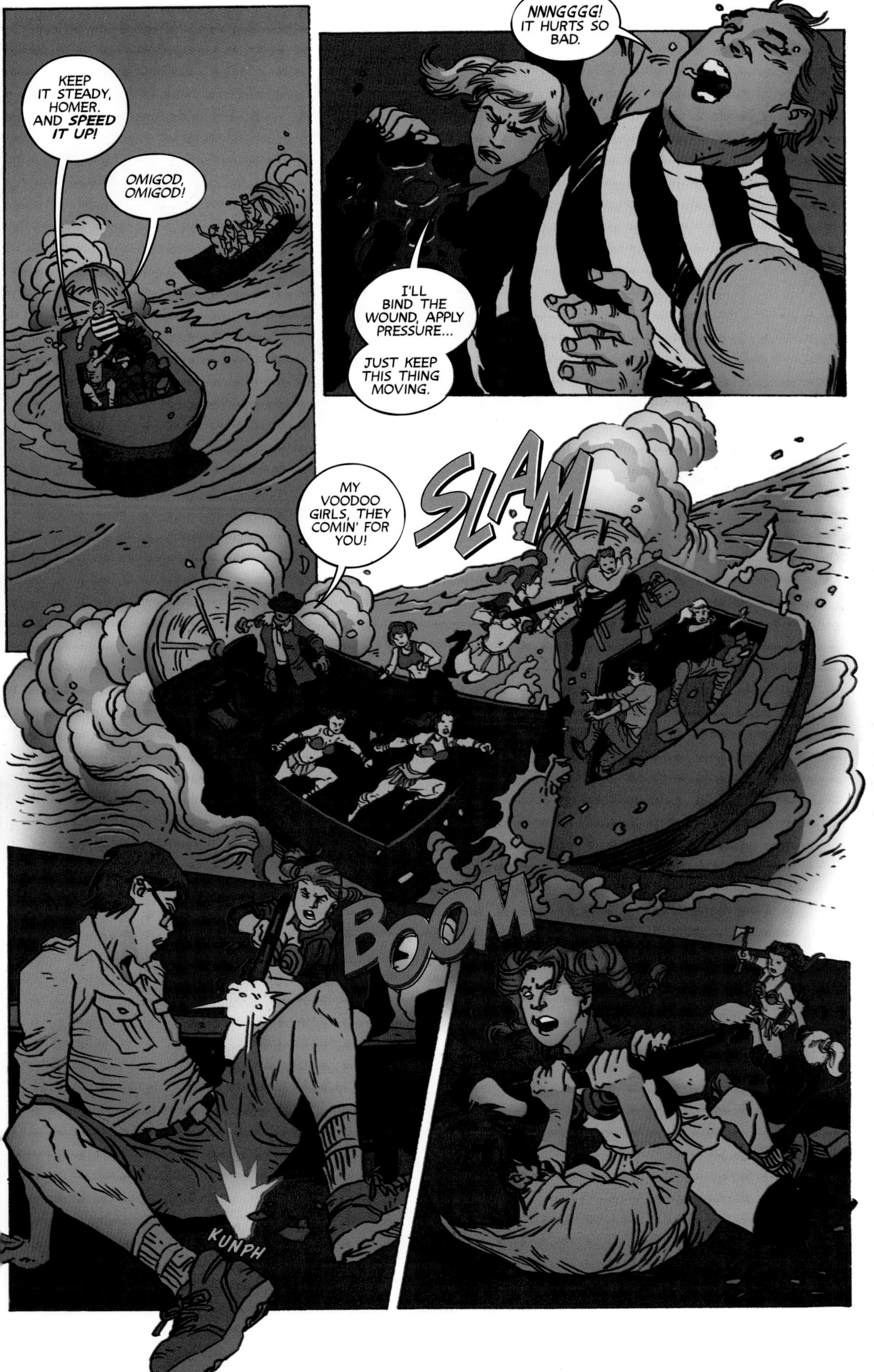
KEEP IT STEADY, HOMER. AND SPEED IT UP!
OMIGOD, OMIGOD!
NNNGGGG! IT HURTS SO BAD.
I'LL BIND THE WOUND, APPLY PRESSURE...
JUST KEEP THIS THING MOVING.
SLAM
MY VOODOO GIRLS, THEY COMIN' FOR YOU!
BOOM
KUNPH

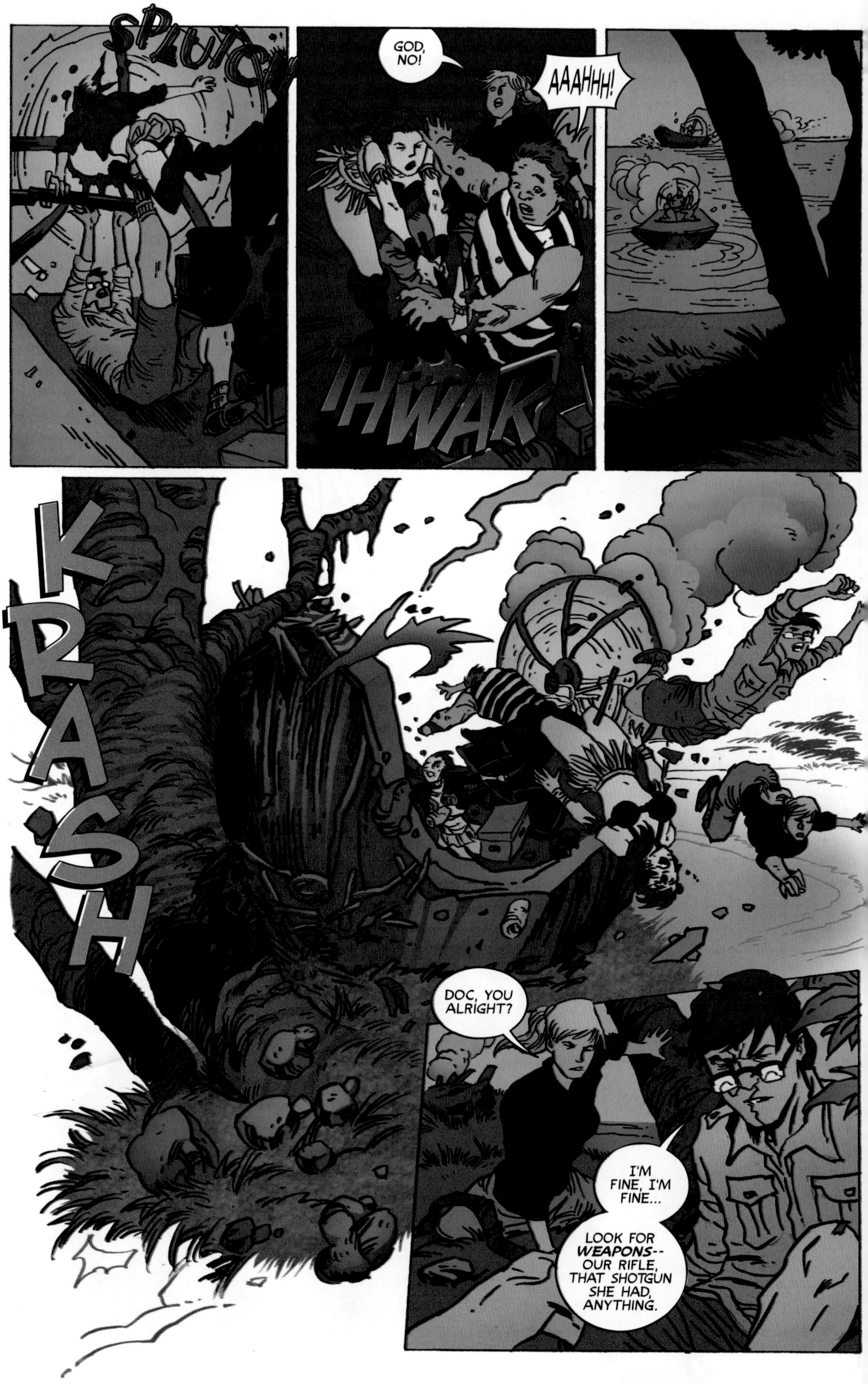
SPLUTCH
GOD, NO!
AAAHHH!
THWAK
KRASH
DOC, YOU ALRIGHT?
I'M FINE, I'M FINE...
LOOK FOR WEAPONS-- OUR RIFLE, THAT SHOTGUN SHE HAD, ANYTHING.

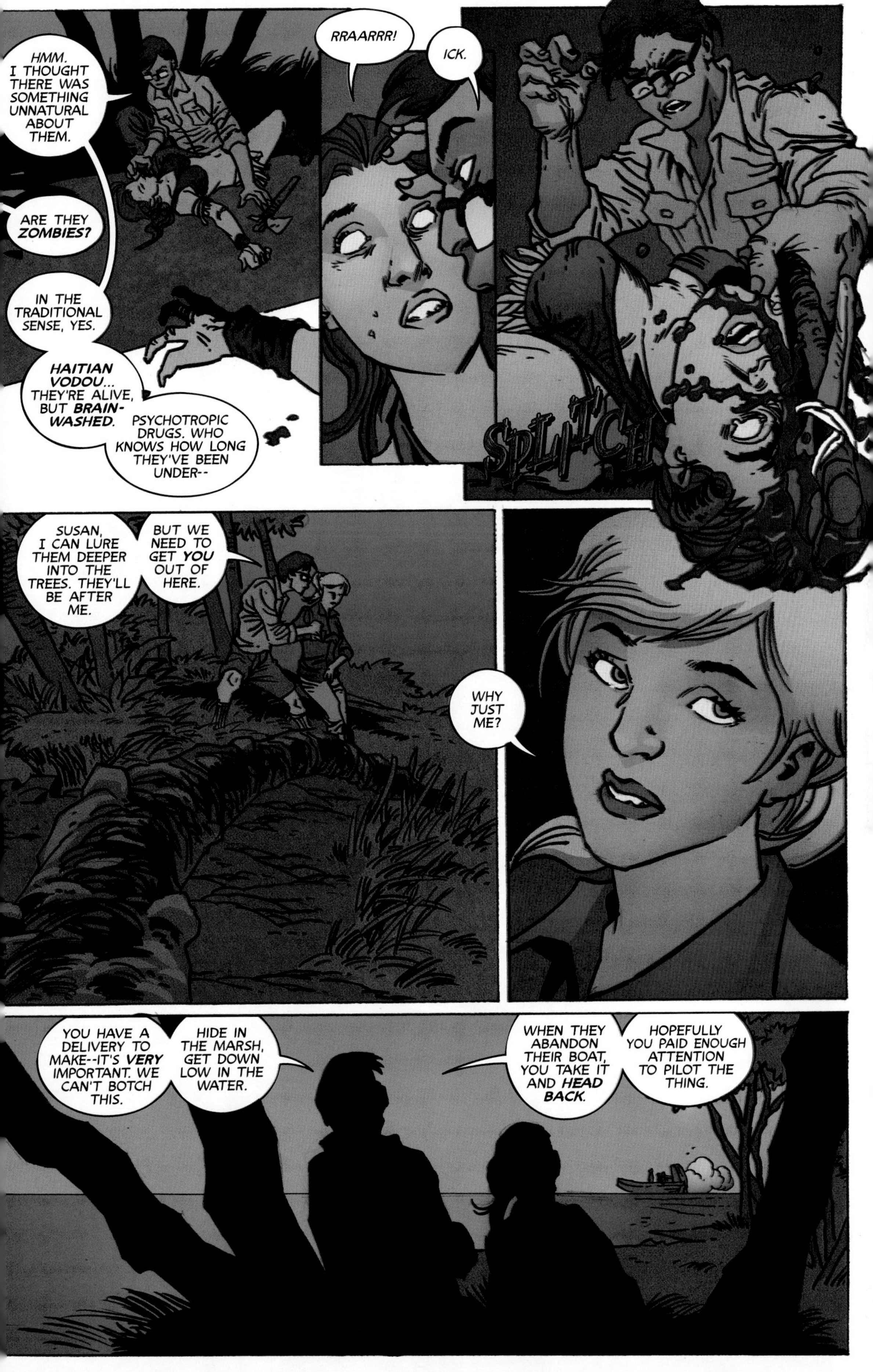
HMM. I THOUGHT THERE WAS SOMETHING UNNATURAL ABOUT THEM.
ARE THEY *ZOMBIES?*
IN THE TRADITIONAL SENSE, YES.
HAITIAN VODOU... THEY'RE ALIVE, BUT *BRAIN-WASHED.*
PSYCHOTROPIC DRUGS. WHO KNOWS HOW LONG THEY'VE BEEN UNDER--
RRAARRR!
ICK.
SPLITCH
SUSAN, I CAN LURE THEM DEEPER INTO THE TREES. THEY'LL BE AFTER ME.
BUT WE NEED TO GET *YOU* OUT OF HERE.
WHY JUST ME?
YOU HAVE A DELIVERY TO MAKE--IT'S *VERY* IMPORTANT. WE CAN'T BOTCH THIS.
HIDE IN THE MARSH, GET DOWN LOW IN THE WATER.
WHEN THEY ABANDON THEIR BOAT, YOU TAKE IT AND *HEAD BACK.*
HOPEFULLY YOU PAID ENOUGH ATTENTION TO PILOT THE THING.

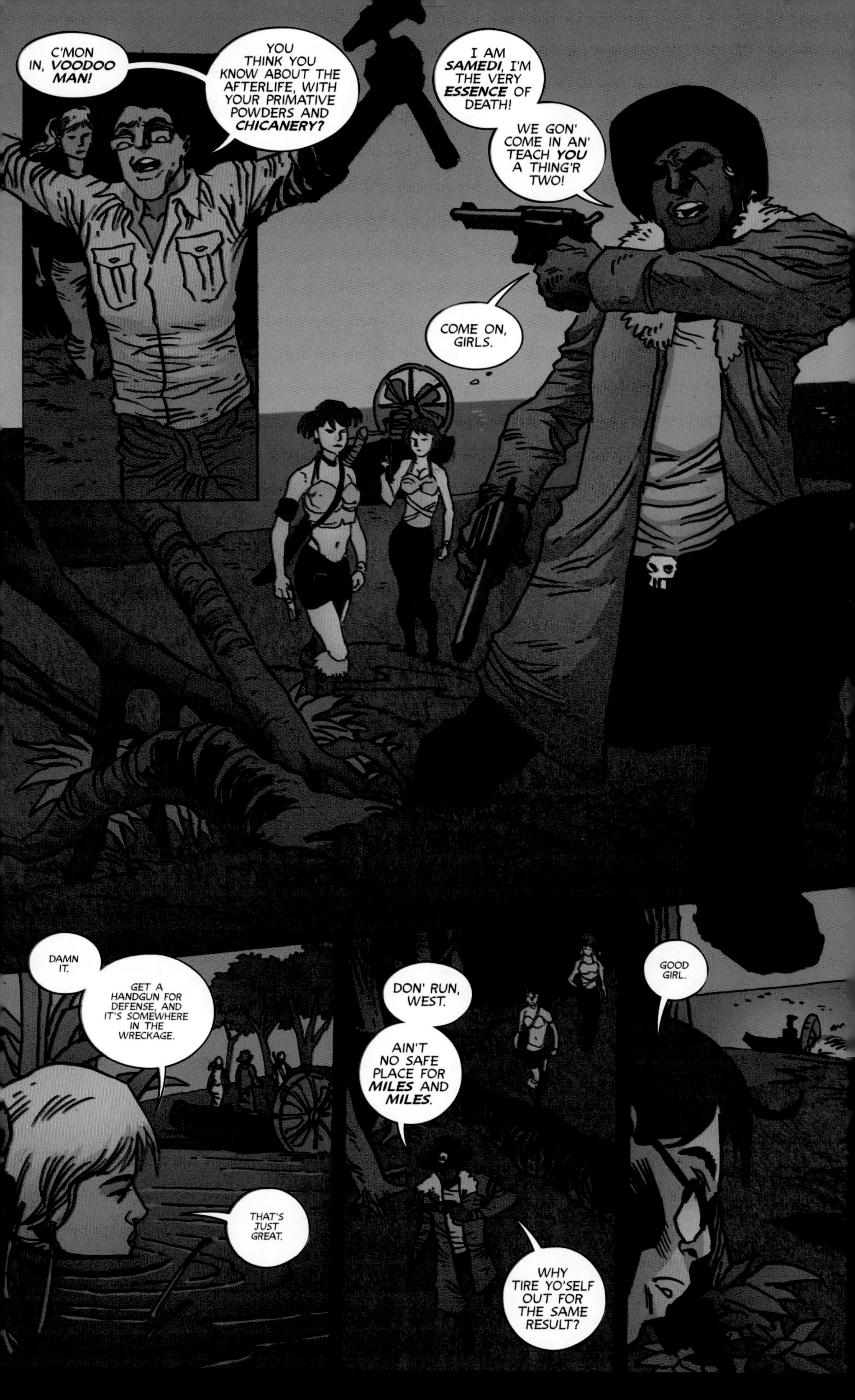
C'MON IN, VOODOO MAN!
YOU THINK YOU KNOW ABOUT THE AFTERLIFE, WITH YOUR PRIMATIVE POWDERS AND CHICANERY?
I AM SAMEDI, I'M THE VERY ESSENCE OF DEATH!
WE GON' COME IN AN' TEACH YOU A THING'R TWO!
COME ON, GIRLS.
DAMN IT.
GET A HANDGUN FOR DEFENSE, AND IT'S SOMEWHERE IN THE WRECKAGE.
THAT'S JUST GREAT.
DON' RUN, WEST.
AIN'T NO SAFE PLACE FOR MILES AND MILES.
WHY TIRE YO'SELF OUT FOR THE SAME RESULT?
GOOD GIRL.

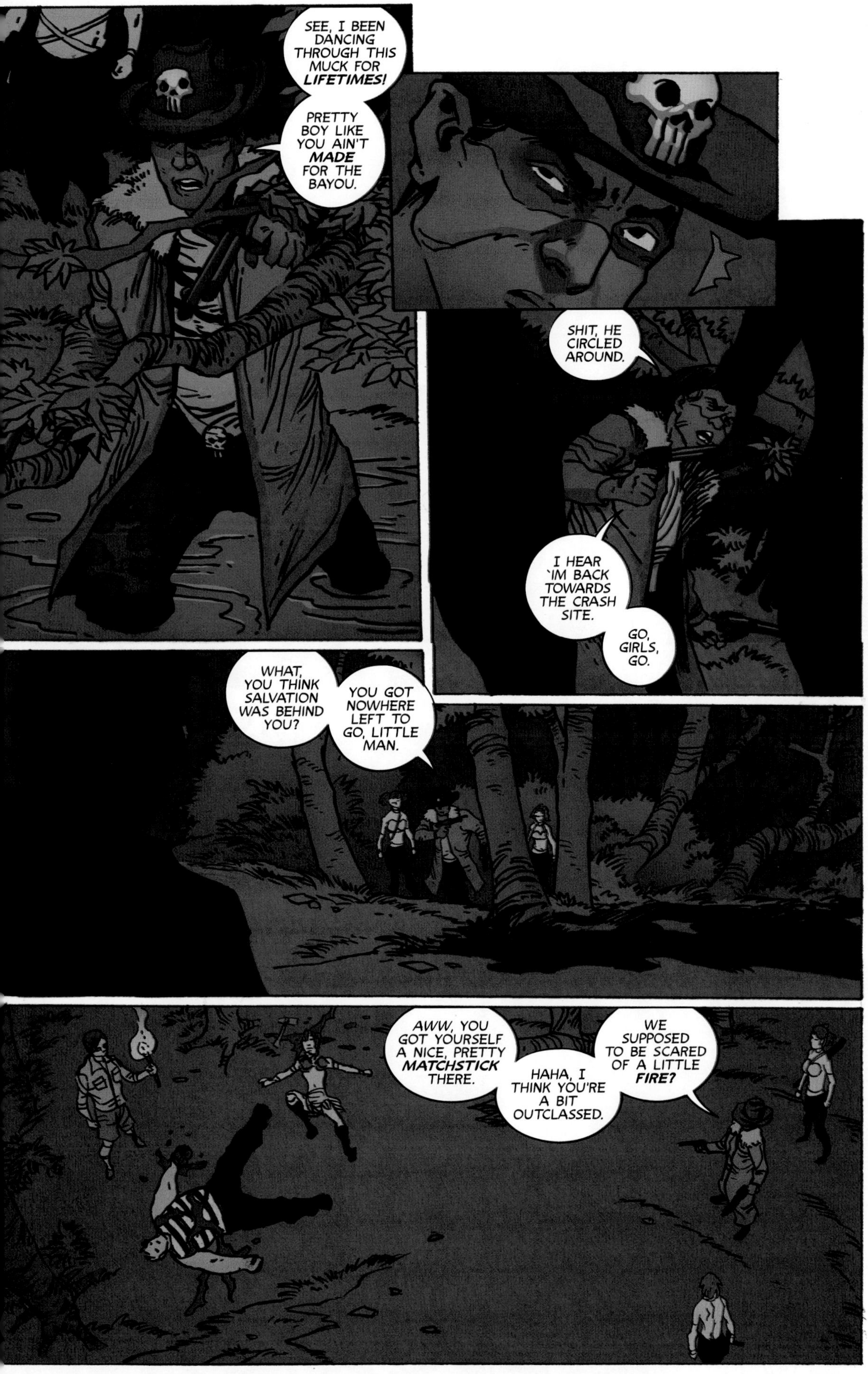
SEE, I BEEN DANCING THROUGH THIS MUCK FOR LIFETIMES!
PRETTY BOY LIKE YOU AIN'T MADE FOR THE BAYOU.
SHIT, HE CIRCLED AROUND.
I HEAR `IM BACK TOWARDS THE CRASH SITE.
GO, GIRLS, GO.
WHAT, YOU THINK SALVATION WAS BEHIND YOU?
YOU GOT NOWHERE LEFT TO GO, LITTLE MAN.
AWW, YOU GOT YOURSELF A NICE, PRETTY MATCHSTICK THERE.
HAHA, I THINK YOU'RE A BIT OUTCLASSED.
WE SUPPOSED TO BE SCARED OF A LITTLE FIRE?

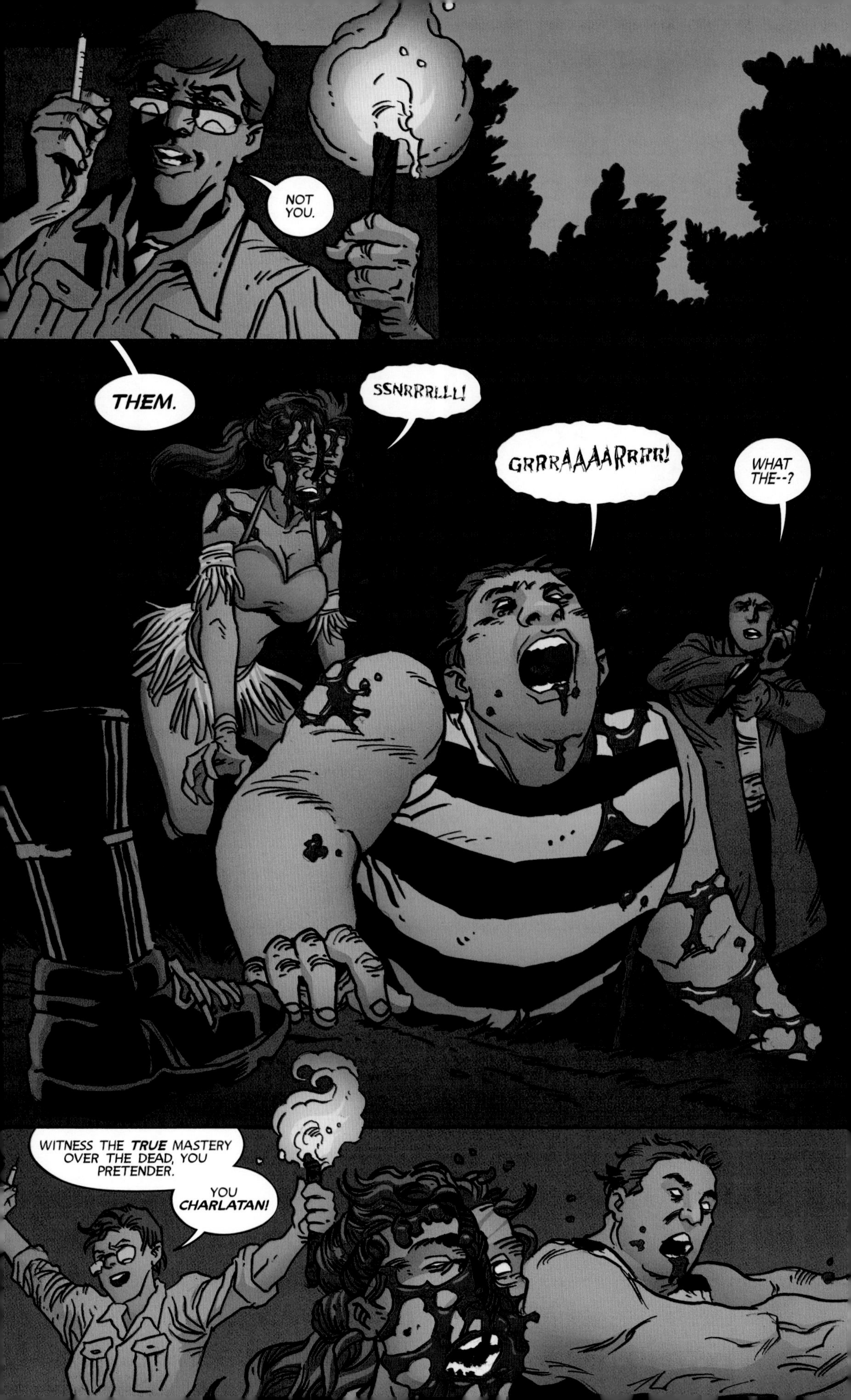
NOT YOU.
THEM.
SSNRRRLLL!
GRRRAAAARRRR!
WHAT THE--?
WITNESS THE **TRUE** MASTERY OVER THE DEAD, YOU PRETENDER.
YOU **CHARLATAN!**

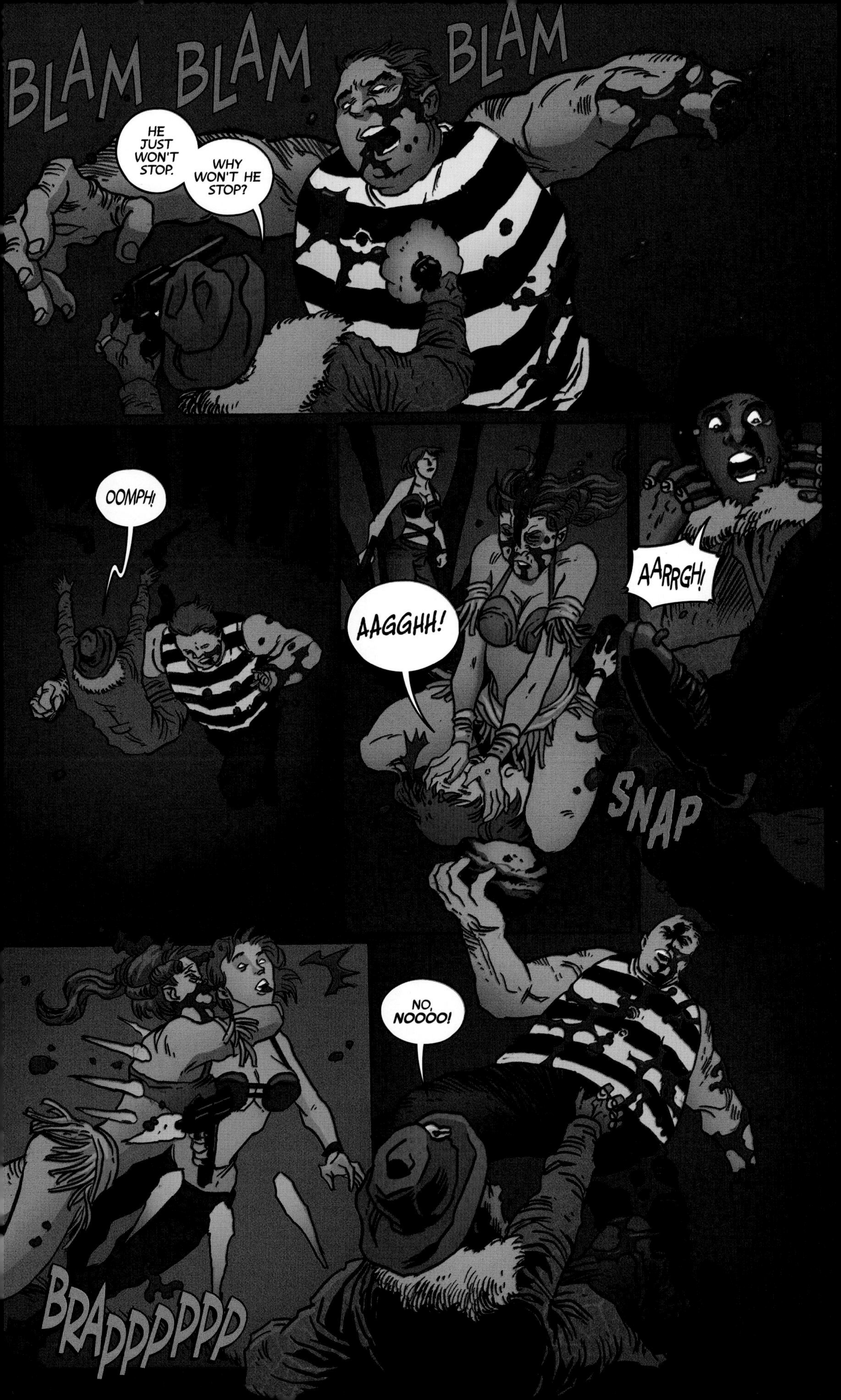
BLAM BLAM
BLAM
HE JUST WON'T STOP.
WHY WON'T HE STOP?
OOMPH!
AAGGHH!
AARRGH!
SNAP
NO, NOOOO!
BRAPPPPPP

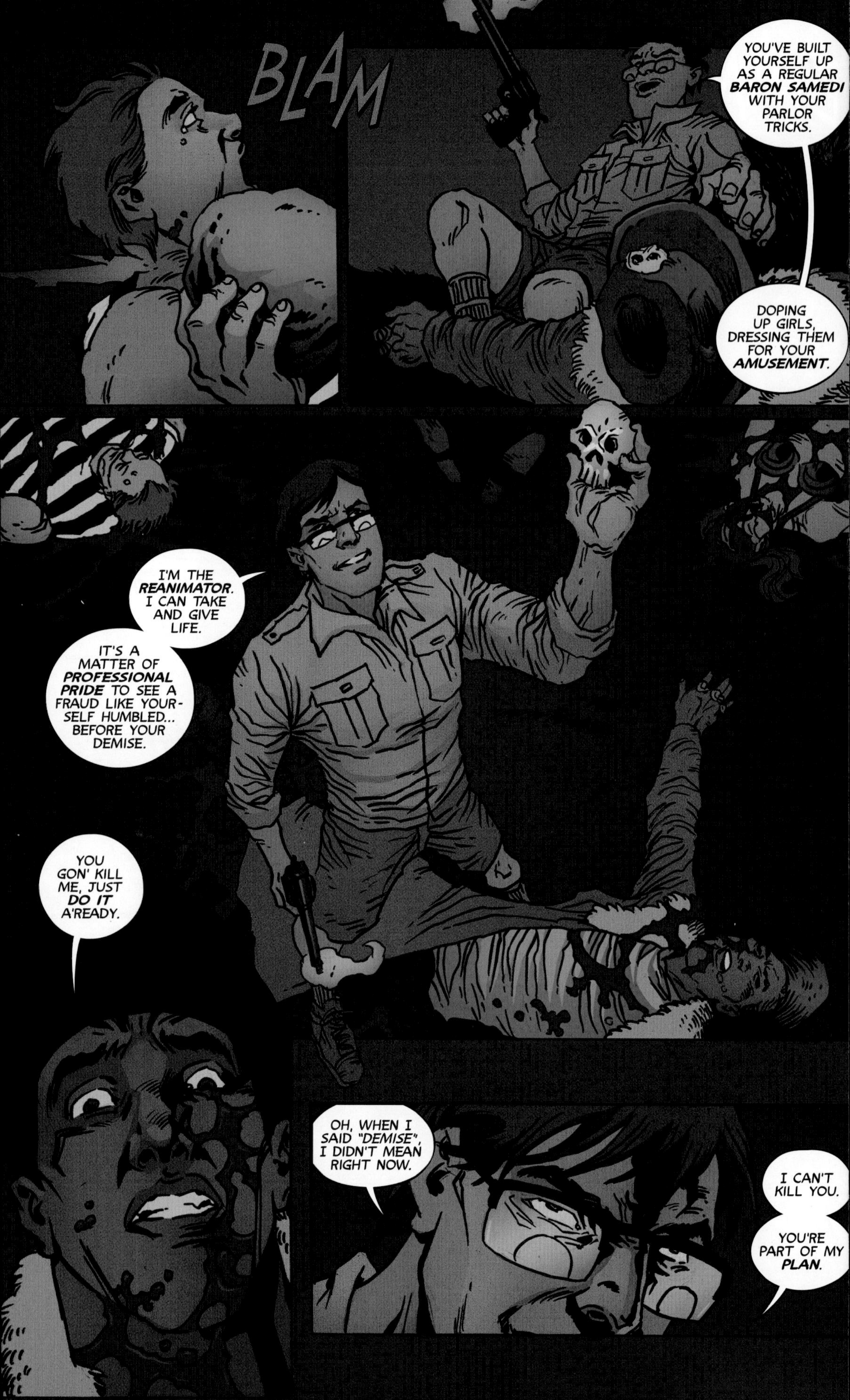
BLAM
YOU'VE BUILT YOURSELF UP AS A REGULAR **BARON SAMEDI** WITH YOUR PARLOR TRICKS.
DOPING UP GIRLS, DRESSING THEM FOR YOUR **AMUSEMENT**.
I'M THE **REANIMATOR**. I CAN TAKE AND GIVE LIFE.
IT'S A MATTER OF **PROFESSIONAL PRIDE** TO SEE A FRAUD LIKE YOUR-SELF HUMBLED... BEFORE YOUR DEMISE.
YOU GON' KILL ME, JUST **DO IT** A'READY.
OH, WHEN I SAID "*DEMISE*", I DIDN'T MEAN RIGHT NOW.
I CAN'T KILL YOU.
YOU'RE PART OF MY **PLAN**.

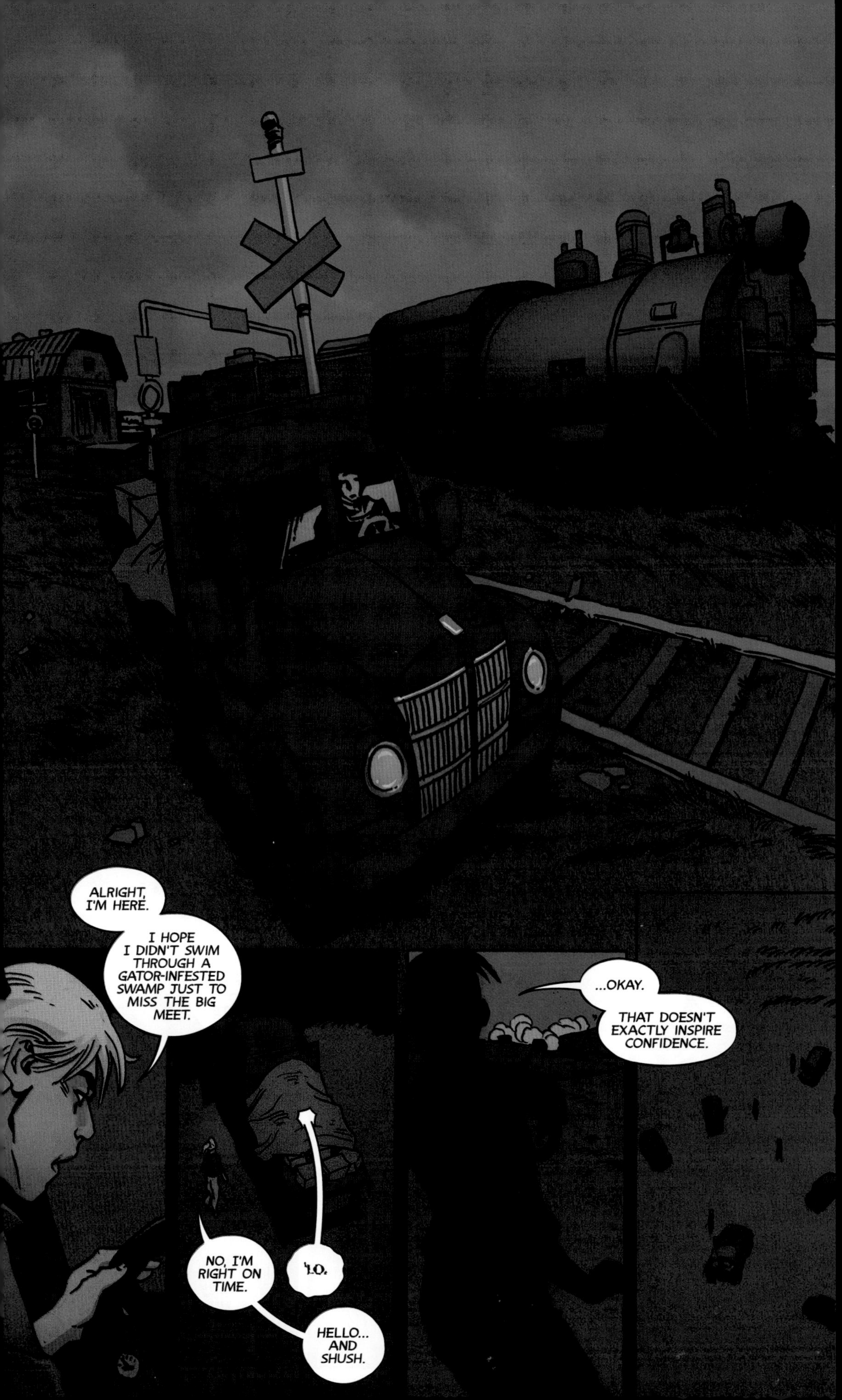
ALRIGHT, I'M HERE.
I HOPE I DIDN'T SWIM THROUGH A GATOR-INFESTED SWAMP JUST TO MISS THE BIG MEET.
NO, I'M RIGHT ON TIME.
YO.
HELLO... AND SHUSH.
...OKAY.
THAT DOESN'T EXACTLY INSPIRE CONFIDENCE.

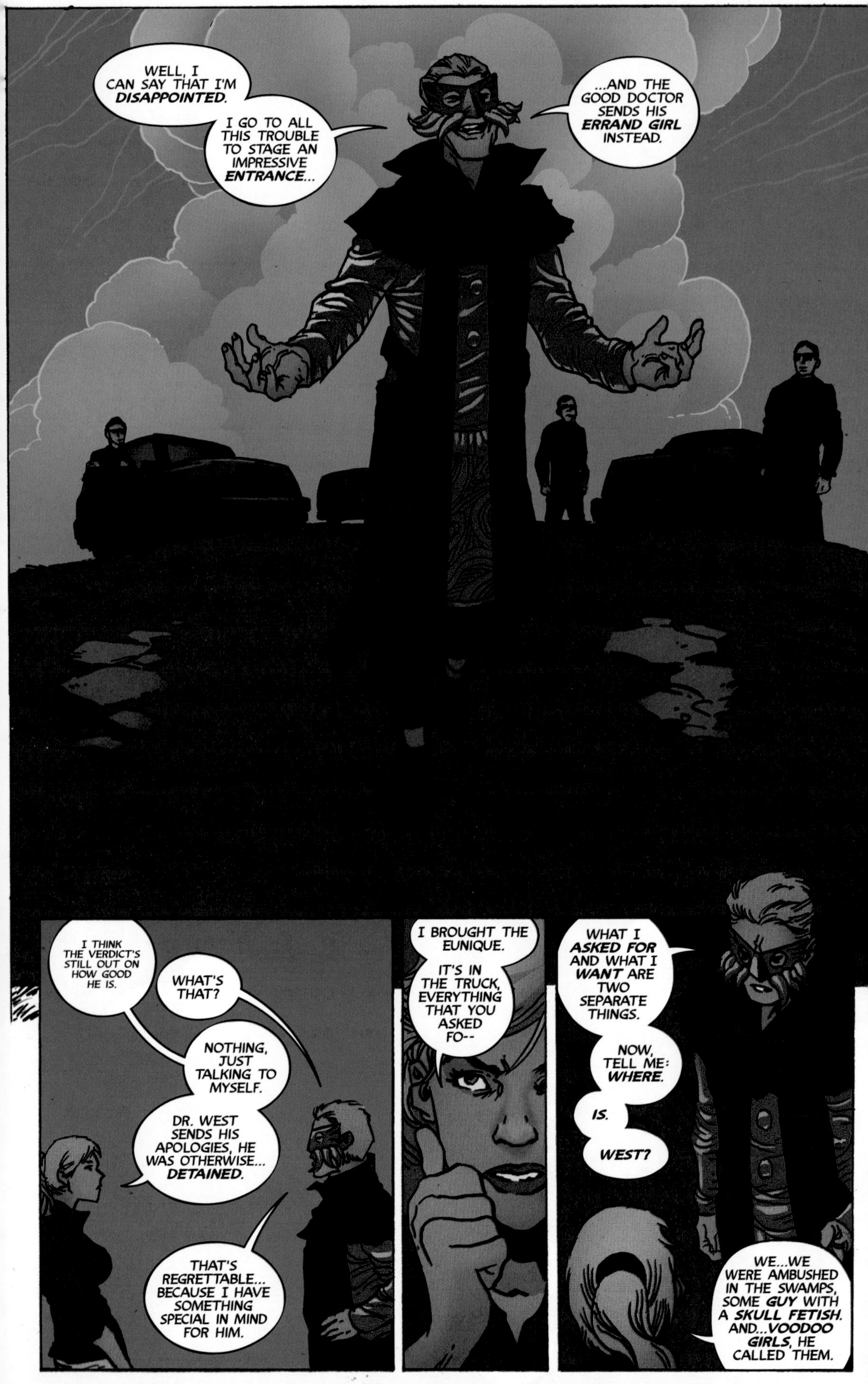

WELL, I CAN SAY THAT I'M DISAPPOINTED.
I GO TO ALL THIS TROUBLE TO STAGE AN IMPRESSIVE ENTRANCE...
...AND THE GOOD DOCTOR SENDS HIS ERRAND GIRL INSTEAD.
I THINK THE VERDICT'S STILL OUT ON HOW GOOD HE IS.
WHAT'S THAT?
NOTHING, JUST TALKING TO MYSELF.
DR. WEST SENDS HIS APOLOGIES, HE WAS OTHERWISE... DETAINED.
THAT'S REGRETTABLE... BECAUSE I HAVE SOMETHING SPECIAL IN MIND FOR HIM.
I BROUGHT THE EUNIQUE.
IT'S IN THE TRUCK, EVERYTHING THAT YOU ASKED FO--
WHAT I ASKED FOR AND WHAT I WANT ARE TWO SEPARATE THINGS.
NOW, TELL ME: WHERE.
IS.
WEST?
WE...WE WERE AMBUSHED IN THE SWAMPS, SOME GUY WITH A SKULL FETISH. AND...VOODOO GIRLS, HE CALLED THEM.

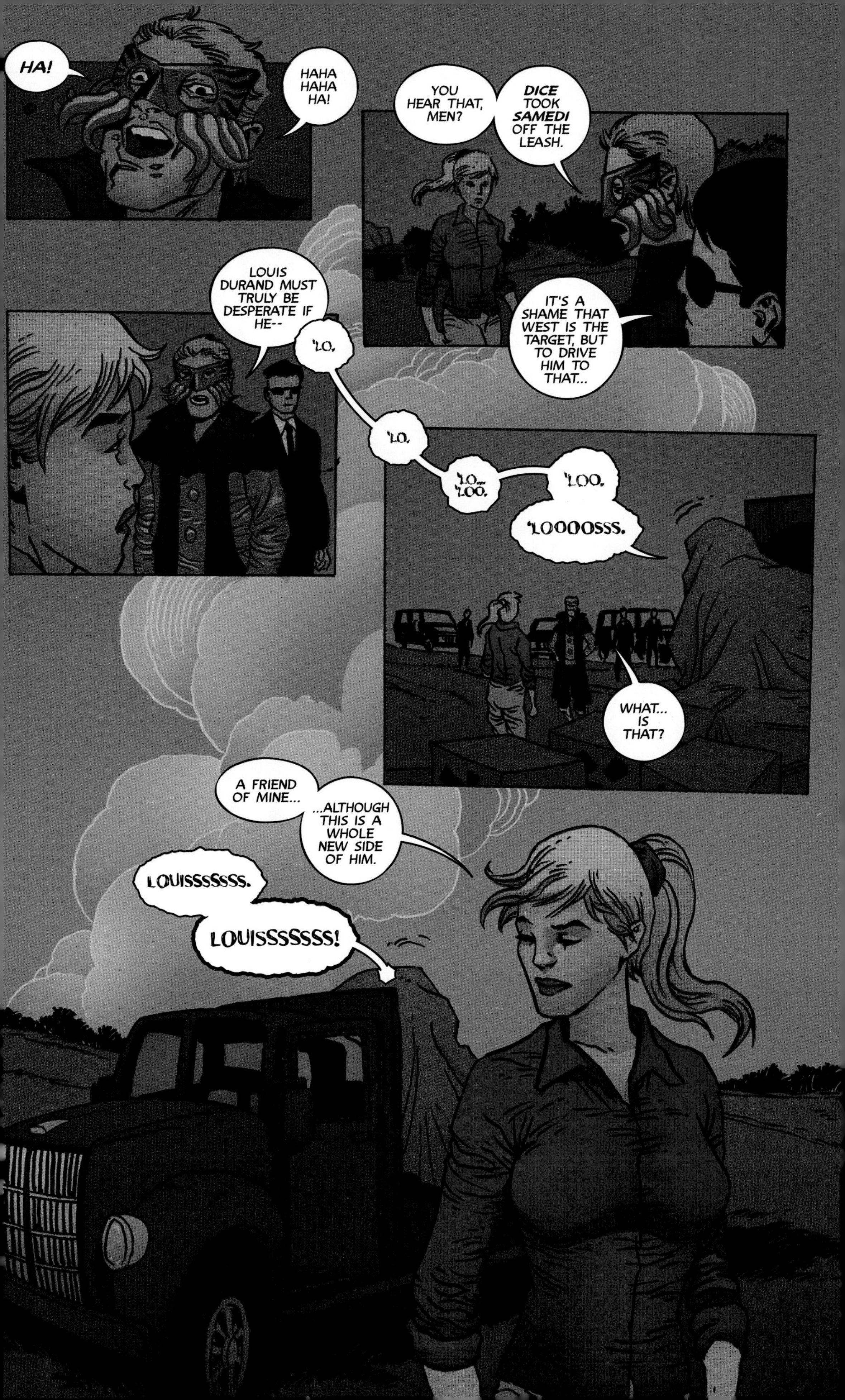
HA!
HAHA HAHA HA!
YOU HEAR THAT, MEN?
DICE TOOK SAMEDI OFF THE LEASH.
IT'S A SHAME THAT WEST IS THE TARGET, BUT TO DRIVE HIM TO THAT...
LOUIS DURAND MUST TRULY BE DESPERATE IF HE--
'LO.
'LO.
'LO... 'LOO.
'LOO.
'LOOOOSSS.
WHAT... IS THAT?
A FRIEND OF MINE...
...ALTHOUGH THIS IS A WHOLE NEW SIDE OF HIM.
LOUISSSSSSS.
LOUISSSSSSS!

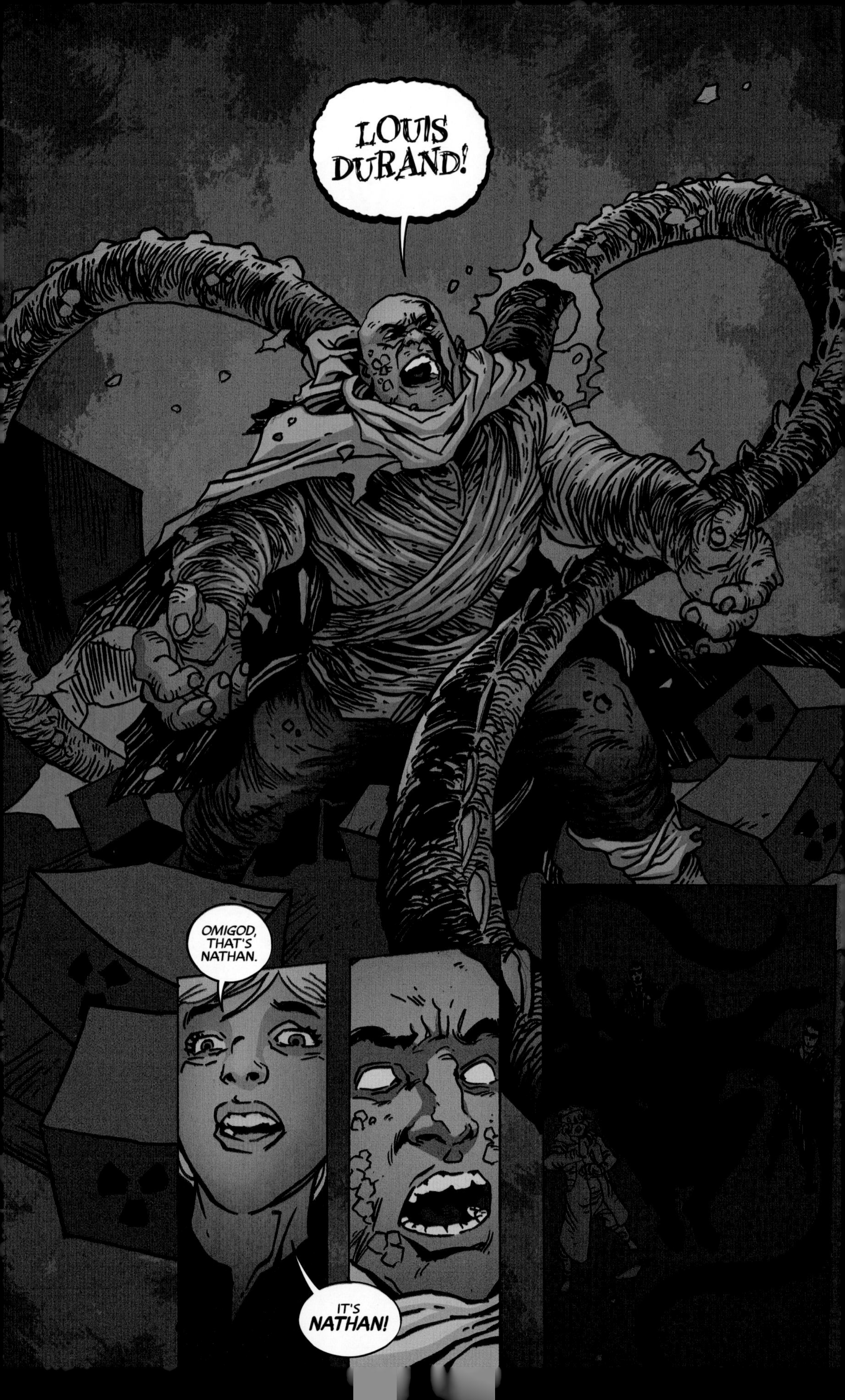
LOUIS DURAND!
OMIGOD, THAT'S NATHAN.
IT'S NATHAN!

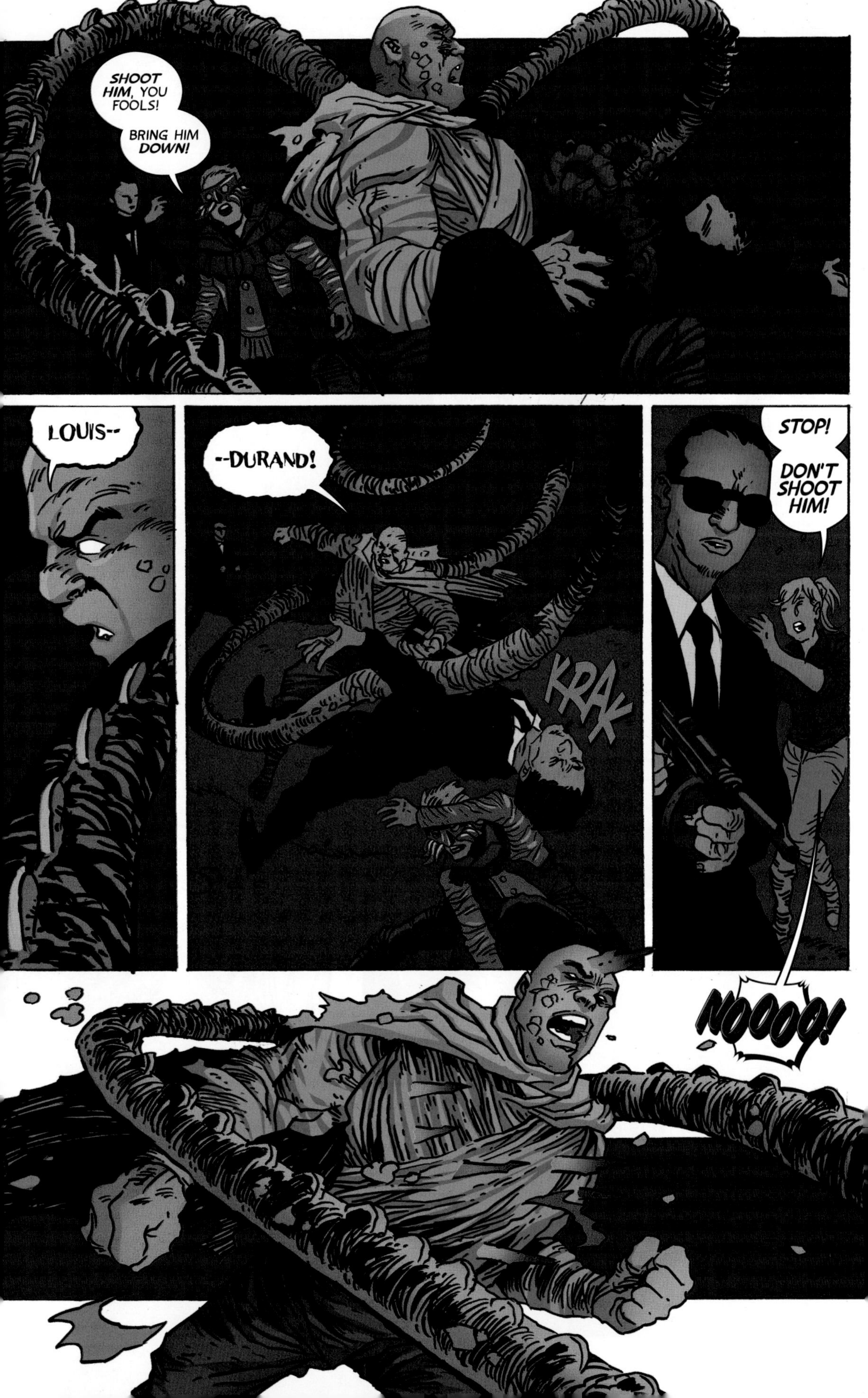
SHOOT HIM, YOU FOOLS!
BRING HIM DOWN!
LOUIS--
--DURAND!
KRAK
STOP!
DON'T SHOOT HIM!
NOOOO!

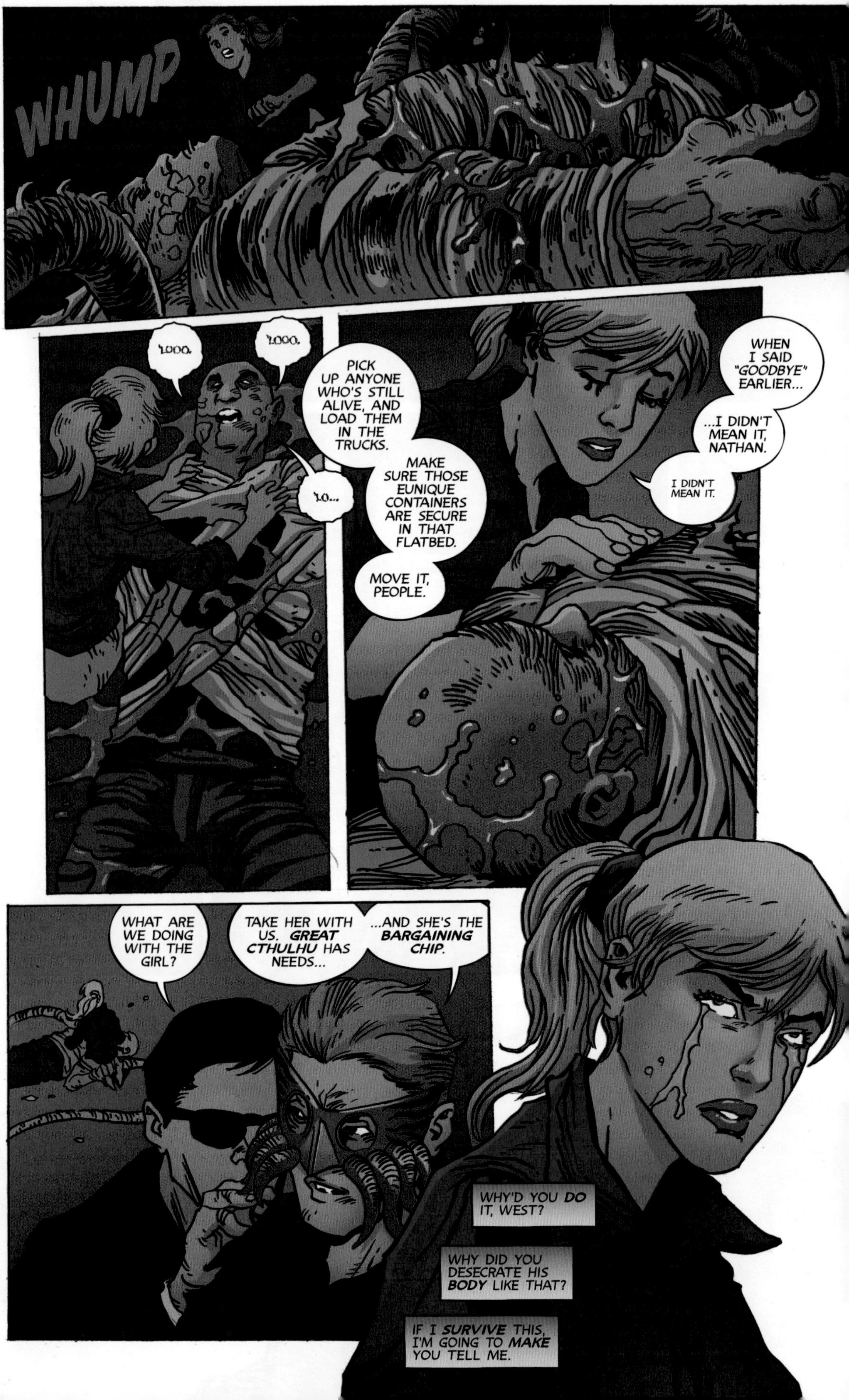
WHUMP
PICK UP ANYONE WHO'S STILL ALIVE, AND LOAD THEM IN THE TRUCKS.
MAKE SURE THOSE EUNIQUE CONTAINERS ARE SECURE IN THAT FLATBED.
MOVE IT, PEOPLE.
WHEN I SAID "GOODBYE" EARLIER...
...I DIDN'T MEAN IT, NATHAN.
I DIDN'T MEAN IT.
WHAT ARE WE DOING WITH THE GIRL?
TAKE HER WITH US. GREAT CTHULHU HAS NEEDS...
...AND SHE'S THE BARGAINING CHIP.
WHY'D YOU DO IT, WEST?
WHY DID YOU DESECRATE HIS BODY LIKE THAT?
IF I SURVIVE THIS, I'M GOING TO MAKE YOU TELL ME.

GREWSOME TALES

THREE

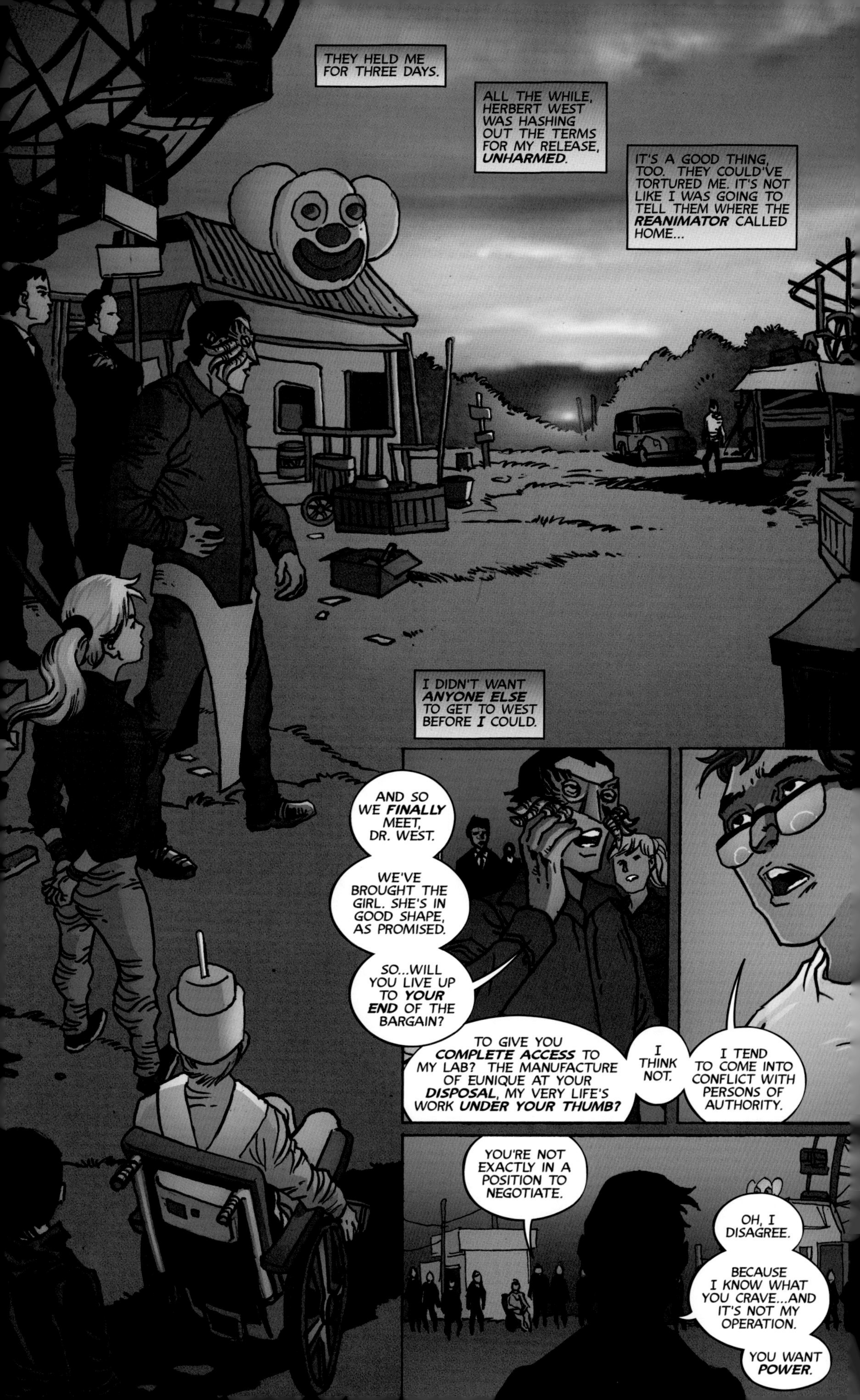
THEY HELD ME FOR THREE DAYS.
ALL THE WHILE, HERBERT WEST WAS HASHING OUT THE TERMS FOR MY RELEASE, UNHARMED.
IT'S A GOOD THING, TOO. THEY COULD'VE TORTURED ME. IT'S NOT LIKE I WAS GOING TO TELL THEM WHERE THE REANIMATOR CALLED HOME...
I DIDN'T WANT ANYONE ELSE TO GET TO WEST BEFORE I COULD.
AND SO WE FINALLY MEET, DR. WEST.
WE'VE BROUGHT THE GIRL. SHE'S IN GOOD SHAPE, AS PROMISED.
SO...WILL YOU LIVE UP TO YOUR END OF THE BARGAIN?
TO GIVE YOU COMPLETE ACCESS TO MY LAB? THE MANUFACTURE OF EUNIQUE AT YOUR DISPOSAL, MY VERY LIFE'S WORK UNDER YOUR THUMB?
I THINK NOT.
I TEND TO COME INTO CONFLICT WITH PERSONS OF AUTHORITY.
YOU'RE NOT EXACTLY IN A POSITION TO NEGOTIATE.
OH, I DISAGREE.
BECAUSE I KNOW WHAT YOU CRAVE...AND IT'S NOT MY OPERATION.
YOU WANT POWER.

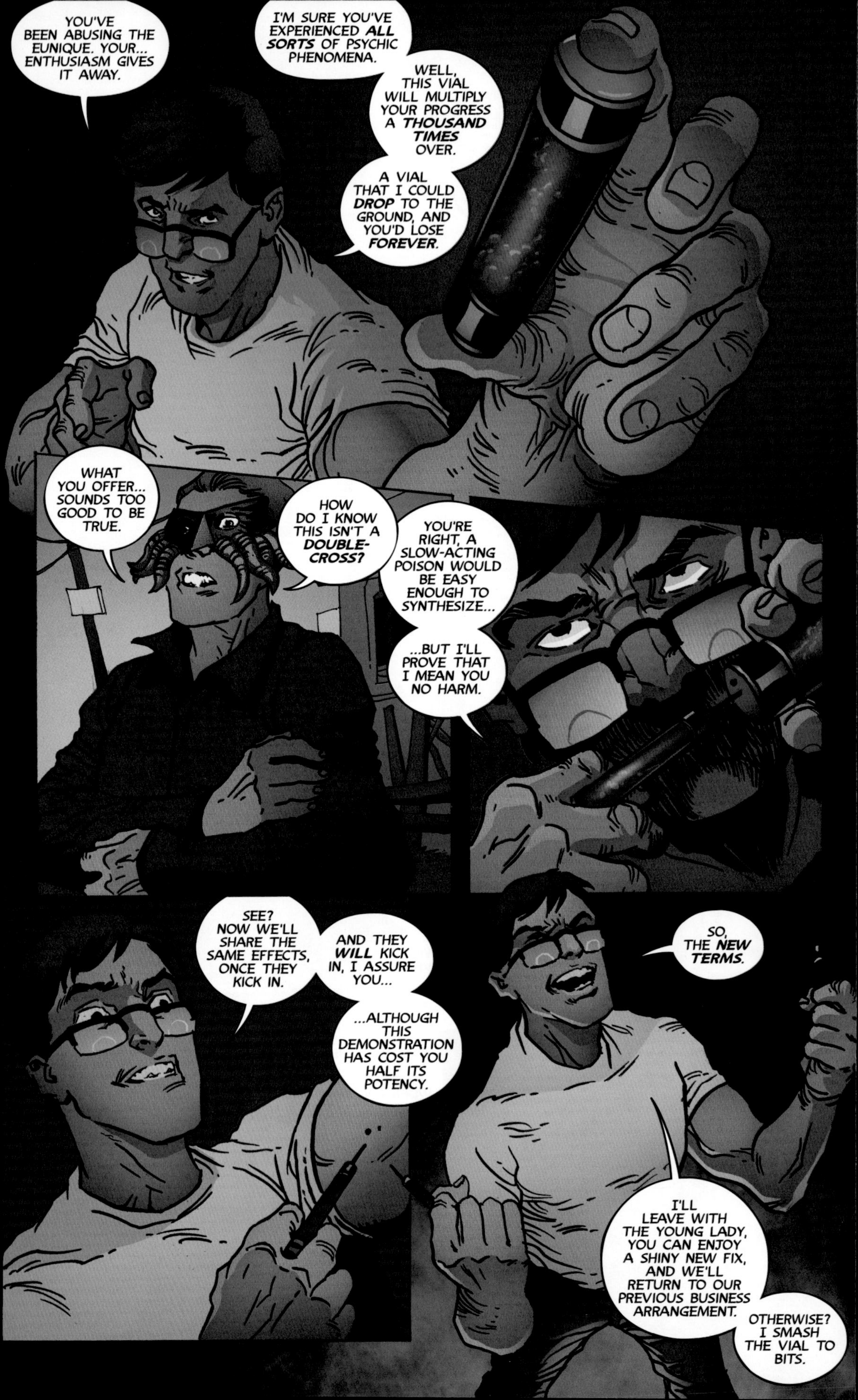
YOU'VE BEEN ABUSING THE EUNIQUE. YOUR... ENTHUSIASM GIVES IT AWAY.
I'M SURE YOU'VE EXPERIENCED ALL SORTS OF PSYCHIC PHENOMENA.
WELL, THIS VIAL WILL MULTIPLY YOUR PROGRESS A THOUSAND TIMES OVER.
A VIAL THAT I COULD DROP TO THE GROUND, AND YOU'D LOSE FOREVER.
WHAT YOU OFFER... SOUNDS TOO GOOD TO BE TRUE.
HOW DO I KNOW THIS ISN'T A DOUBLE-CROSS?
YOU'RE RIGHT, A SLOW-ACTING POISON WOULD BE EASY ENOUGH TO SYNTHESIZE...
...BUT I'LL PROVE THAT I MEAN YOU NO HARM.
SEE? NOW WE'LL SHARE THE SAME EFFECTS, ONCE THEY KICK IN.
AND THEY WILL KICK IN, I ASSURE YOU...
...ALTHOUGH THIS DEMONSTRATION HAS COST YOU HALF ITS POTENCY.
SO, THE NEW TERMS.
I'LL LEAVE WITH THE YOUNG LADY, YOU CAN ENJOY A SHINY NEW FIX, AND WE'LL RETURN TO OUR PREVIOUS BUSINESS ARRANGEMENT.
OTHERWISE? I SMASH THE VIAL TO BITS.

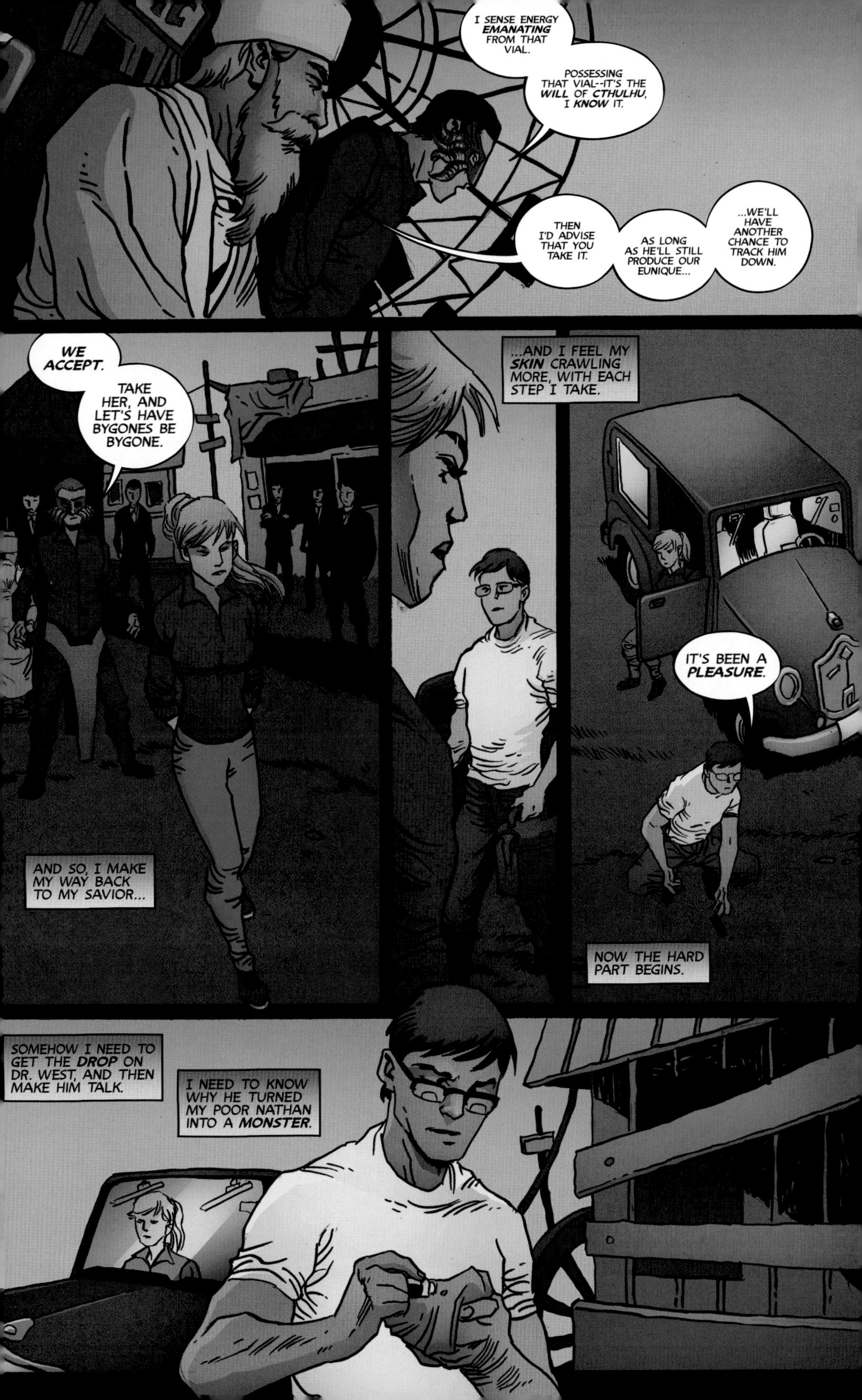
I SENSE ENERGY EMANATING FROM THAT VIAL.
POSSESSING THAT VIAL--IT'S THE WILL OF CTHULHU, I KNOW IT.
THEN I'D ADVISE THAT YOU TAKE IT.
AS LONG AS HE'LL STILL PRODUCE OUR EUNIQUE...
...WE'LL HAVE ANOTHER CHANCE TO TRACK HIM DOWN.
WE ACCEPT.
TAKE HER, AND LET'S HAVE BYGONES BE BYGONE.
AND SO, I MAKE MY WAY BACK TO MY SAVIOR...
...AND I FEEL MY SKIN CRAWLING MORE, WITH EACH STEP I TAKE.
IT'S BEEN A PLEASURE.
NOW THE HARD PART BEGINS.
SOMEHOW I NEED TO GET THE DROP ON DR. WEST, AND THEN MAKE HIM TALK.
I NEED TO KNOW WHY HE TURNED MY POOR NATHAN INTO A MONSTER.

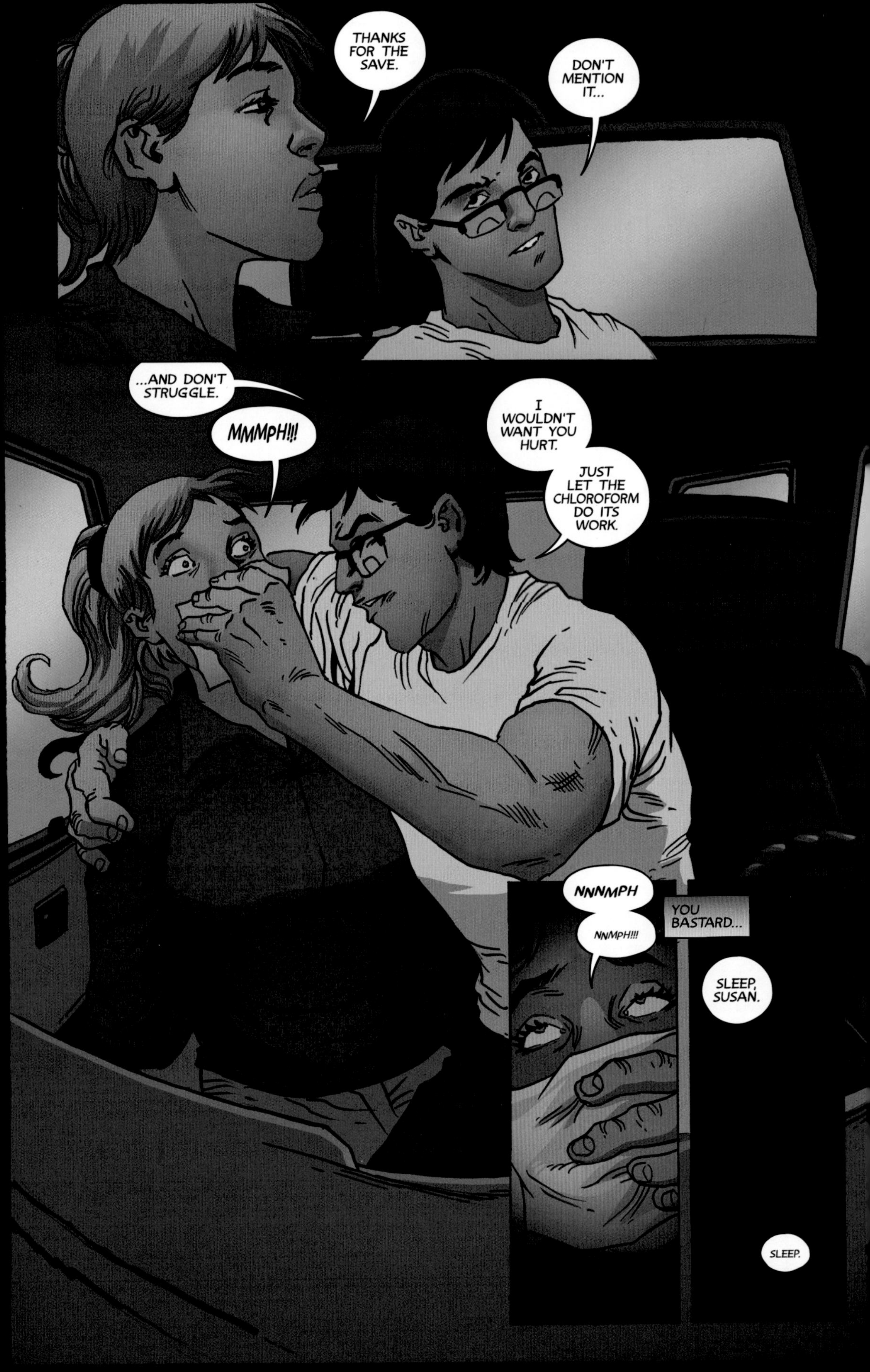
THANKS FOR THE SAVE.
DON'T MENTION IT...
...AND DON'T STRUGGLE.
MMMPH!!!
I WOULDN'T WANT YOU HURT.
JUST LET THE CHLOROFORM DO ITS WORK.
NNNMPH
NNMPH!!!
YOU BASTARD...
SLEEP, SUSAN.
SLEEP.

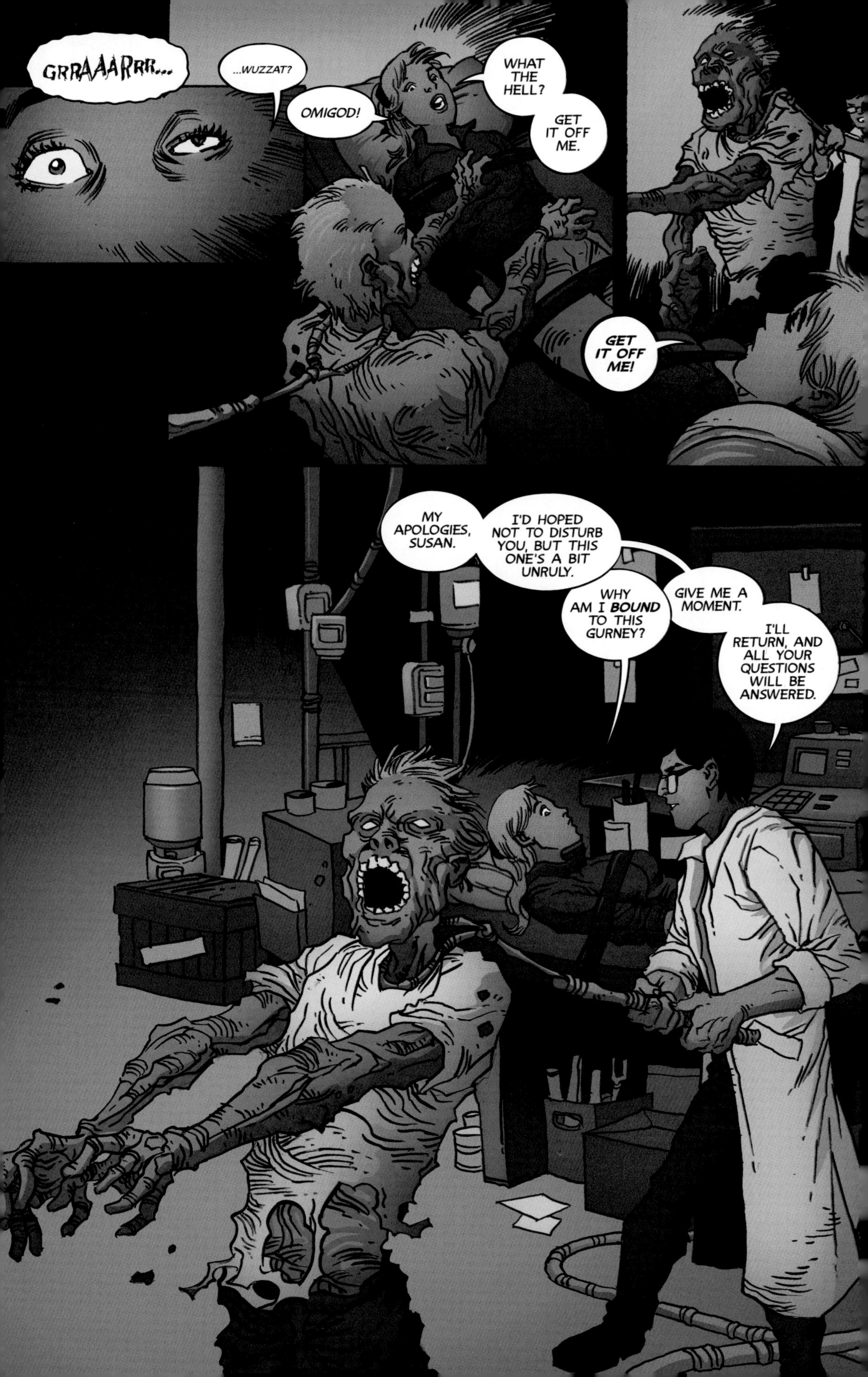
GRRAAARRR...
...WUZZAT?
OMIGOD!
WHAT THE HELL?
GET IT OFF ME.
GET IT OFF ME!
MY APOLOGIES, SUSAN.
I'D HOPED NOT TO DISTURB YOU, BUT THIS ONE'S A BIT UNRULY.
WHY AM I BOUND TO THIS GURNEY?
GIVE ME A MOMENT.
I'LL RETURN, AND ALL YOUR QUESTIONS WILL BE ANSWERED.

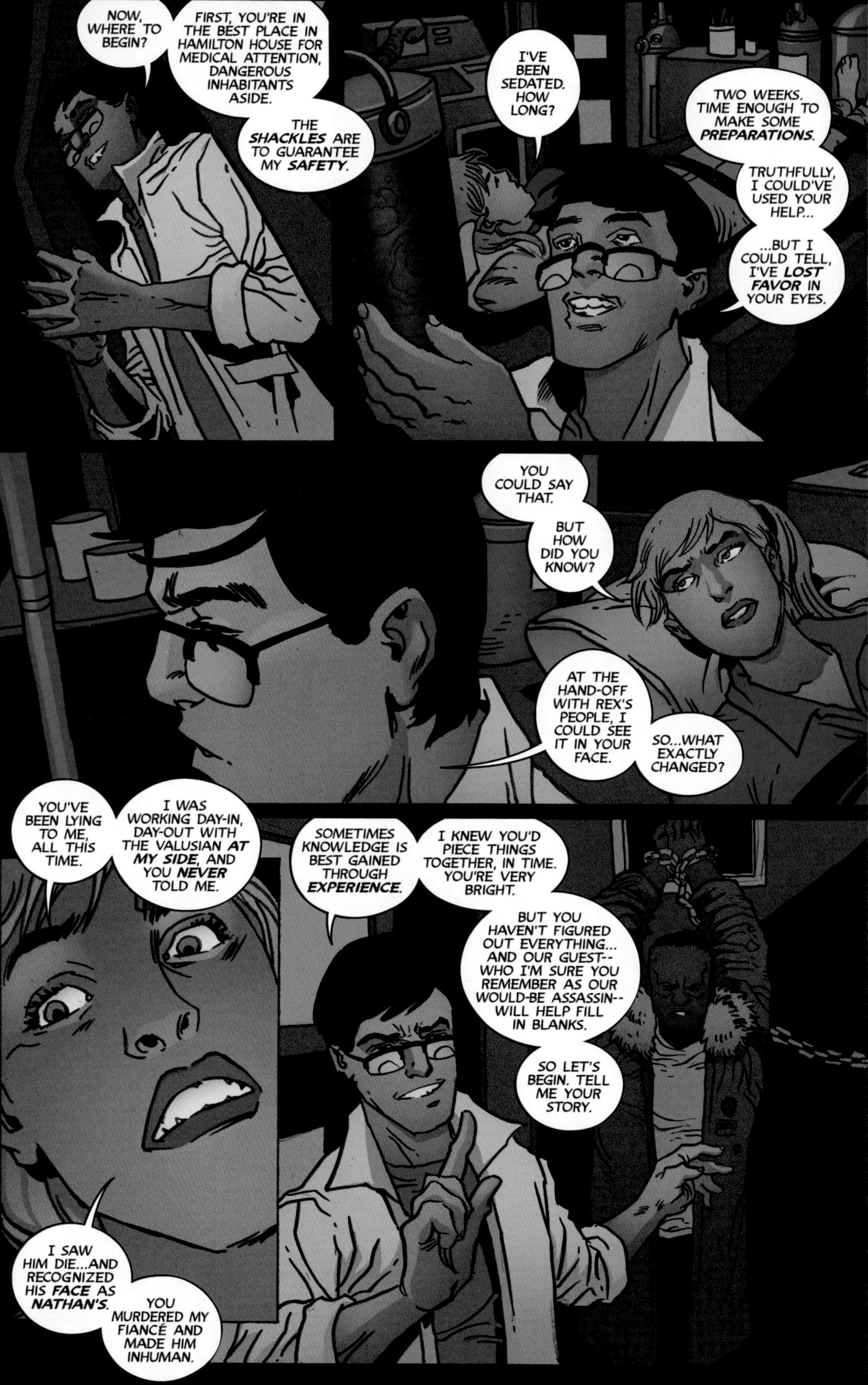
NOW, WHERE TO BEGIN?
FIRST, YOU'RE IN THE BEST PLACE IN HAMILTON HOUSE FOR MEDICAL ATTENTION, DANGEROUS INHABITANTS ASIDE.
THE *SHACKLES* ARE TO GUARANTEE MY *SAFETY*.
I'VE BEEN SEDATED. HOW LONG?
TWO WEEKS. TIME ENOUGH TO MAKE SOME *PREPARATIONS*.
TRUTHFULLY, I COULD'VE USED YOUR HELP...
...BUT I COULD TELL, I'VE *LOST FAVOR* IN YOUR EYES.
YOU COULD SAY THAT.
BUT HOW DID YOU KNOW?
AT THE HAND-OFF WITH REX'S PEOPLE, I COULD SEE IT IN YOUR FACE.
SO...WHAT EXACTLY CHANGED?
YOU'VE BEEN LYING TO ME, ALL THIS TIME.
I WAS WORKING DAY-IN, DAY-OUT WITH THE VALUSIAN *AT MY SIDE*, AND YOU *NEVER* TOLD ME.
I SAW HIM DIE...AND RECOGNIZED HIS *FACE* AS *NATHAN'S*.
YOU MURDERED MY FIANCÉ AND MADE HIM INHUMAN.
SOMETIMES KNOWLEDGE IS BEST GAINED THROUGH *EXPERIENCE*.
I KNEW YOU'D PIECE THINGS TOGETHER, IN TIME. YOU'RE VERY BRIGHT.
BUT YOU HAVEN'T FIGURED OUT EVERYTHING... AND OUR GUEST-- WHO I'M SURE YOU REMEMBER AS OUR WOULD-BE ASSASSIN-- WILL HELP FILL IN BLANKS.
SO LET'S BEGIN. TELL ME YOUR STORY.

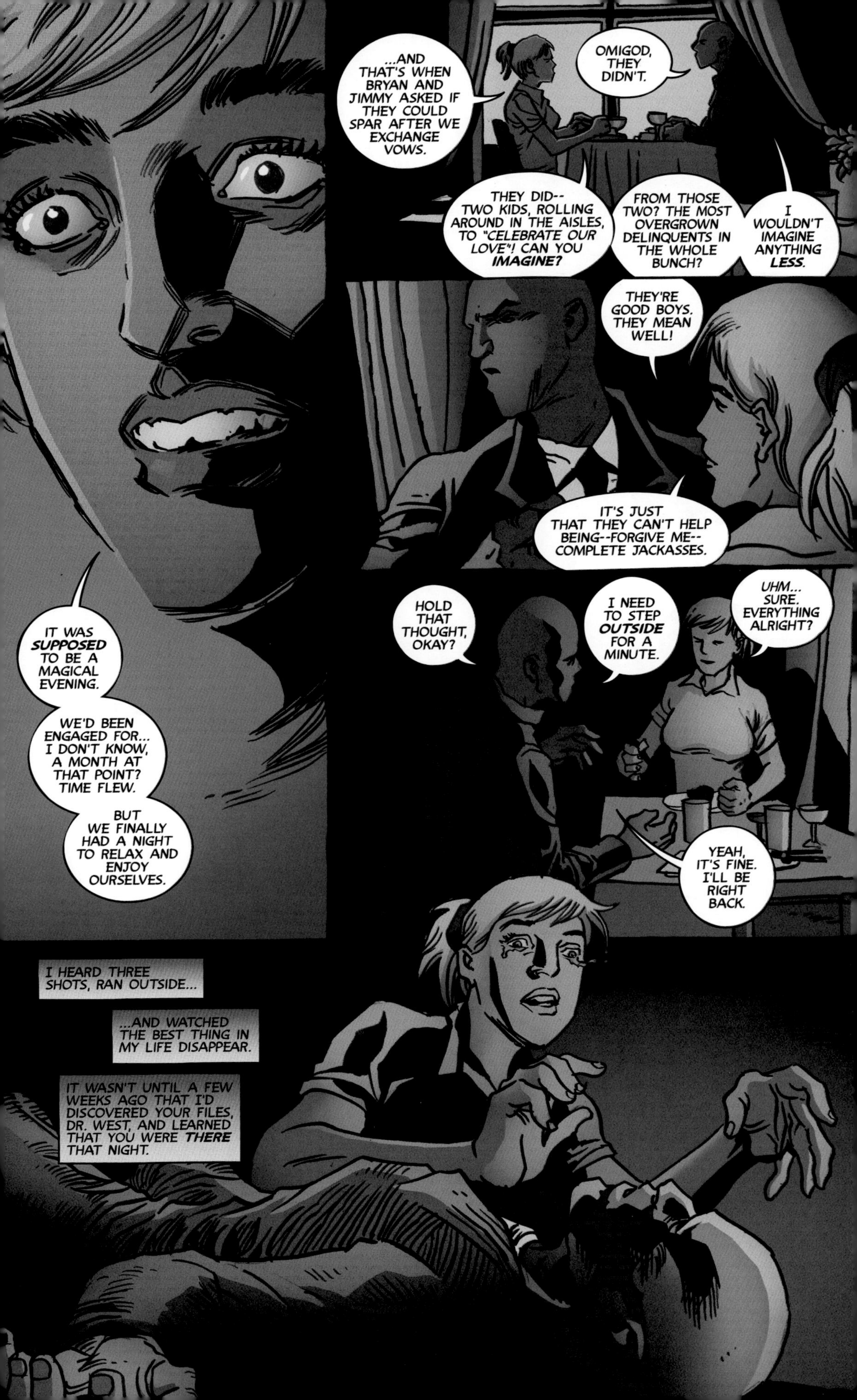
...AND THAT'S WHEN BRYAN AND JIMMY ASKED IF THEY COULD SPAR AFTER WE EXCHANGE VOWS.
OMIGOD, THEY DIDN'T.
THEY DID-- TWO KIDS, ROLLING AROUND IN THE AISLES, TO "CELEBRATE OUR LOVE"! CAN YOU IMAGINE?
FROM THOSE TWO? THE MOST OVERGROWN DELINQUENTS IN THE WHOLE BUNCH?
I WOULDN'T IMAGINE ANYTHING LESS.
THEY'RE GOOD BOYS. THEY MEAN WELL!
IT'S JUST THAT THEY CAN'T HELP BEING--FORGIVE ME-- COMPLETE JACKASSES.
IT WAS SUPPOSED TO BE A MAGICAL EVENING.
WE'D BEEN ENGAGED FOR... I DON'T KNOW, A MONTH AT THAT POINT? TIME FLEW.
BUT WE FINALLY HAD A NIGHT TO RELAX AND ENJOY OURSELVES.
HOLD THAT THOUGHT, OKAY?
I NEED TO STEP OUTSIDE FOR A MINUTE.
UHM... SURE. EVERYTHING ALRIGHT?
YEAH, IT'S FINE. I'LL BE RIGHT BACK.
I HEARD THREE SHOTS, RAN OUTSIDE...
...AND WATCHED THE BEST THING IN MY LIFE DISAPPEAR.
IT WASN'T UNTIL A FEW WEEKS AGO THAT I'D DISCOVERED YOUR FILES, DR. WEST, AND LEARNED THAT YOU WERE THERE THAT NIGHT.

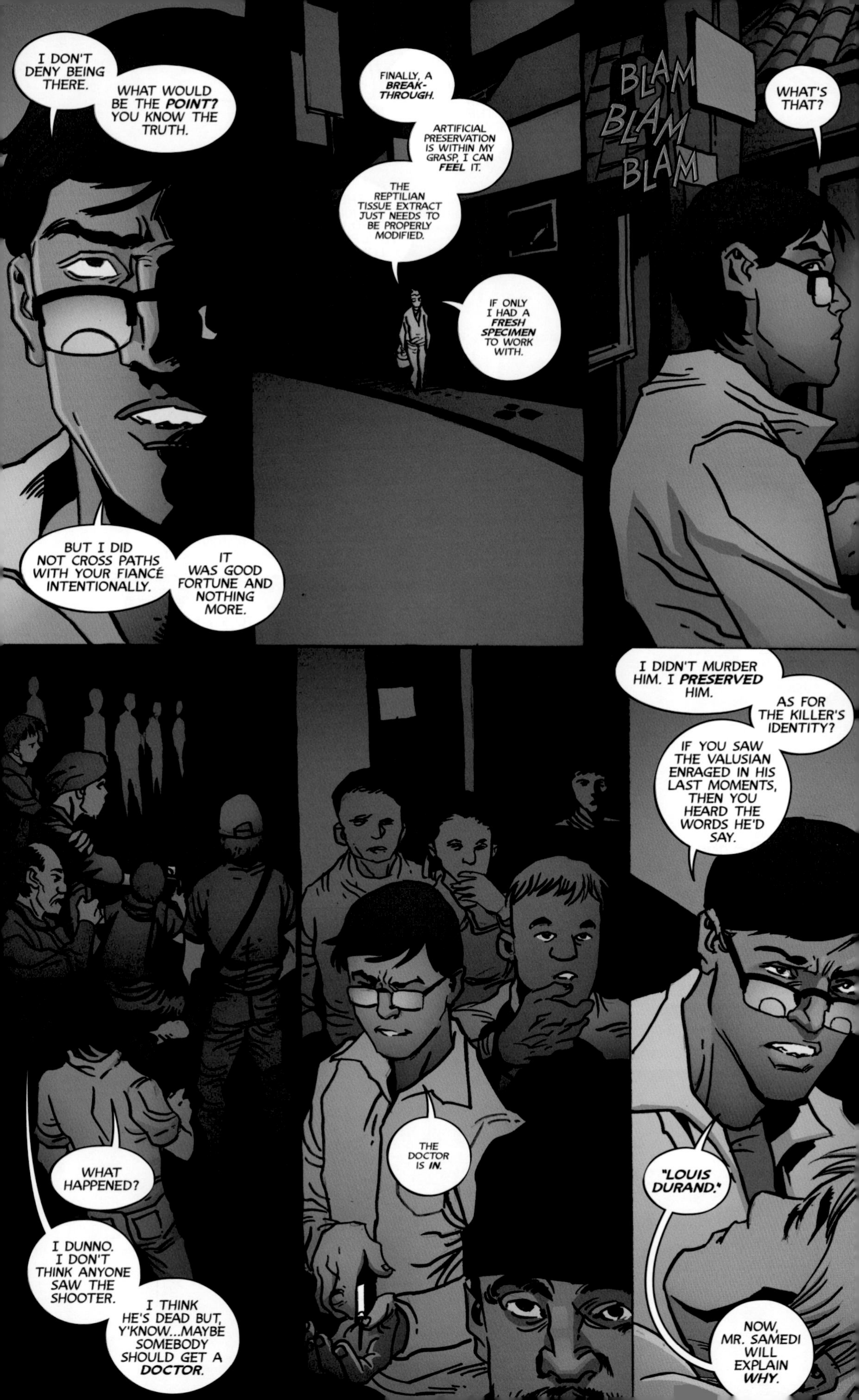
I DON'T DENY BEING THERE.
WHAT WOULD BE THE POINT? YOU KNOW THE TRUTH.
BUT I DID NOT CROSS PATHS WITH YOUR FIANCÉ INTENTIONALLY.
IT WAS GOOD FORTUNE AND NOTHING MORE.
FINALLY, A BREAK-THROUGH.
ARTIFICIAL PRESERVATION IS WITHIN MY GRASP, I CAN FEEL IT.
THE REPTILIAN TISSUE EXTRACT JUST NEEDS TO BE PROPERLY MODIFIED.
IF ONLY I HAD A FRESH SPECIMEN TO WORK WITH.
BLAM BLAM BLAM
WHAT'S THAT?
WHAT HAPPENED?
I DUNNO. I DON'T THINK ANYONE SAW THE SHOOTER.
I THINK HE'S DEAD BUT, Y'KNOW...MAYBE SOMEBODY SHOULD GET A DOCTOR.
THE DOCTOR IS IN.
I DIDN'T MURDER HIM. I PRESERVED HIM.
AS FOR THE KILLER'S IDENTITY?
IF YOU SAW THE VALUSIAN ENRAGED IN HIS LAST MOMENTS, THEN YOU HEARD THE WORDS HE'D SAY.
"LOUIS DURAND."
NOW, MR. SAMEDI WILL EXPLAIN WHY.

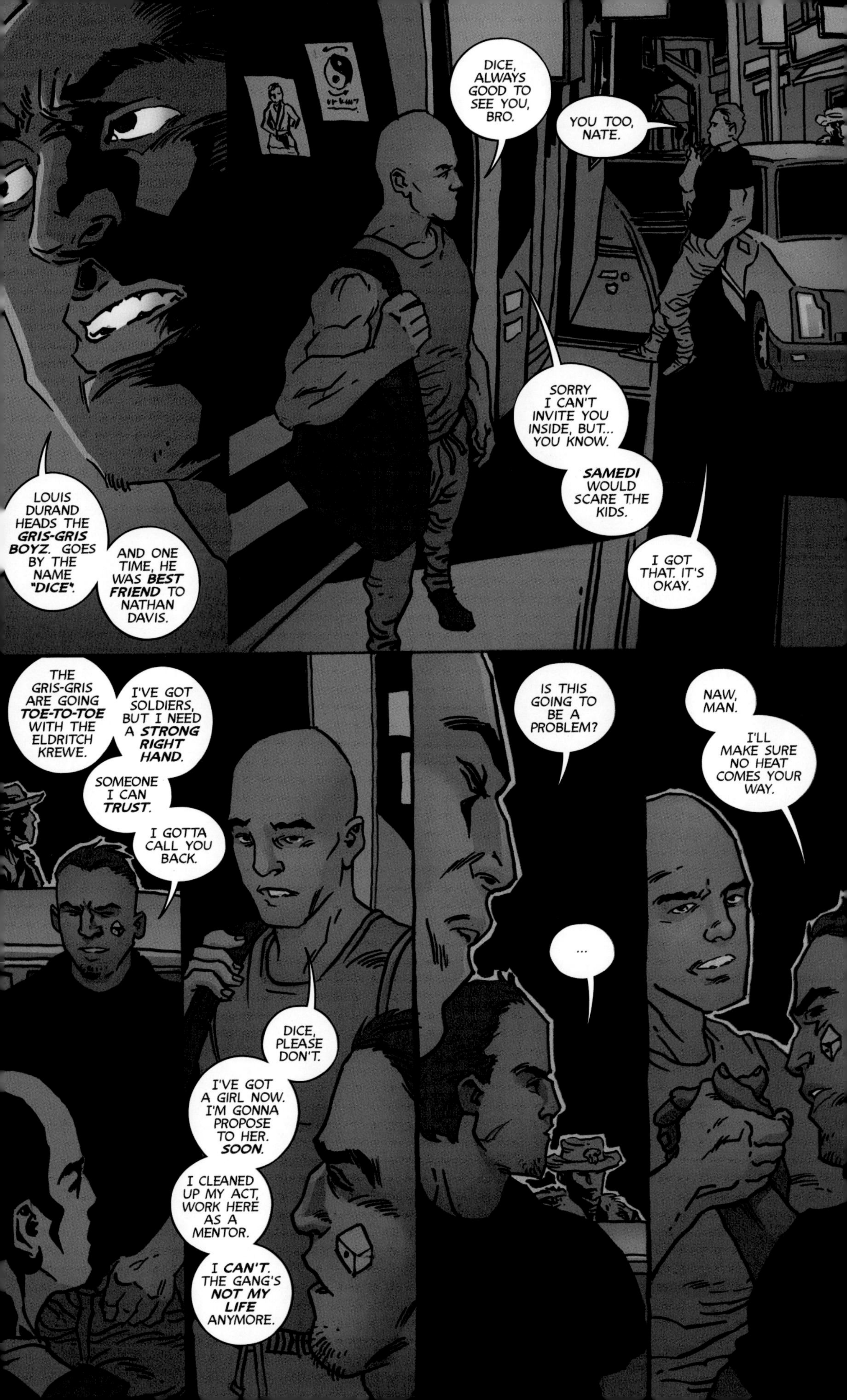

LOUIS DURAND HEADS THE **GRIS-GRIS BOYZ**. GOES BY THE NAME **"DICE"**.
AND ONE TIME, HE WAS **BEST FRIEND** TO NATHAN DAVIS.
DICE, ALWAYS GOOD TO SEE YOU, BRO.
YOU TOO, NATE.
SORRY I CAN'T INVITE YOU INSIDE, BUT... YOU KNOW.
SAMEDI WOULD SCARE THE KIDS.
I GOT THAT. IT'S OKAY.
THE GRIS-GRIS ARE GOING **TOE-TO-TOE** WITH THE ELDRITCH KREWE.
I'VE GOT SOLDIERS, BUT I NEED A **STRONG RIGHT HAND**.
SOMEONE I CAN **TRUST**.
I GOTTA CALL YOU BACK.
DICE, PLEASE DON'T.
I'VE GOT A GIRL NOW. I'M GONNA PROPOSE TO HER. **SOON**.
I CLEANED UP MY ACT, WORK HERE AS A MENTOR.
I **CAN'T**. THE GANG'S **NOT MY LIFE** ANYMORE.
IS THIS GOING TO BE A PROBLEM?
...
NAW, MAN.
I'LL MAKE SURE NO HEAT COMES YOUR WAY.

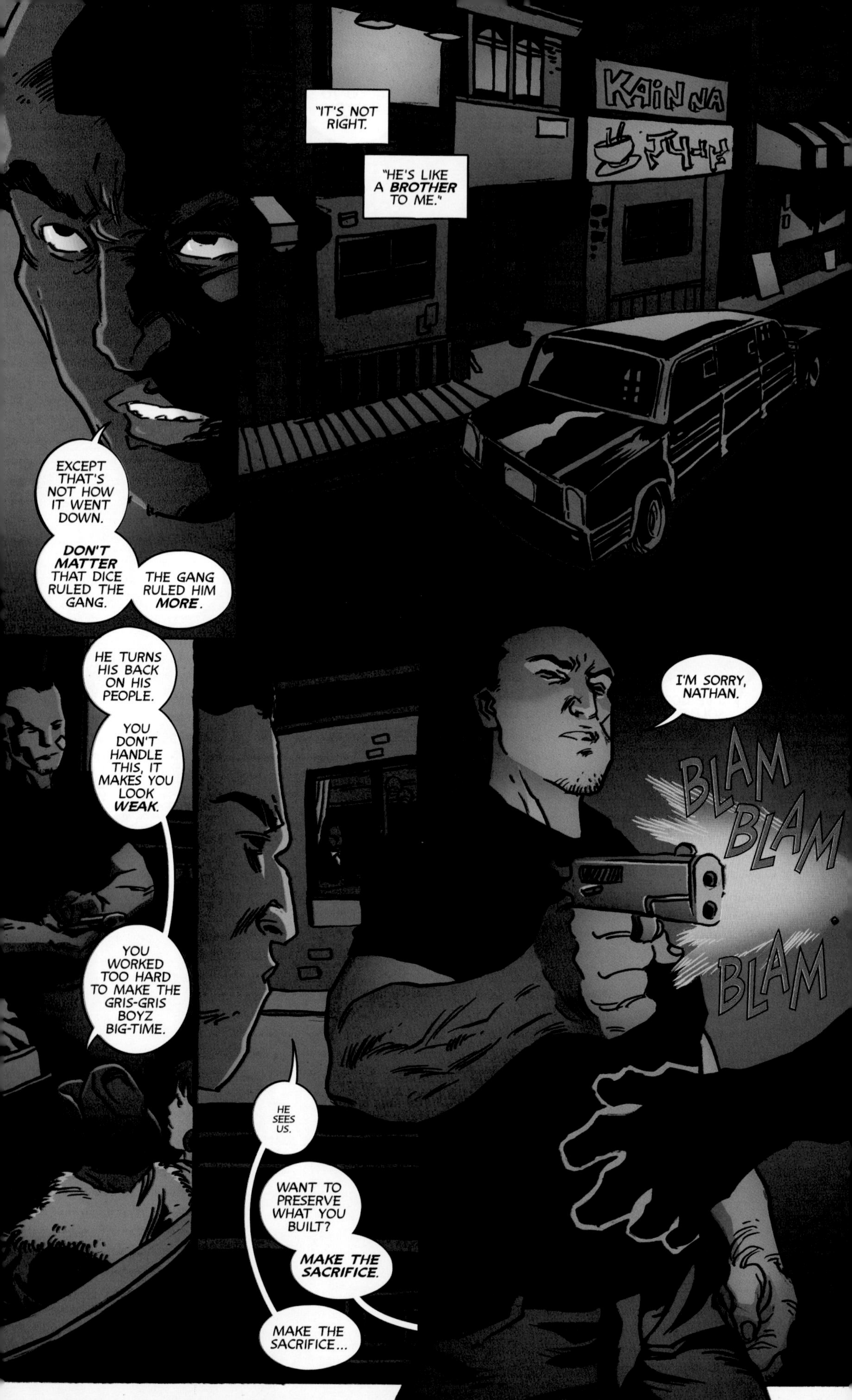

"IT'S NOT RIGHT.
"HE'S LIKE A BROTHER TO ME."
KAIN NA
EXCEPT THAT'S NOT HOW IT WENT DOWN.
DON'T MATTER THAT DICE RULED THE GANG.
THE GANG RULED HIM MORE.
HE TURNS HIS BACK ON HIS PEOPLE.
YOU DON'T HANDLE THIS, IT MAKES YOU LOOK WEAK.
YOU WORKED TOO HARD TO MAKE THE GRIS-GRIS BOYZ BIG-TIME.
I'M SORRY, NATHAN.
BLAM BLAM
BLAM
HE SEES US.
WANT TO PRESERVE WHAT YOU BUILT?
MAKE THE SACRIFICE.
MAKE THE SACRIFICE...

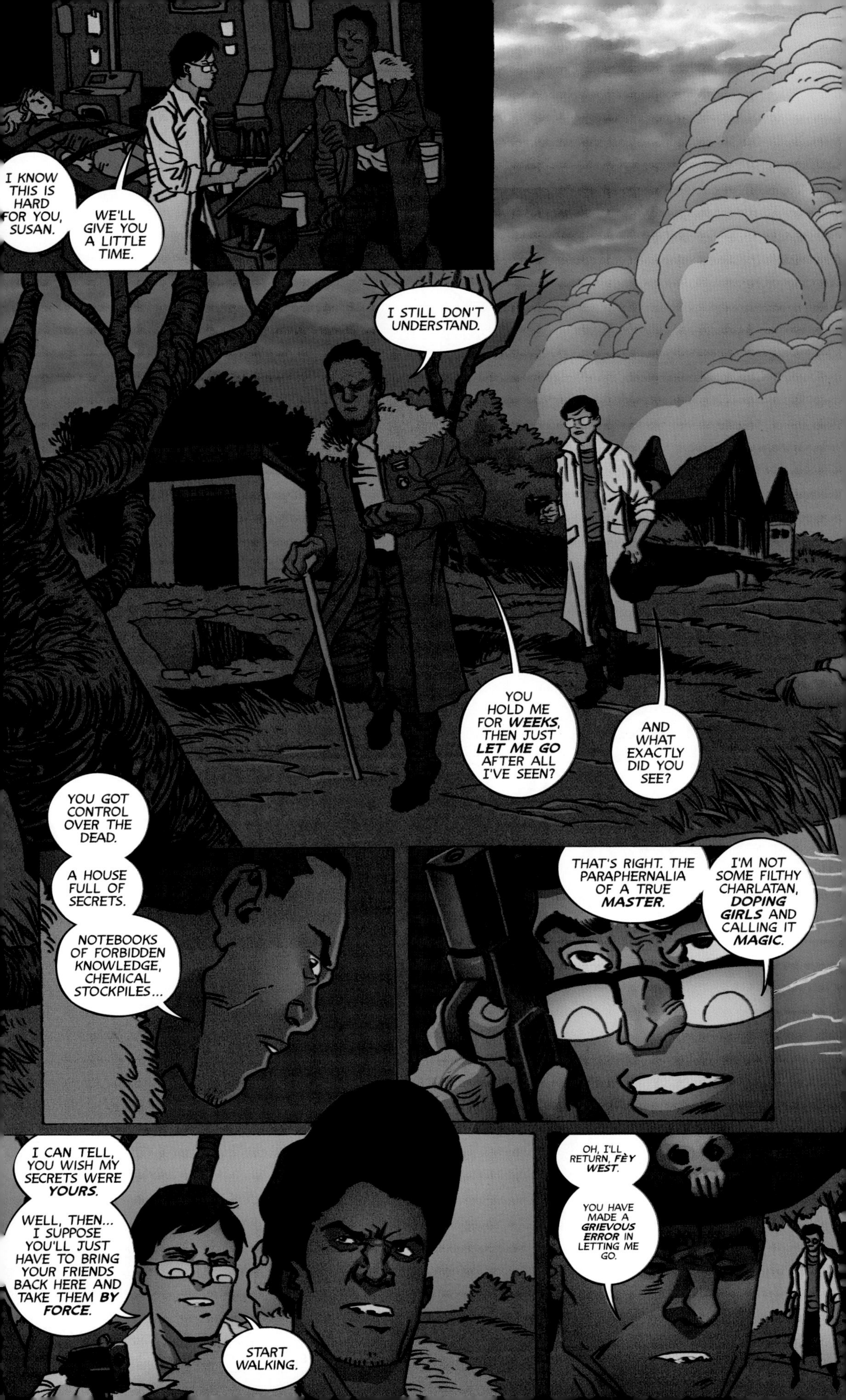
I KNOW THIS IS HARD FOR YOU, SUSAN.
WE'LL GIVE YOU A LITTLE TIME.
I STILL DON'T UNDERSTAND.
YOU HOLD ME FOR *WEEKS*, THEN JUST *LET ME GO* AFTER ALL I'VE SEEN?
AND WHAT EXACTLY DID YOU SEE?
YOU GOT CONTROL OVER THE DEAD.
A HOUSE FULL OF SECRETS.
NOTEBOOKS OF FORBIDDEN KNOWLEDGE, CHEMICAL STOCKPILES...
THAT'S RIGHT. THE PARAPHERNALIA OF A TRUE *MASTER*.
I'M NOT SOME FILTHY CHARLATAN, *DOPING GIRLS* AND CALLING IT *MAGIC*.
I CAN TELL, YOU WISH MY SECRETS WERE *YOURS*.
WELL, THEN... I SUPPOSE YOU'LL JUST HAVE TO BRING YOUR FRIENDS BACK HERE AND TAKE THEM *BY FORCE*.
START WALKING.
OH, I'LL RETURN, *FÈY WEST*.
YOU HAVE MADE A *GRIEVOUS ERROR* IN LETTING ME GO.

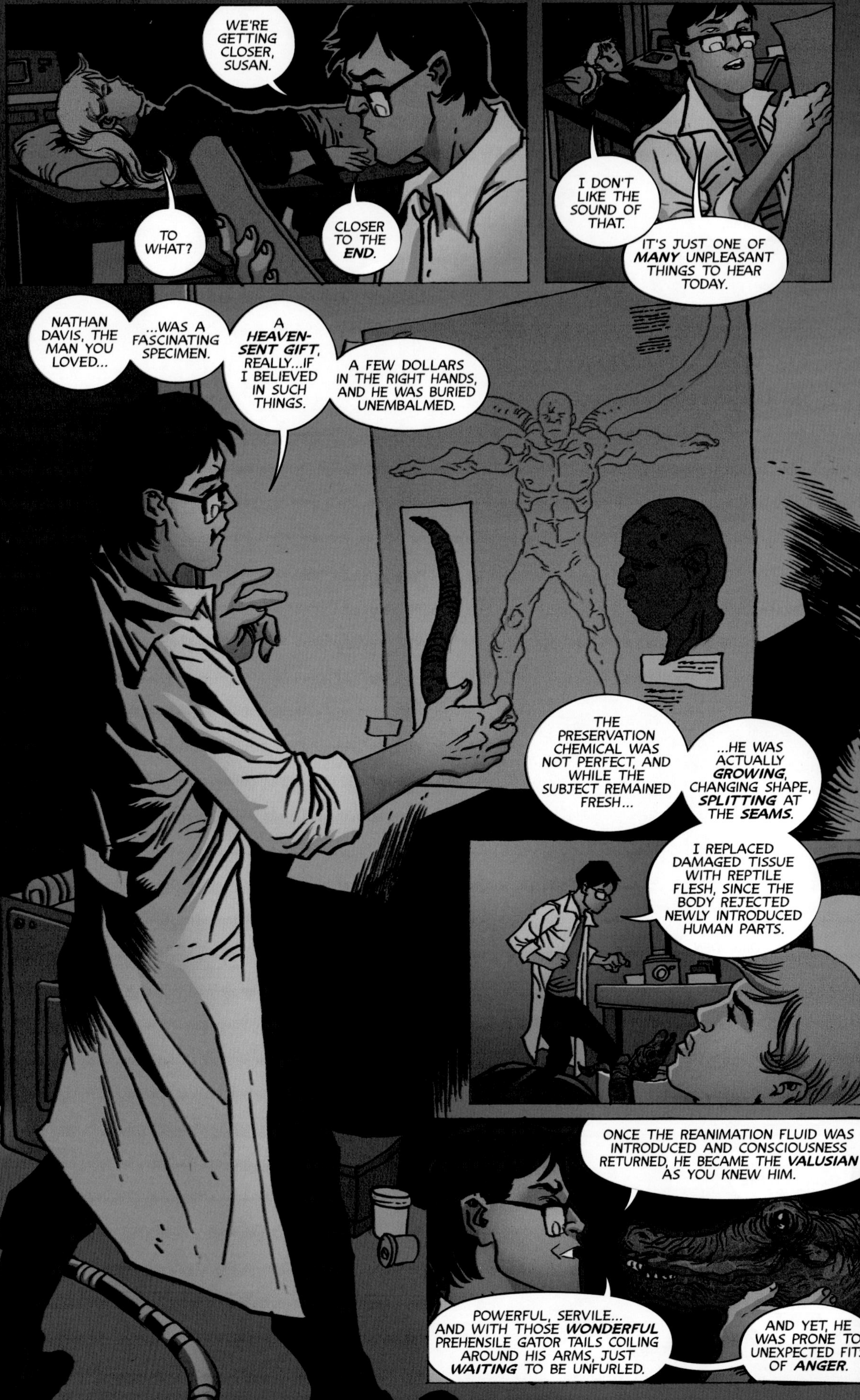
WE'RE GETTING CLOSER, SUSAN.
TO WHAT?
CLOSER TO THE *END.*
I DON'T LIKE THE SOUND OF THAT.
IT'S JUST ONE OF *MANY* UNPLEASANT THINGS TO HEAR TODAY.
NATHAN DAVIS, THE MAN YOU LOVED...
...WAS A FASCINATING SPECIMEN.
A *HEAVEN-SENT GIFT*, REALLY...IF I BELIEVED IN SUCH THINGS.
A FEW DOLLARS IN THE RIGHT HANDS, AND HE WAS BURIED UNEMBALMED.
THE PRESERVATION CHEMICAL WAS NOT PERFECT, AND WHILE THE SUBJECT REMAINED FRESH...
...HE WAS ACTUALLY *GROWING*, CHANGING SHAPE, *SPLITTING* AT THE *SEAMS*.
I REPLACED DAMAGED TISSUE WITH REPTILE FLESH, SINCE THE BODY REJECTED NEWLY INTRODUCED HUMAN PARTS.
ONCE THE REANIMATION FLUID WAS INTRODUCED AND CONSCIOUSNESS RETURNED, HE BECAME THE *VALUSIAN* AS YOU KNEW HIM.
POWERFUL, SERVILE... AND WITH THOSE *WONDERFUL* PREHENSILE GATOR TAILS COILING AROUND HIS ARMS, JUST *WAITING* TO BE UNFURLED.
AND YET, HE WAS PRONE TO UNEXPECTED FITS OF *ANGER*.

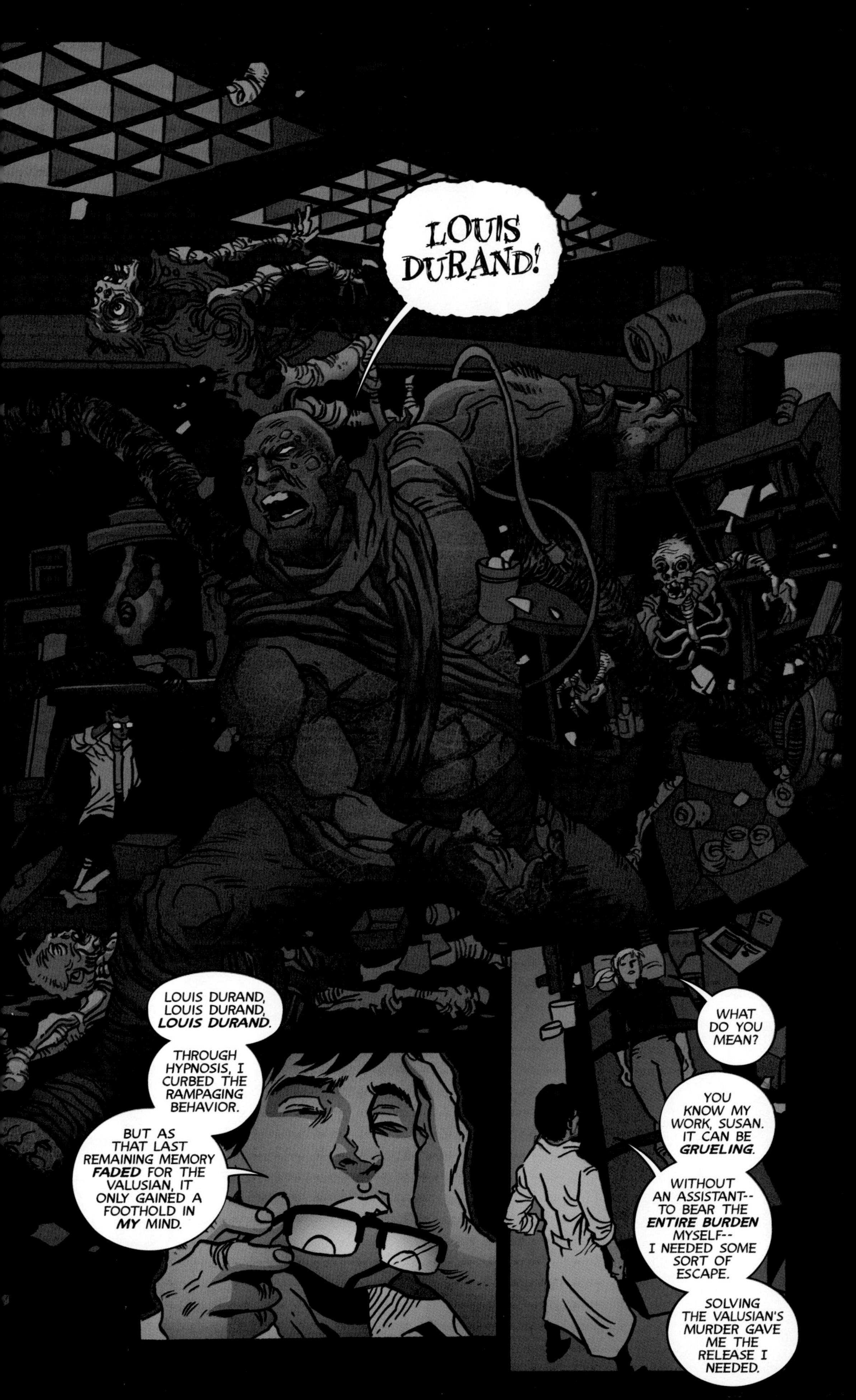
LOUIS DURAND!
LOUIS DURAND, LOUIS DURAND, LOUIS DURAND.
THROUGH HYPNOSIS, I CURBED THE RAMPAGING BEHAVIOR.
BUT AS THAT LAST REMAINING MEMORY FADED FOR THE VALUSIAN, IT ONLY GAINED A FOOTHOLD IN MY MIND.
WHAT DO YOU MEAN?
YOU KNOW MY WORK, SUSAN. IT CAN BE GRUELING.
WITHOUT AN ASSISTANT-- TO BEAR THE ENTIRE BURDEN MYSELF-- I NEEDED SOME SORT OF ESCAPE.
SOLVING THE VALUSIAN'S MURDER GAVE ME THE RELEASE I NEEDED.

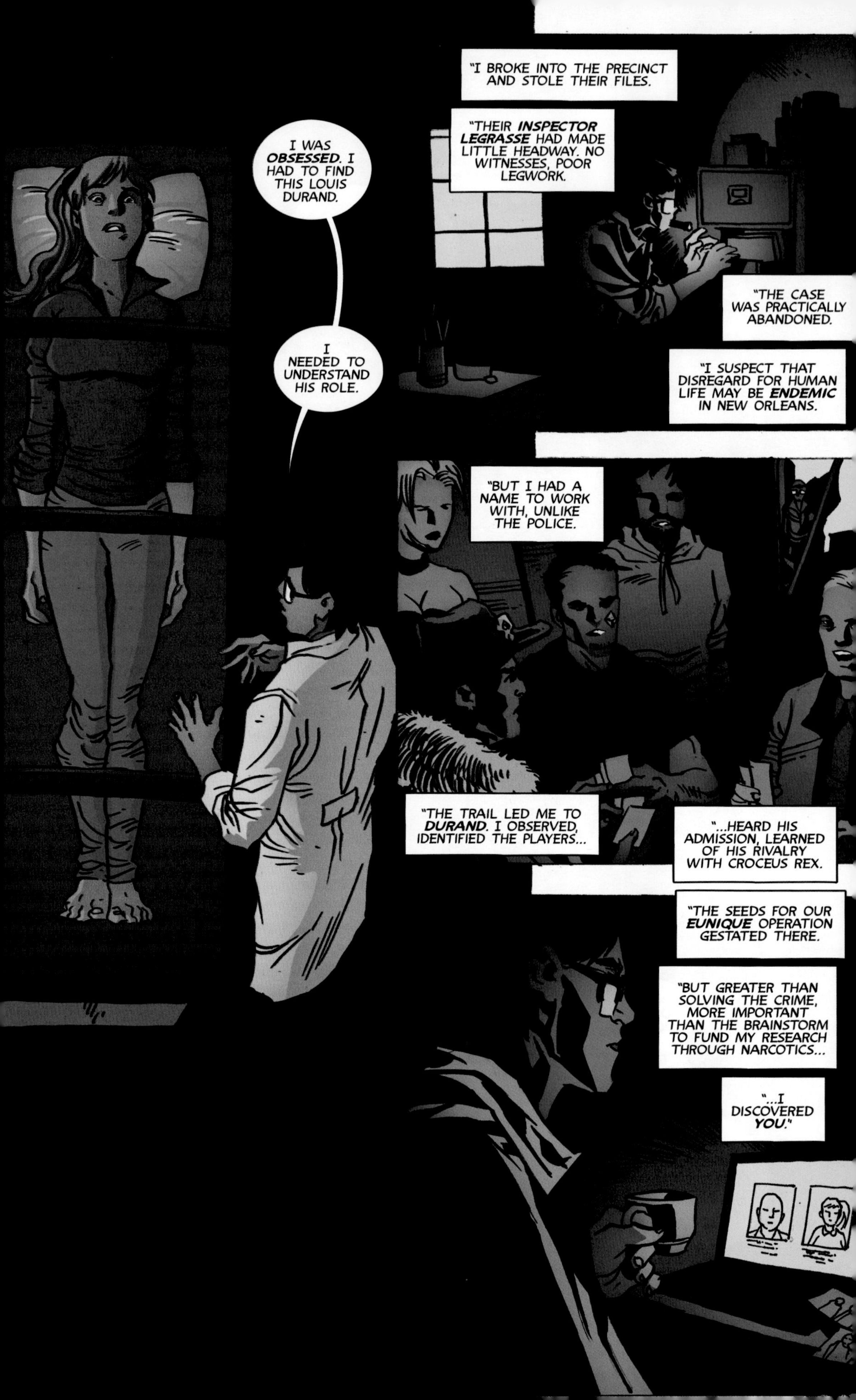
I WAS OBSESSED. I HAD TO FIND THIS LOUIS DURAND.
I NEEDED TO UNDERSTAND HIS ROLE.
"I BROKE INTO THE PRECINCT AND STOLE THEIR FILES.
"THEIR INSPECTOR LEGRASSE HAD MADE LITTLE HEADWAY. NO WITNESSES, POOR LEGWORK.
"THE CASE WAS PRACTICALLY ABANDONED.
"I SUSPECT THAT DISREGARD FOR HUMAN LIFE MAY BE ENDEMIC IN NEW ORLEANS.
"BUT I HAD A NAME TO WORK WITH, UNLIKE THE POLICE.
"THE TRAIL LED ME TO DURAND. I OBSERVED, IDENTIFIED THE PLAYERS...
"...HEARD HIS ADMISSION, LEARNED OF HIS RIVALRY WITH CROCEUS REX.
"THE SEEDS FOR OUR EUNIQUE OPERATION GESTATED THERE.
"BUT GREATER THAN SOLVING THE CRIME, MORE IMPORTANT THAN THE BRAINSTORM TO FUND MY RESEARCH THROUGH NARCOTICS...
"...I DISCOVERED YOU."

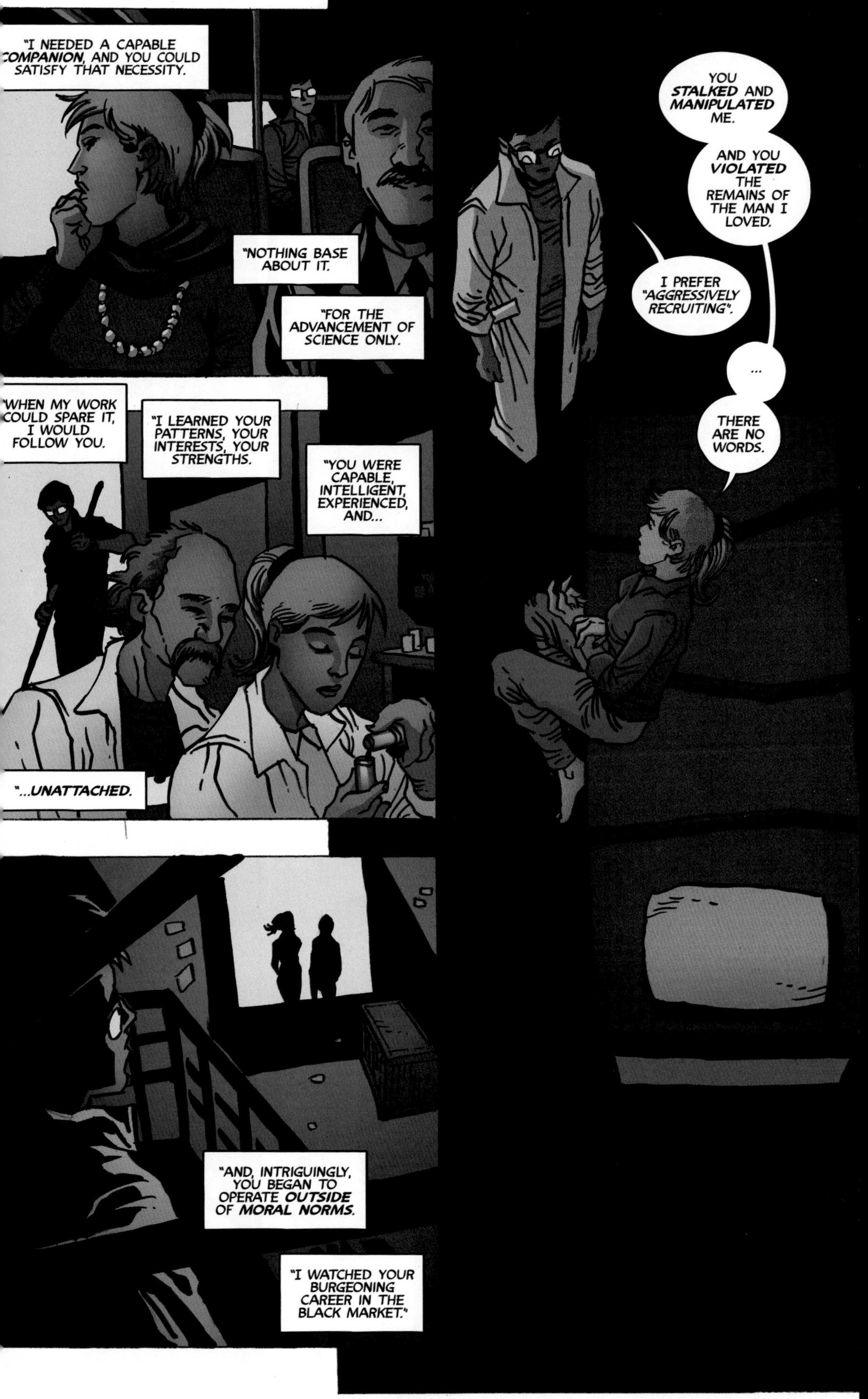
"I NEEDED A CAPABLE COMPANION, AND YOU COULD SATISFY THAT NECESSITY.
"NOTHING BASE ABOUT IT.
"FOR THE ADVANCEMENT OF SCIENCE ONLY.
"WHEN MY WORK COULD SPARE IT, I WOULD FOLLOW YOU.
"I LEARNED YOUR PATTERNS, YOUR INTERESTS, YOUR STRENGTHS.
"YOU WERE CAPABLE, INTELLIGENT, EXPERIENCED, AND...
"...UNATTACHED.
"AND, INTRIGUINGLY, YOU BEGAN TO OPERATE OUTSIDE OF MORAL NORMS.
"I WATCHED YOUR BURGEONING CAREER IN THE BLACK MARKET."
YOU STALKED AND MANIPULATED ME.
AND YOU VIOLATED THE REMAINS OF THE MAN I LOVED.
I PREFER "AGGRESSIVELY RECRUITING".
...
THERE ARE NO WORDS.

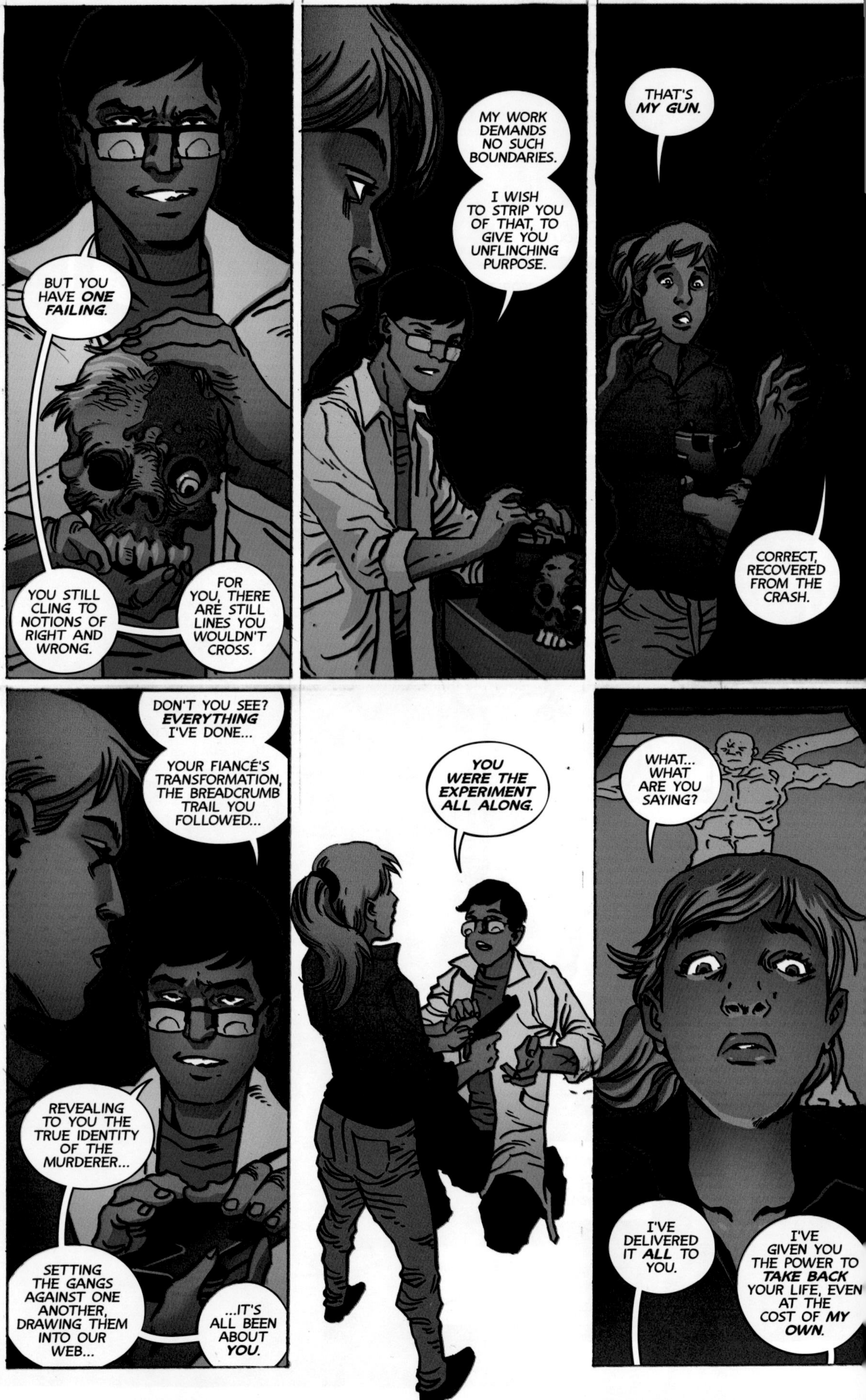
BUT YOU HAVE ONE FAILING.
YOU STILL CLING TO NOTIONS OF RIGHT AND WRONG.
FOR YOU, THERE ARE STILL LINES YOU WOULDN'T CROSS.
MY WORK DEMANDS NO SUCH BOUNDARIES.
I WISH TO STRIP YOU OF THAT, TO GIVE YOU UNFLINCHING PURPOSE.
THAT'S MY GUN.
CORRECT, RECOVERED FROM THE CRASH.
DON'T YOU SEE? EVERYTHING I'VE DONE...
YOUR FIANCÉ'S TRANSFORMATION, THE BREADCRUMB TRAIL YOU FOLLOWED...
REVEALING TO YOU THE TRUE IDENTITY OF THE MURDERER...
SETTING THE GANGS AGAINST ONE ANOTHER, DRAWING THEM INTO OUR WEB...
...IT'S ALL BEEN ABOUT YOU.
YOU WERE THE EXPERIMENT ALL ALONG.
WHAT... WHAT ARE YOU SAYING?
I'VE DELIVERED IT ALL TO YOU.
I'VE GIVEN YOU THE POWER TO TAKE BACK YOUR LIFE, EVEN AT THE COST OF MY OWN.

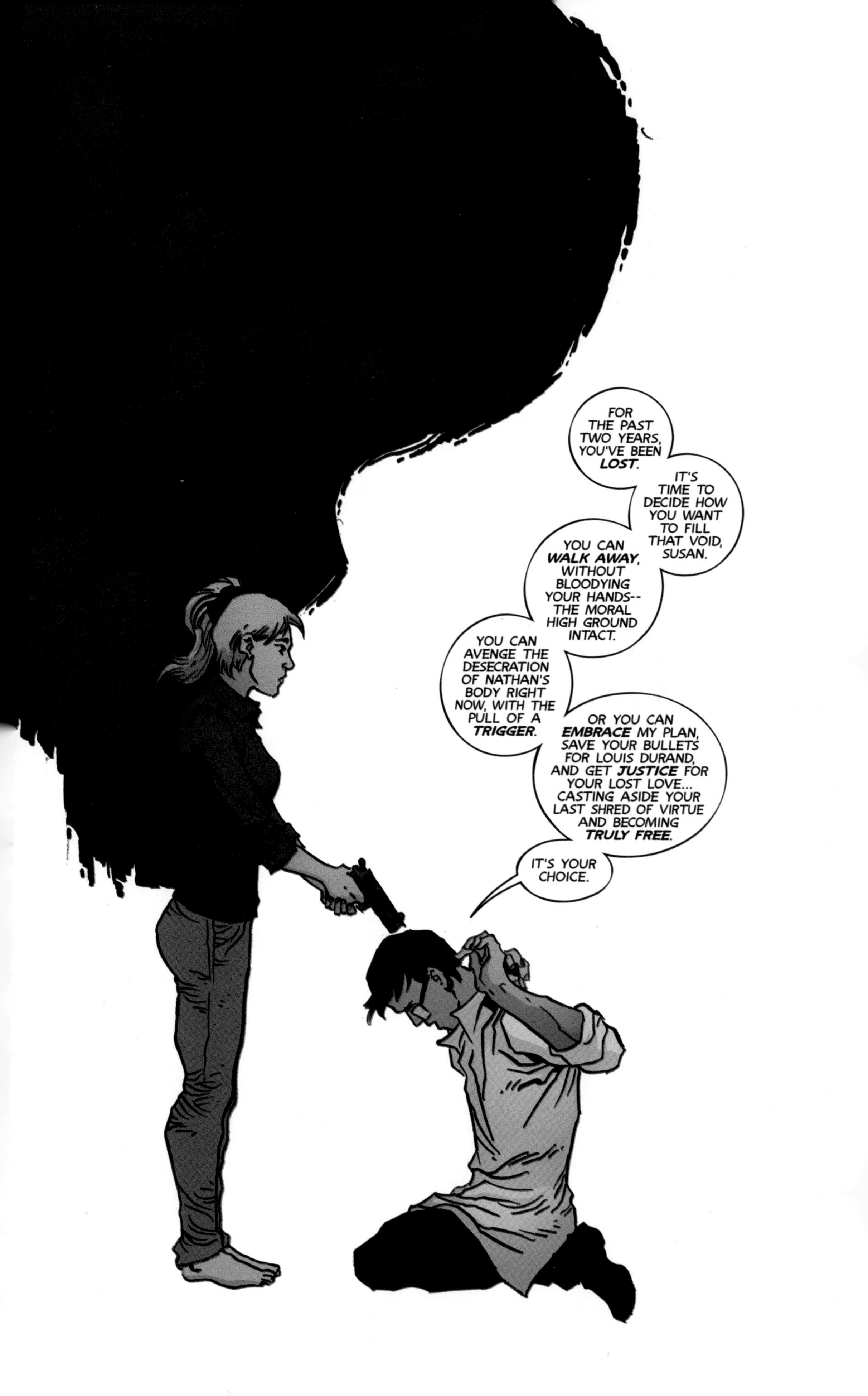
FOR THE PAST TWO YEARS, YOU'VE BEEN LOST.
IT'S TIME TO DECIDE HOW YOU WANT TO FILL THAT VOID, SUSAN.
YOU CAN WALK AWAY, WITHOUT BLOODYING YOUR HANDS-- THE MORAL HIGH GROUND INTACT.
YOU CAN AVENGE THE DESECRATION OF NATHAN'S BODY RIGHT NOW, WITH THE PULL OF A TRIGGER.
OR YOU CAN EMBRACE MY PLAN, SAVE YOUR BULLETS FOR LOUIS DURAND, AND GET JUSTICE FOR YOUR LOST LOVE... CASTING ASIDE YOUR LAST SHRED OF VIRTUE AND BECOMING TRULY FREE.
IT'S YOUR CHOICE.

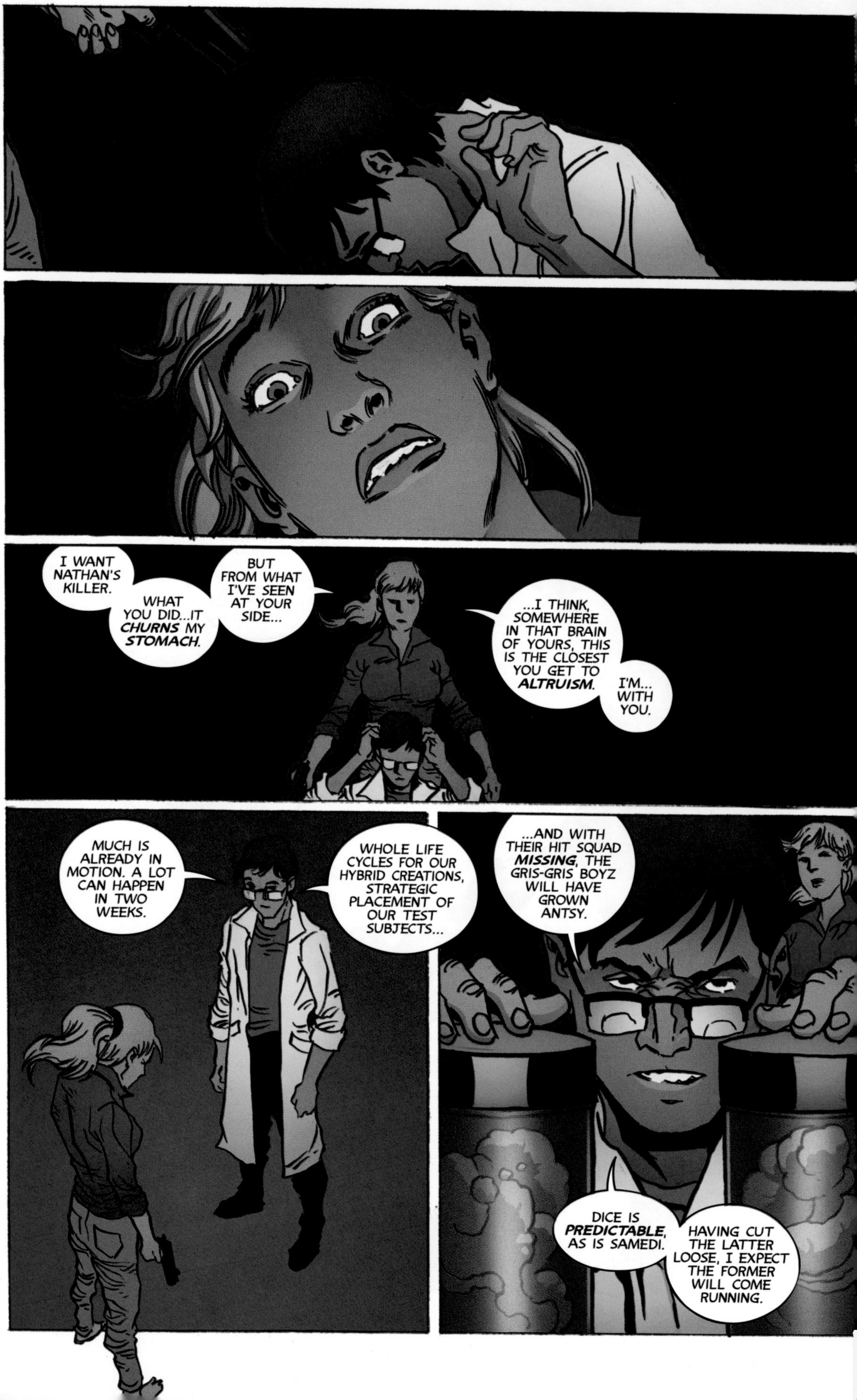
I WANT NATHAN'S KILLER.
WHAT YOU DID...IT CHURNS MY STOMACH.
BUT FROM WHAT I'VE SEEN AT YOUR SIDE...
...I THINK, SOMEWHERE IN THAT BRAIN OF YOURS, THIS IS THE CLOSEST YOU GET TO ALTRUISM.
I'M... WITH YOU.
MUCH IS ALREADY IN MOTION. A LOT CAN HAPPEN IN TWO WEEKS.
WHOLE LIFE CYCLES FOR OUR HYBRID CREATIONS, STRATEGIC PLACEMENT OF OUR TEST SUBJECTS...
...AND WITH THEIR HIT SQUAD MISSING, THE GRIS-GRIS BOYZ WILL HAVE GROWN ANTSY.
DICE IS PREDICTABLE, AS IS SAMEDI.
HAVING CUT THE LATTER LOOSE, I EXPECT THE FORMER WILL COME RUNNING.

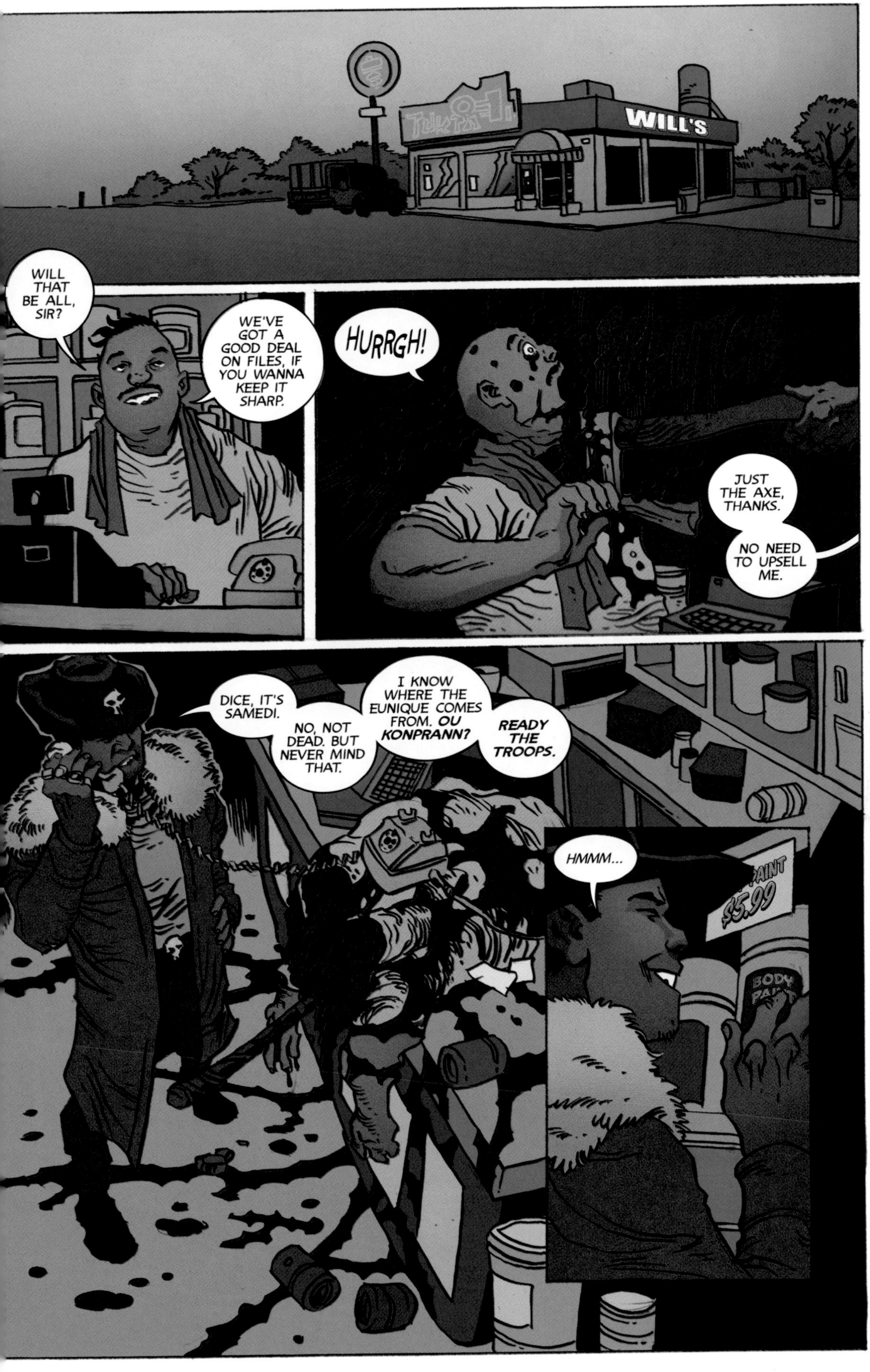
WILL'S
WILL THAT BE ALL, SIR?
WE'VE GOT A GOOD DEAL ON FILES, IF YOU WANNA KEEP IT SHARP.
HURRGH!
JUST THE AXE, THANKS.
NO NEED TO UPSELL ME.
DICE, IT'S SAMEDI.
NO, NOT DEAD. BUT NEVER MIND THAT.
I KNOW WHERE THE EUNIQUE COMES FROM. *OU KONPRANN?*
READY THE TROOPS.
HMMM...
PAINT
$5.99
BODY

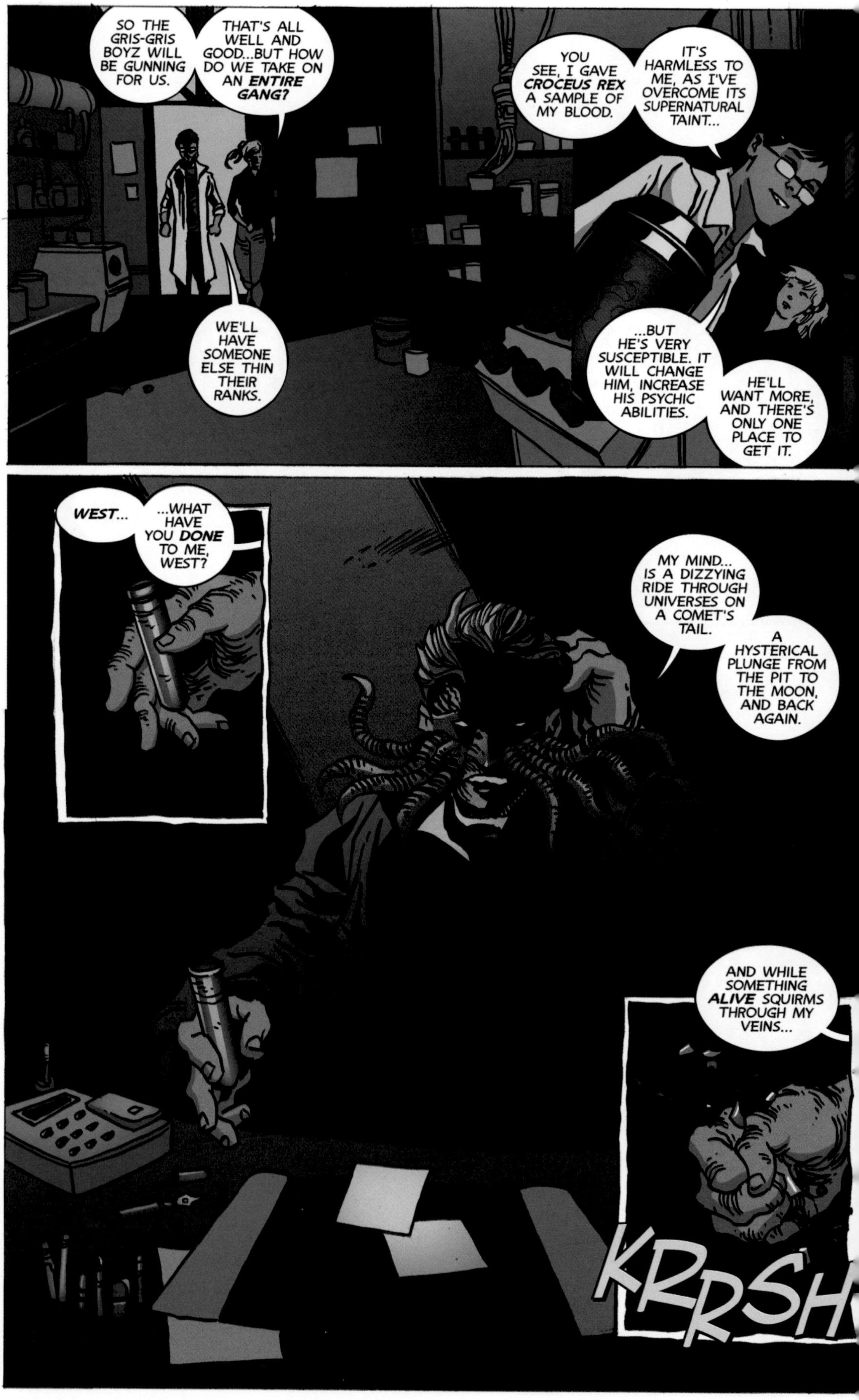
SO THE GRIS-GRIS BOYZ WILL BE GUNNING FOR US.
THAT'S ALL WELL AND GOOD...BUT HOW DO WE TAKE ON AN ENTIRE GANG?
WE'LL HAVE SOMEONE ELSE THIN THEIR RANKS.
YOU SEE, I GAVE CROCEUS REX A SAMPLE OF MY BLOOD.
IT'S HARMLESS TO ME, AS I'VE OVERCOME ITS SUPERNATURAL TAINT...
...BUT HE'S VERY SUSCEPTIBLE. IT WILL CHANGE HIM, INCREASE HIS PSYCHIC ABILITIES.
HE'LL WANT MORE, AND THERE'S ONLY ONE PLACE TO GET IT.
WEST...
...WHAT HAVE YOU DONE TO ME, WEST?
MY MIND... IS A DIZZYING RIDE THROUGH UNIVERSES ON A COMET'S TAIL.
A HYSTERICAL PLUNGE FROM THE PIT TO THE MOON, AND BACK AGAIN.
AND WHILE SOMETHING ALIVE SQUIRMS THROUGH MY VEINS...
KRRSH

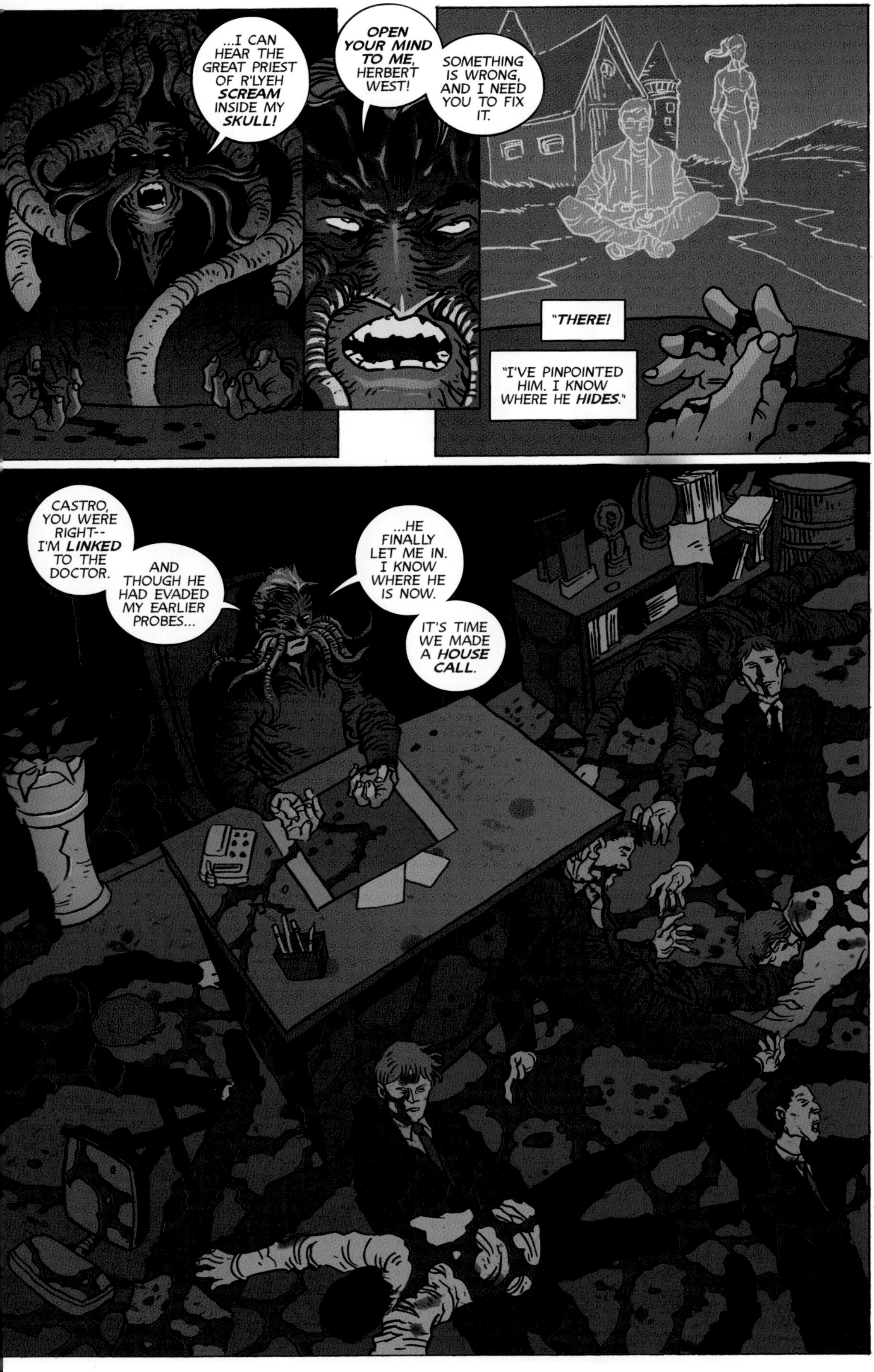
...I CAN HEAR THE GREAT PRIEST OF R'LYEH **SCREAM** INSIDE MY **SKULL!**
OPEN YOUR MIND TO ME, HERBERT WEST!
SOMETHING IS WRONG, AND I NEED YOU TO FIX IT.
"**THERE!**
"I'VE PINPOINTED HIM. I KNOW WHERE HE **HIDES**."
CASTRO, YOU WERE RIGHT-- I'M **LINKED** TO THE DOCTOR.
AND THOUGH HE HAD EVADED MY EARLIER PROBES...
...HE FINALLY LET ME IN. I KNOW WHERE HE IS NOW.
IT'S TIME WE MADE A **HOUSE CALL**.

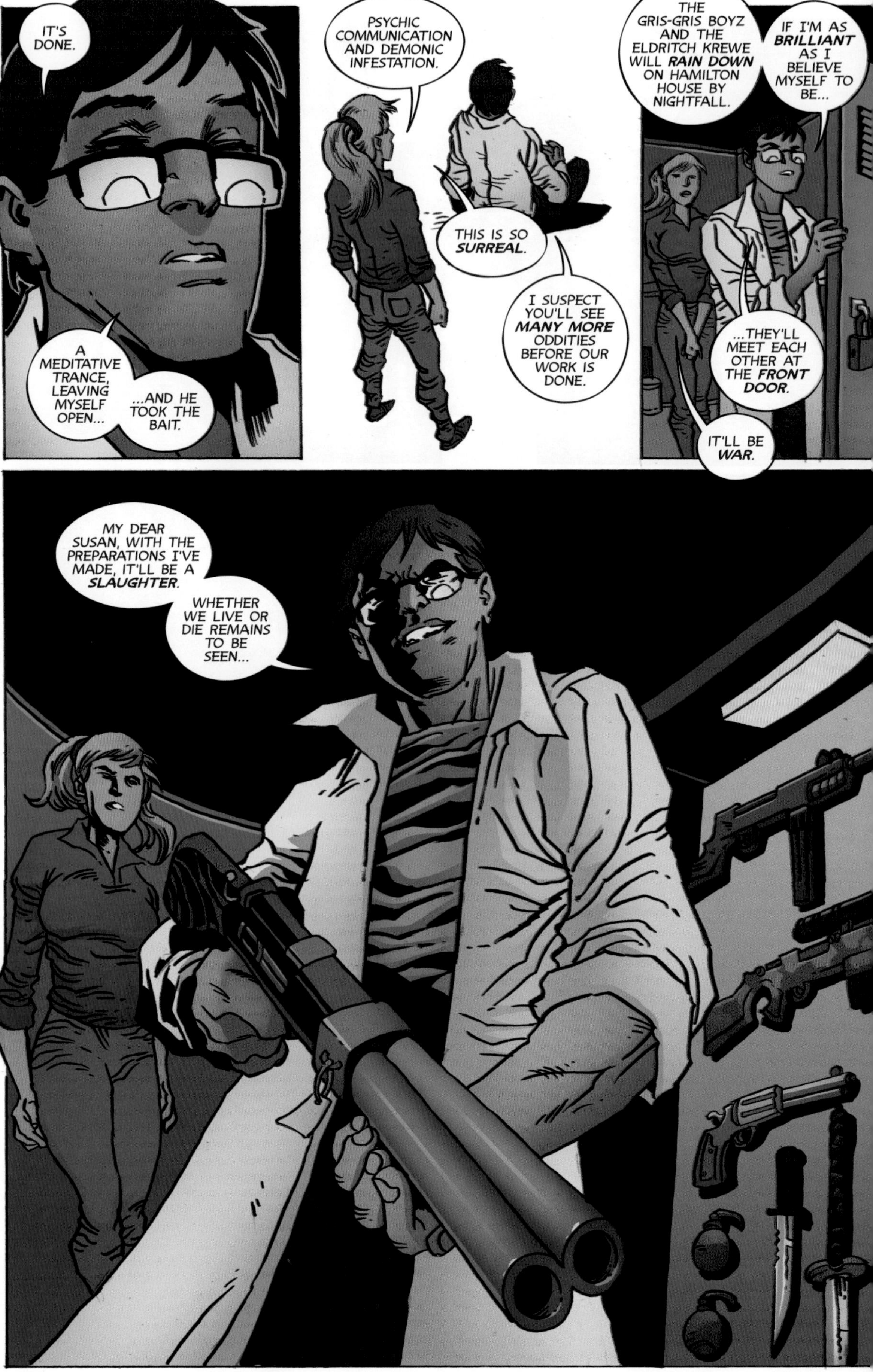
IT'S DONE.
A MEDITATIVE TRANCE, LEAVING MYSELF OPEN...
...AND HE TOOK THE BAIT.
PSYCHIC COMMUNICATION AND DEMONIC INFESTATION.
THIS IS SO SURREAL.
I SUSPECT YOU'LL SEE MANY MORE ODDITIES BEFORE OUR WORK IS DONE.
THE GRIS-GRIS BOYZ AND THE ELDRITCH KREWE WILL RAIN DOWN ON HAMILTON HOUSE BY NIGHTFALL.
IF I'M AS BRILLIANT AS I BELIEVE MYSELF TO BE...
...THEY'LL MEET EACH OTHER AT THE FRONT DOOR.
IT'LL BE WAR.
MY DEAR SUSAN, WITH THE PREPARATIONS I'VE MADE, IT'LL BE A SLAUGHTER.
WHETHER WE LIVE OR DIE REMAINS TO BE SEEN...

FOUR

Beyond Good and Evil

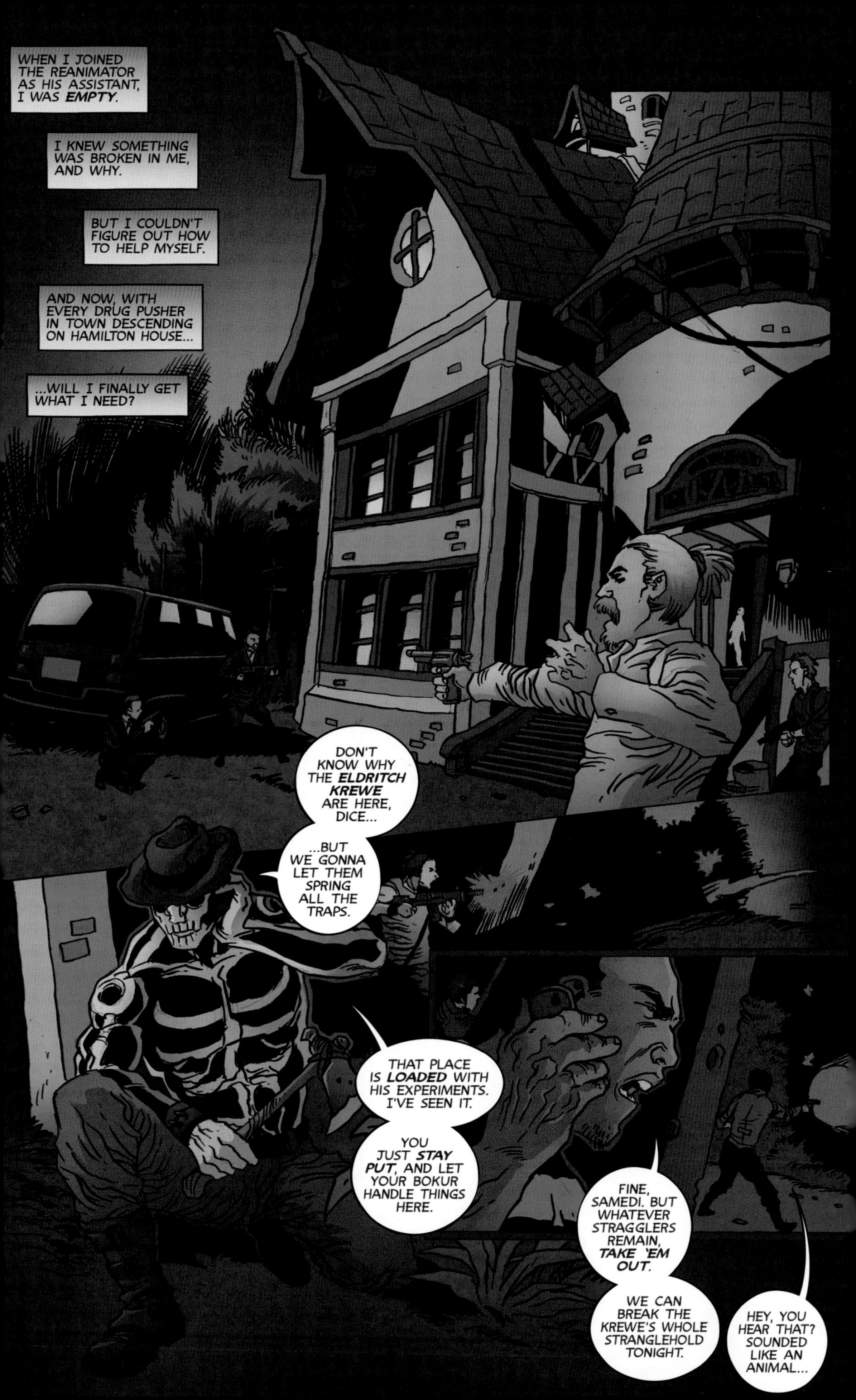
WHEN I JOINED THE REANIMATOR AS HIS ASSISTANT, I WAS EMPTY.
I KNEW SOMETHING WAS BROKEN IN ME, AND WHY.
BUT I COULDN'T FIGURE OUT HOW TO HELP MYSELF.
AND NOW, WITH EVERY DRUG PUSHER IN TOWN DESCENDING ON HAMILTON HOUSE...
...WILL I FINALLY GET WHAT I NEED?
DON'T KNOW WHY THE ELDRITCH KREWE ARE HERE, DICE...
...BUT WE GONNA LET THEM SPRING ALL THE TRAPS.
THAT PLACE IS LOADED WITH HIS EXPERIMENTS. I'VE SEEN IT.
YOU JUST STAY PUT, AND LET YOUR BOKUR HANDLE THINGS HERE.
FINE, SAMEDI. BUT WHATEVER STRAGGLERS REMAIN, TAKE 'EM OUT.
WE CAN BREAK THE KREWE'S WHOLE STRANGLEHOLD TONIGHT.
HEY, YOU HEAR THAT? SOUNDED LIKE AN ANIMAL...

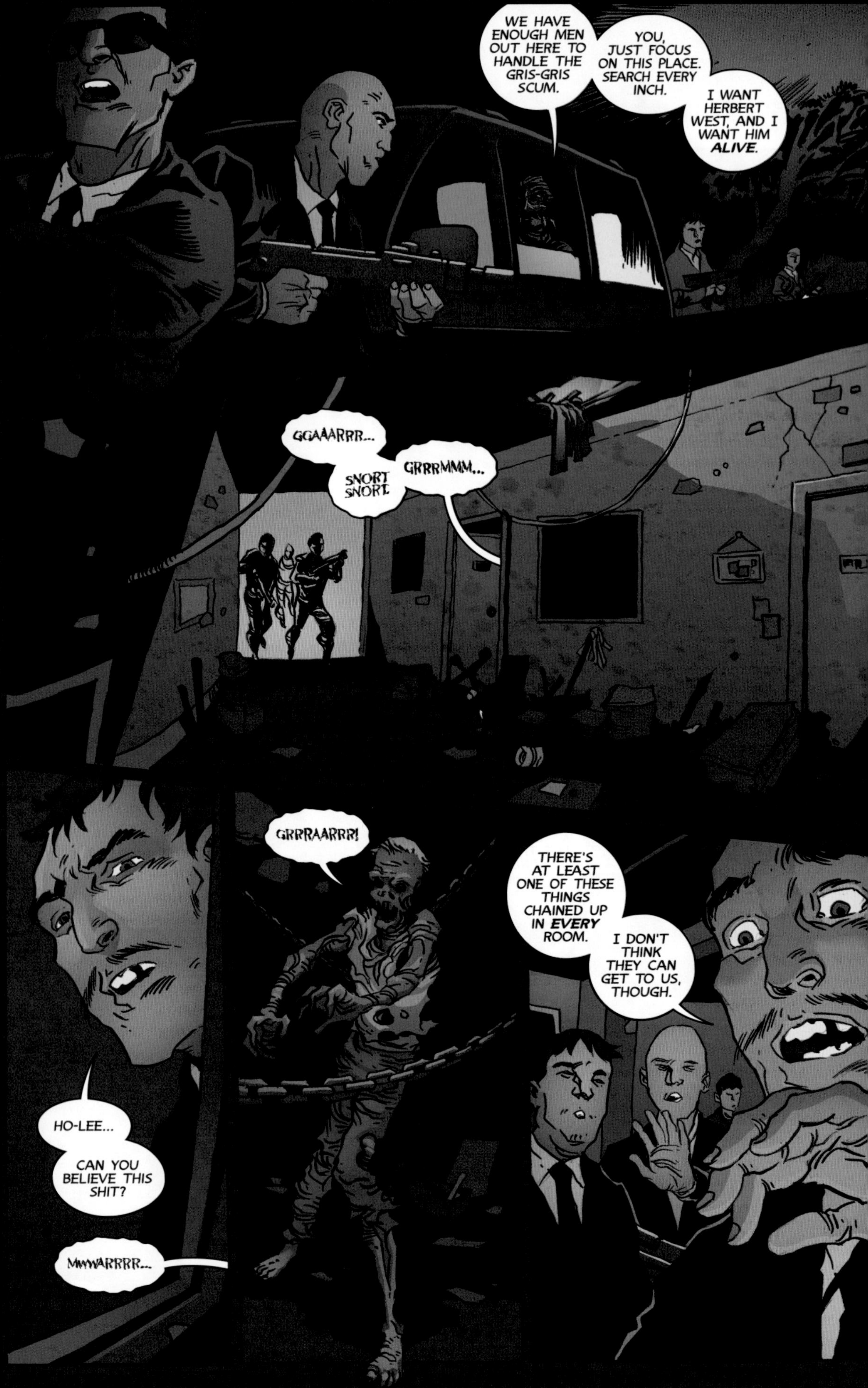

WE HAVE ENOUGH MEN OUT HERE TO HANDLE THE GRIS-GRIS SCUM.
YOU, JUST FOCUS ON THIS PLACE. SEARCH EVERY INCH.
I WANT HERBERT WEST, AND I WANT HIM *ALIVE*.
GGAAARRR...
SNORT SNORT.
GRRRMMM...
GRRRAARRR!
THERE'S AT LEAST ONE OF THESE THINGS CHAINED UP IN *EVERY* ROOM.
I DON'T THINK THEY CAN GET TO US, THOUGH.
HO-LEE...
CAN YOU BELIEVE THIS SHIT?
MWWARRRR...

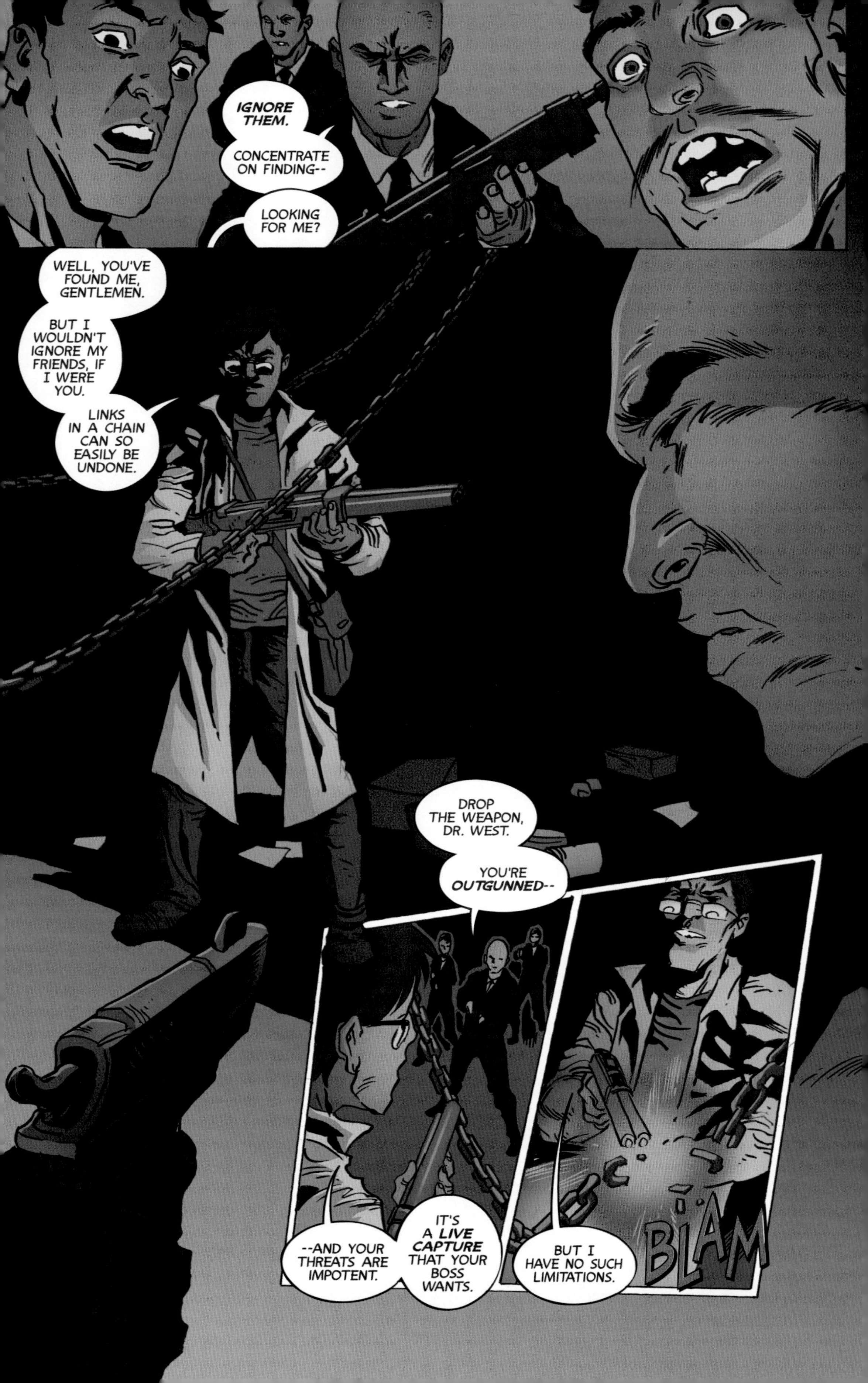
IGNORE THEM.
CONCENTRATE ON FINDING--
LOOKING FOR ME?
WELL, YOU'VE FOUND ME, GENTLEMEN.
BUT I WOULDN'T IGNORE MY FRIENDS, IF I WERE YOU.
LINKS IN A CHAIN CAN SO EASILY BE UNDONE.
DROP THE WEAPON, DR. WEST.
YOU'RE OUTGUNNED--
--AND YOUR THREATS ARE IMPOTENT.
IT'S A LIVE CAPTURE THAT YOUR BOSS WANTS.
BUT I HAVE NO SUCH LIMITATIONS.
BLAM

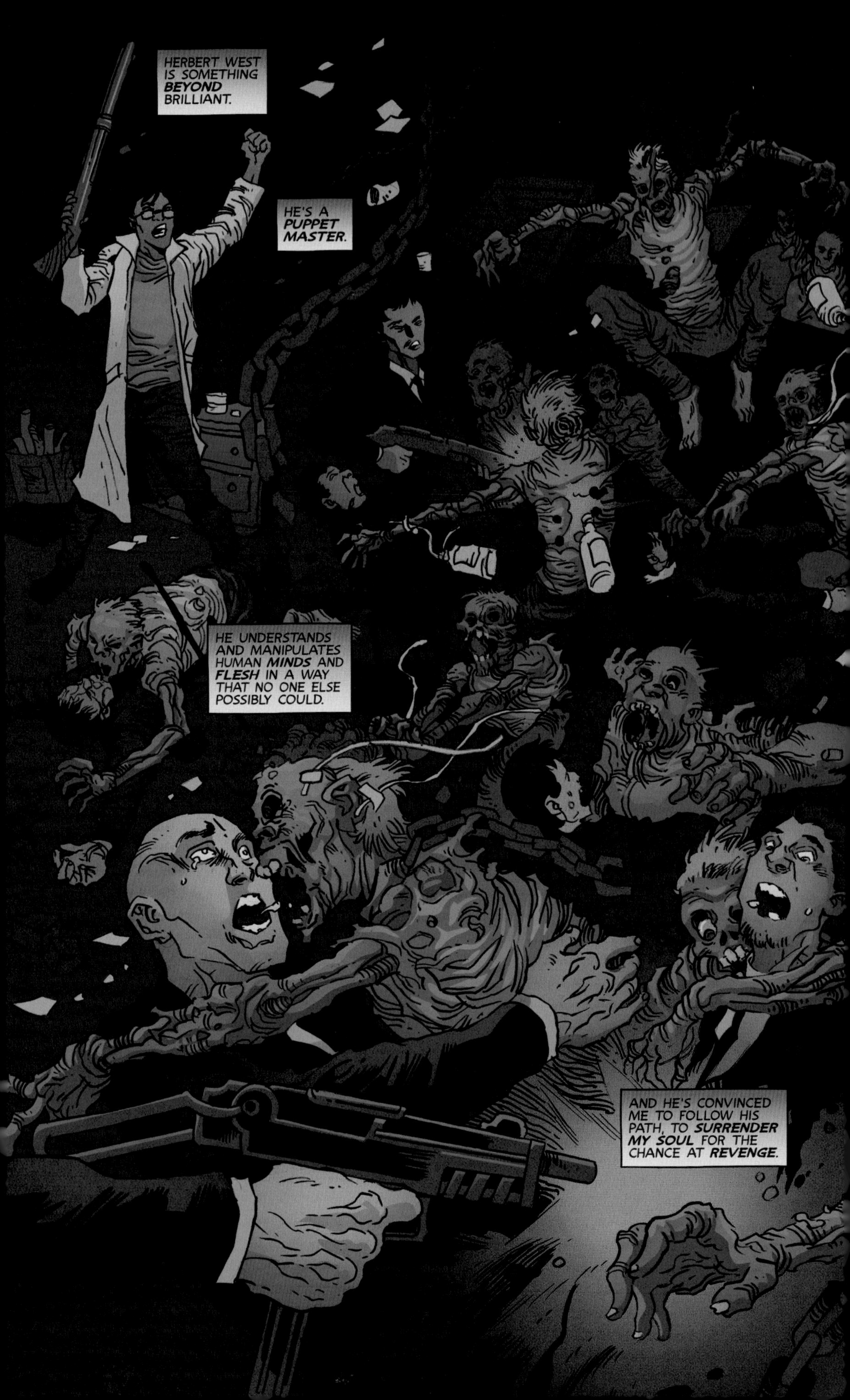
HERBERT WEST IS SOMETHING BEYOND BRILLIANT.
HE'S A PUPPET MASTER.
HE UNDERSTANDS AND MANIPULATES HUMAN MINDS AND FLESH IN A WAY THAT NO ONE ELSE POSSIBLY COULD.
AND HE'S CONVINCED ME TO FOLLOW HIS PATH, TO SURRENDER MY SOUL FOR THE CHANCE AT REVENGE.

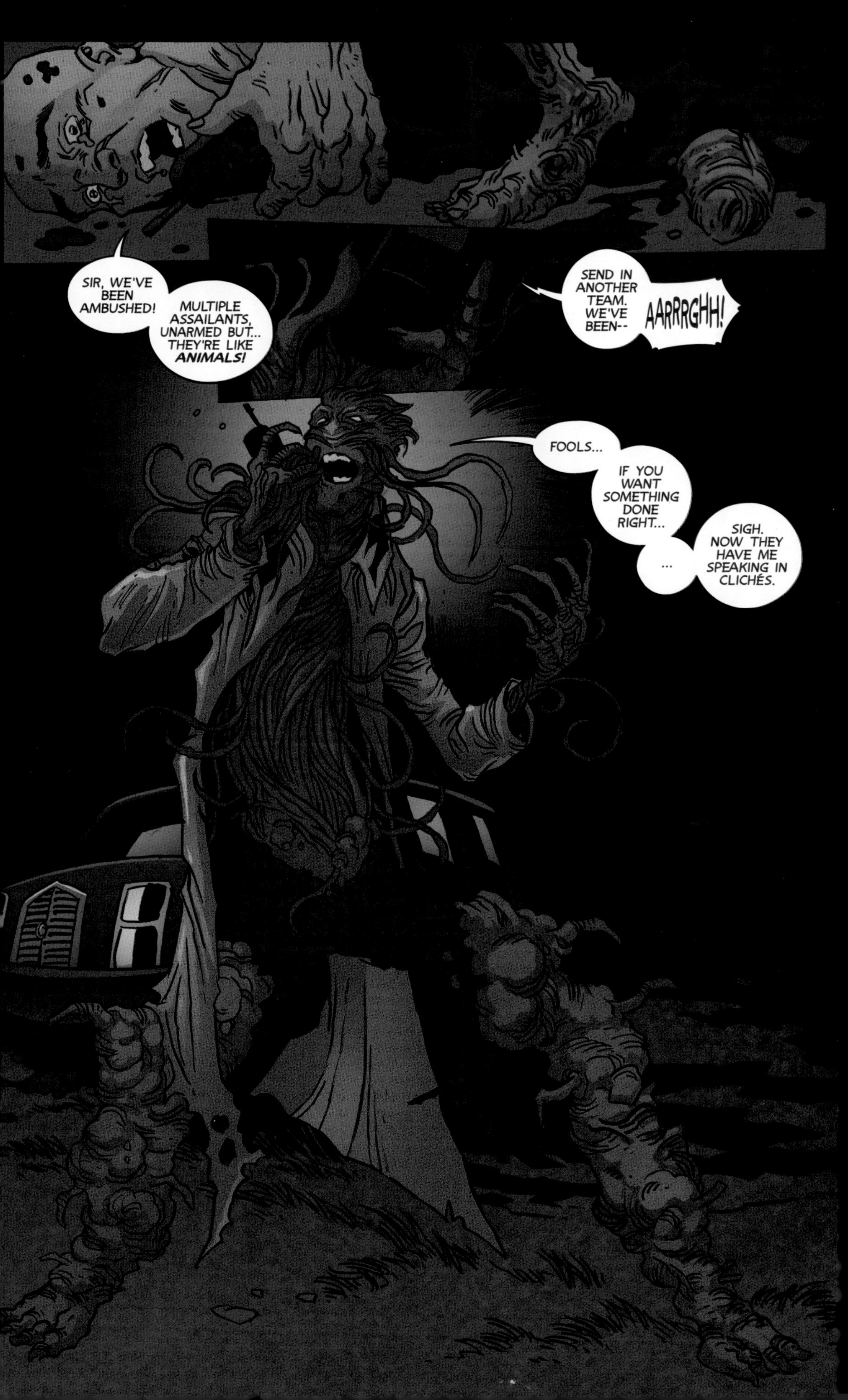
SIR, WE'VE BEEN AMBUSHED!
MULTIPLE ASSAILANTS, UNARMED BUT... THEY'RE LIKE ANIMALS!
SEND IN ANOTHER TEAM. WE'VE BEEN--
AARRRGHH!
FOOLS...
IF YOU WANT SOMETHING DONE RIGHT...
...
SIGH. NOW THEY HAVE ME SPEAKING IN CLICHÉS.

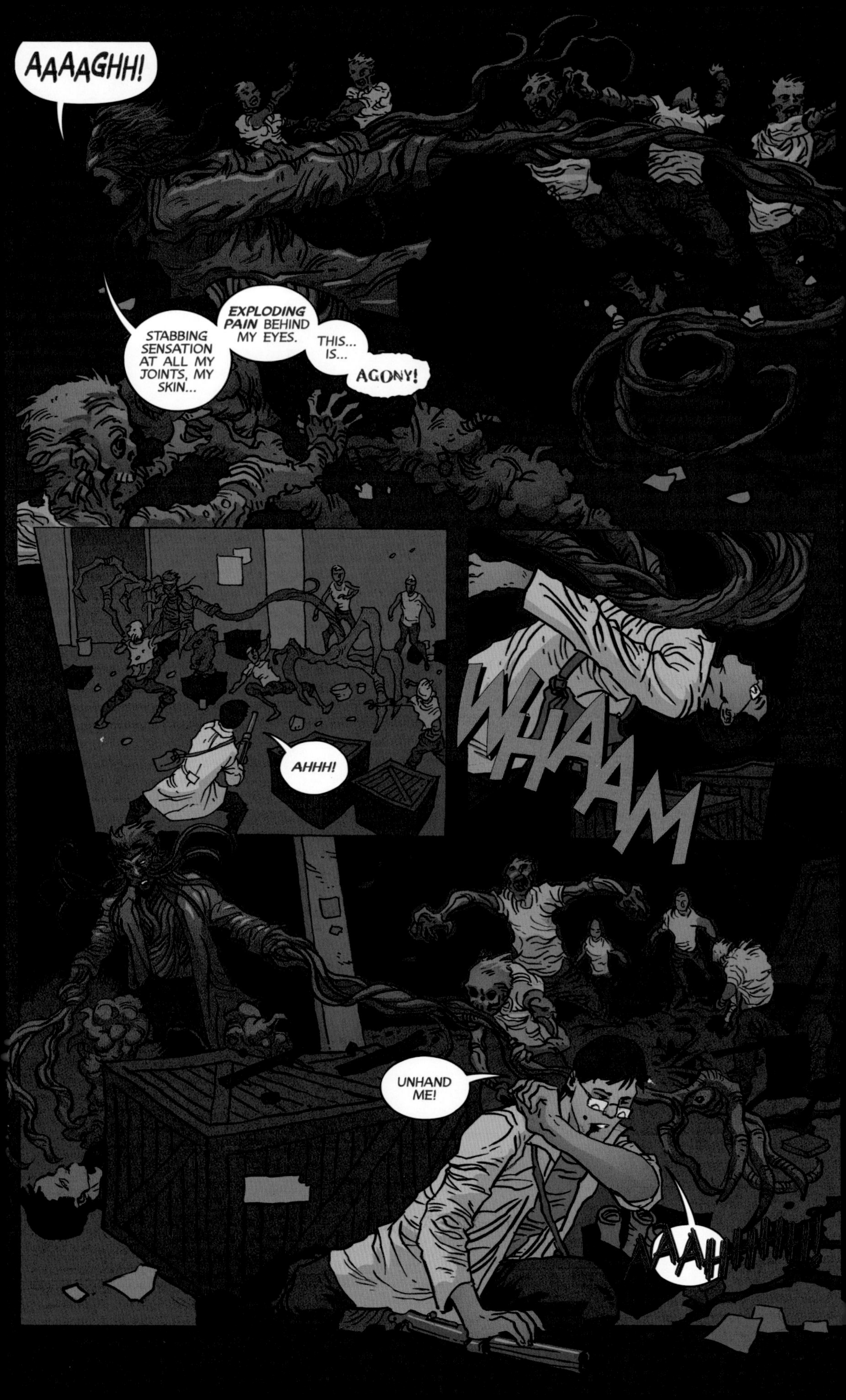
AAAAGHH!
STABBING SENSATION AT ALL MY JOINTS, MY SKIN...
EXPLODING PAIN BEHIND MY EYES.
THIS... IS...
AGONY!
AHHH!
WHAAM
UNHAND ME!
AAAHHHHHHH!

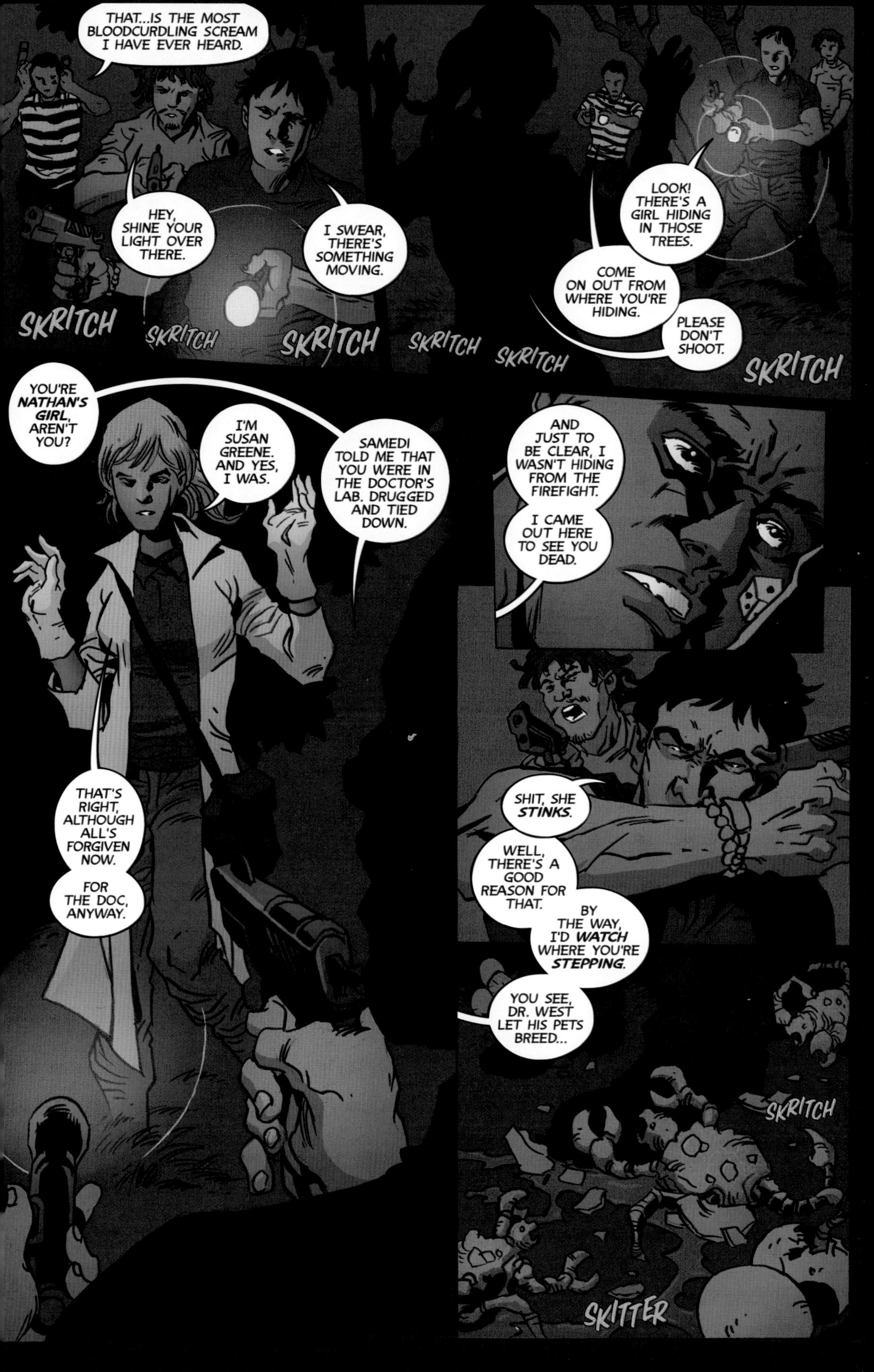
THAT...IS THE MOST BLOODCURDLING SCREAM I HAVE EVER HEARD.
HEY, SHINE YOUR LIGHT OVER THERE.
I SWEAR, THERE'S SOMETHING MOVING.
SKRITCH
SKRITCH
SKRITCH
LOOK! THERE'S A GIRL HIDING IN THOSE TREES.
COME ON OUT FROM WHERE YOU'RE HIDING.
PLEASE DON'T SHOOT.
SKRITCH
SKRITCH
SKRITCH
YOU'RE *NATHAN'S GIRL*, AREN'T YOU?
I'M SUSAN GREENE. AND YES, I WAS.
SAMEDI TOLD ME THAT YOU WERE IN THE DOCTOR'S LAB. DRUGGED AND TIED DOWN.
THAT'S RIGHT, ALTHOUGH ALL'S FORGIVEN NOW.
FOR THE DOC, ANYWAY.
AND JUST TO BE CLEAR, I WASN'T HIDING FROM THE FIREFIGHT.
I CAME OUT HERE TO SEE YOU DEAD.
SHIT, SHE *STINKS*.
WELL, THERE'S A GOOD REASON FOR THAT.
BY THE WAY, I'D *WATCH* WHERE YOU'RE *STEPPING*.
YOU SEE, DR. WEST LET HIS PETS BREED...
SKRITCH
SKITTER

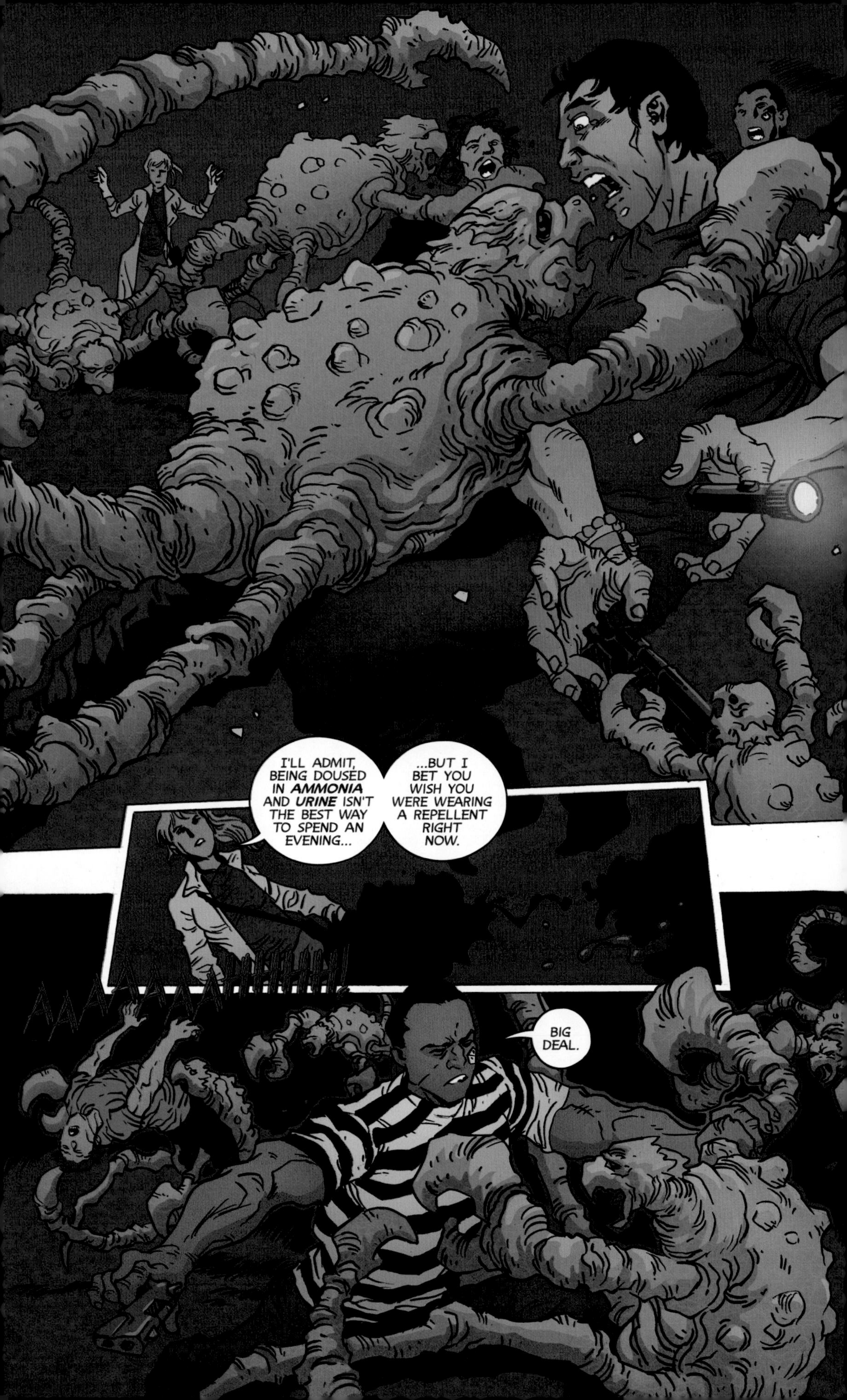
I'LL ADMIT, BEING DOUSED IN AMMONIA AND URINE ISN'T THE BEST WAY TO SPEND AN EVENING...
...BUT I BET YOU WISH YOU WERE WEARING A REPELLENT RIGHT NOW.
AAAAAAAHHHHH!
BIG DEAL.

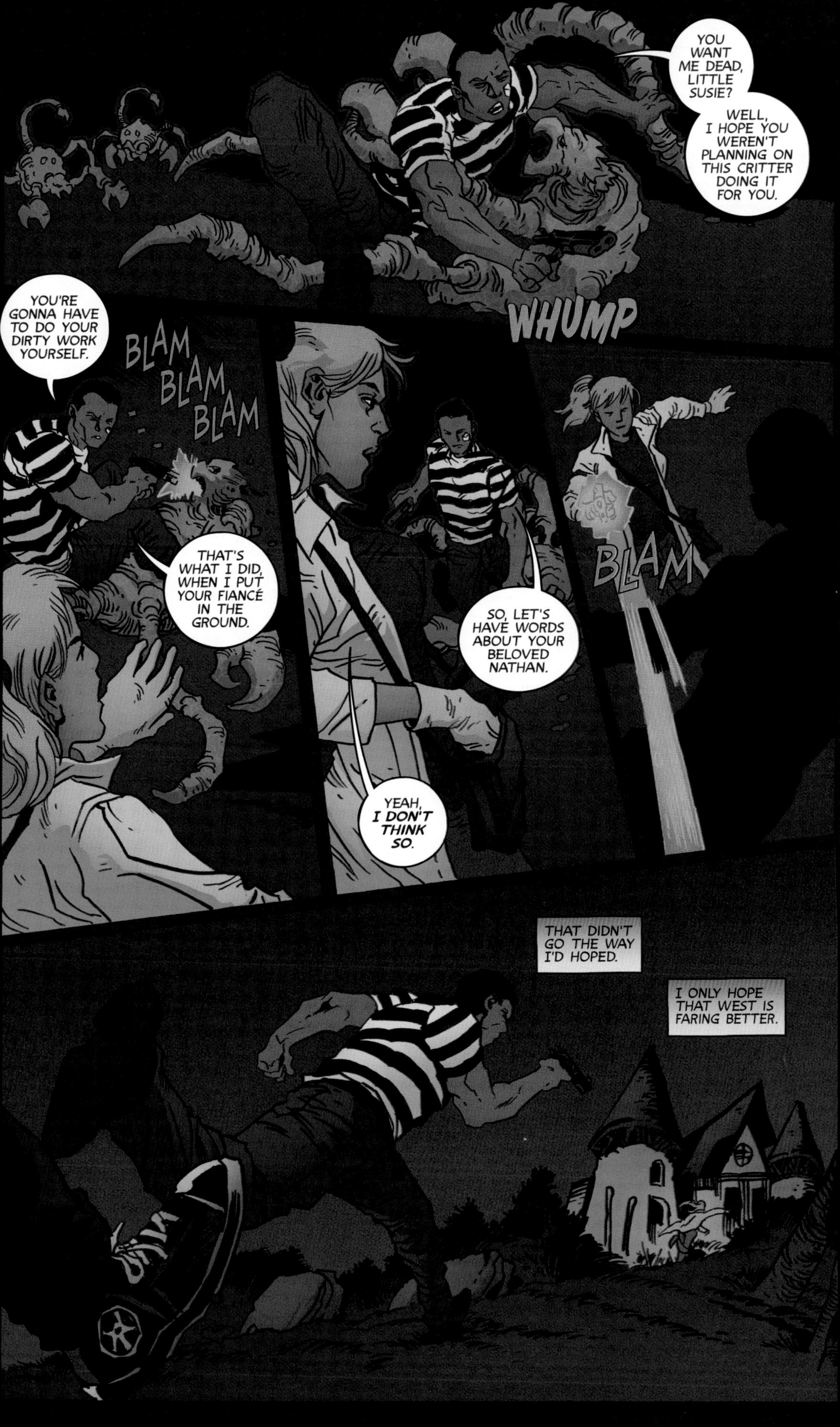
YOU WANT ME DEAD, LITTLE SUSIE?
WELL, I HOPE YOU WEREN'T PLANNING ON THIS CRITTER DOING IT FOR YOU.
WHUMP
YOU'RE GONNA HAVE TO DO YOUR DIRTY WORK YOURSELF.
BLAM BLAM BLAM
THAT'S WHAT I DID, WHEN I PUT YOUR FIANCÉ IN THE GROUND.
SO, LET'S HAVE WORDS ABOUT YOUR BELOVED NATHAN.
YEAH, I DON'T THINK SO.
BLAM
THAT DIDN'T GO THE WAY I'D HOPED.
I ONLY HOPE THAT WEST IS FARING BETTER.

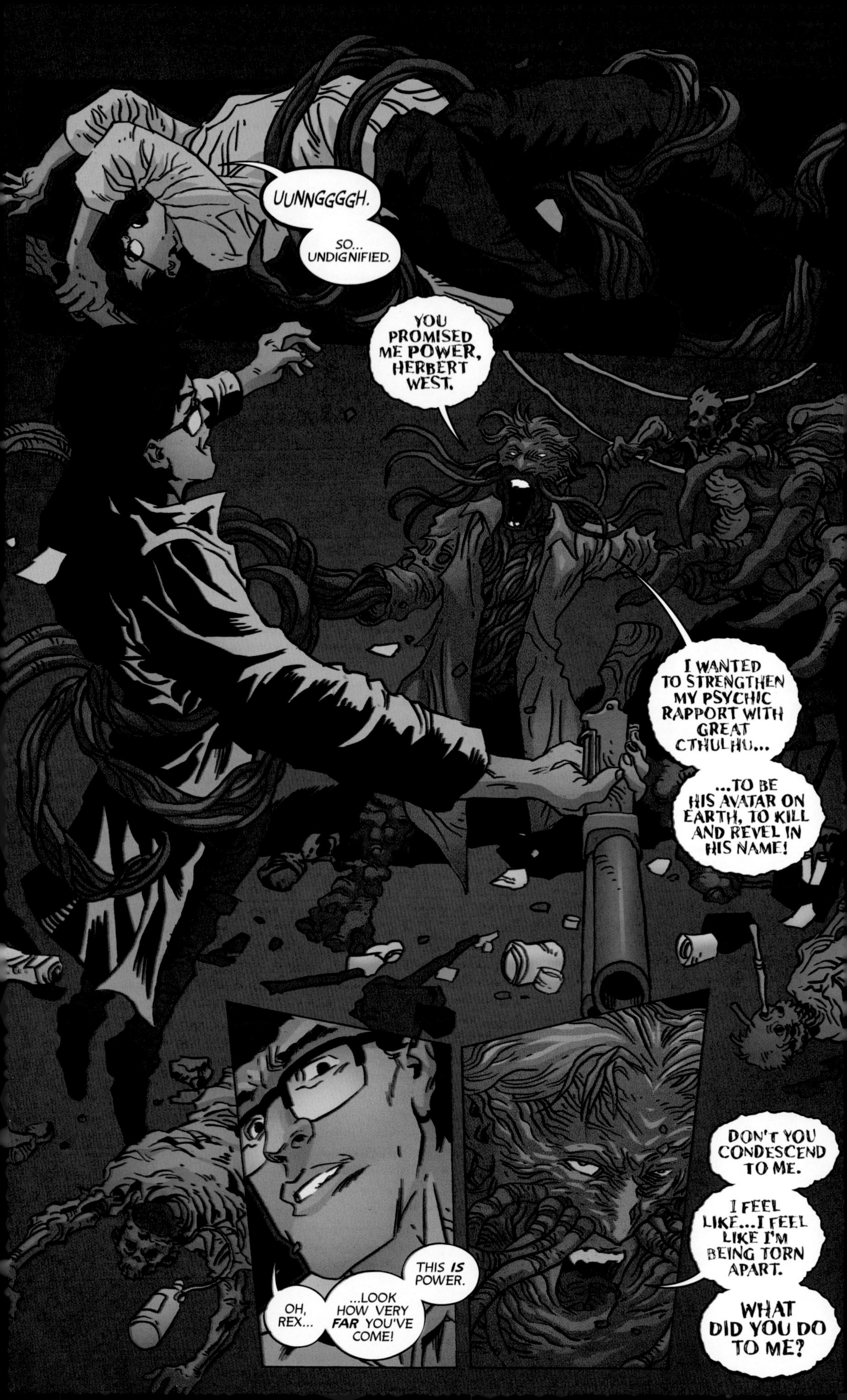
UUNNGGGGH.
SO... UNDIGNIFIED.
YOU PROMISED ME POWER, HERBERT WEST.
I WANTED TO STRENGTHEN MY PSYCHIC RAPPORT WITH GREAT CTHULHU...
...TO BE HIS AVATAR ON EARTH, TO KILL AND REVEL IN HIS NAME!
OH, REX...
...LOOK HOW VERY FAR YOU'VE COME!
THIS IS POWER.
DON'T YOU CONDESCEND TO ME.
I FEEL LIKE...I FEEL LIKE I'M BEING TORN APART.
WHAT DID YOU DO TO ME?

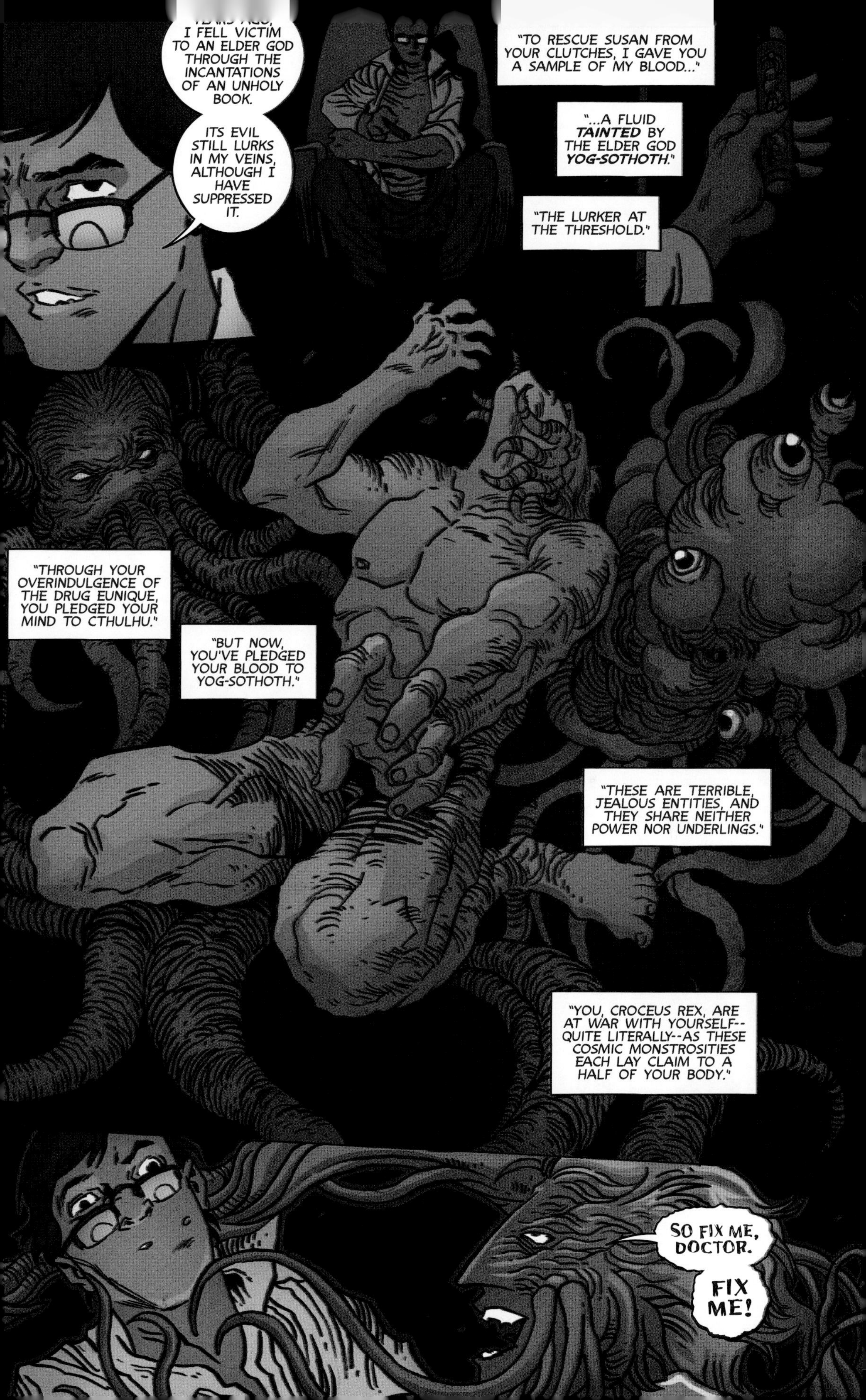
I FELL VICTIM TO AN ELDER GOD THROUGH THE INCANTATIONS OF AN UNHOLY BOOK.
ITS EVIL STILL LURKS IN MY VEINS, ALTHOUGH I HAVE SUPPRESSED IT.
"TO RESCUE SUSAN FROM YOUR CLUTCHES, I GAVE YOU A SAMPLE OF MY BLOOD..."
"...A FLUID **TAINTED** BY THE ELDER GOD ***YOG-SOTHOTH.***"
"THE LURKER AT THE THRESHOLD."
"THROUGH YOUR OVERINDULGENCE OF THE DRUG EUNIQUE, YOU PLEDGED YOUR MIND TO CTHULHU."
"BUT NOW, YOU'VE PLEDGED YOUR BLOOD TO YOG-SOTHOTH."
"THESE ARE TERRIBLE, JEALOUS ENTITIES, AND THEY SHARE NEITHER POWER NOR UNDERLINGS."
"YOU, CROCEUS REX, ARE AT WAR WITH YOURSELF--QUITE LITERALLY--AS THESE COSMIC MONSTROSITIES EACH LAY CLAIM TO A HALF OF YOUR BODY."
SO FIX ME, DOCTOR.
FIX ME!

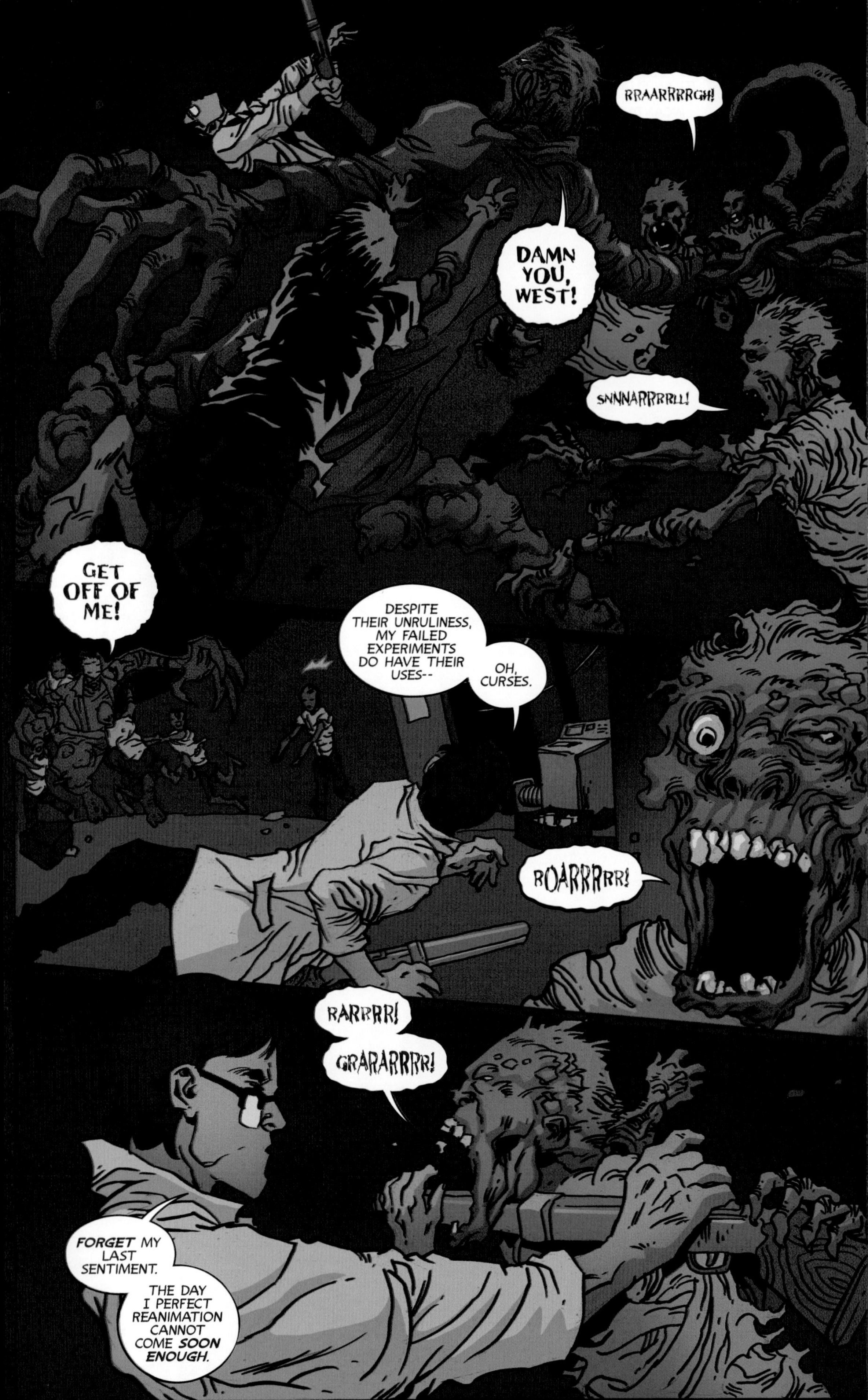
RRAARRRRGH!
DAMN YOU, WEST!
SNNNARRRRLL!
GET OFF OF ME!
DESPITE THEIR UNRULINESS, MY FAILED EXPERIMENTS DO HAVE THEIR USES--
OH, CURSES.
ROARRRRR!
RARRRR!
GRARARRRR!
FORGET MY LAST SENTIMENT.
THE DAY I PERFECT REANIMATION CANNOT COME SOON ENOUGH.

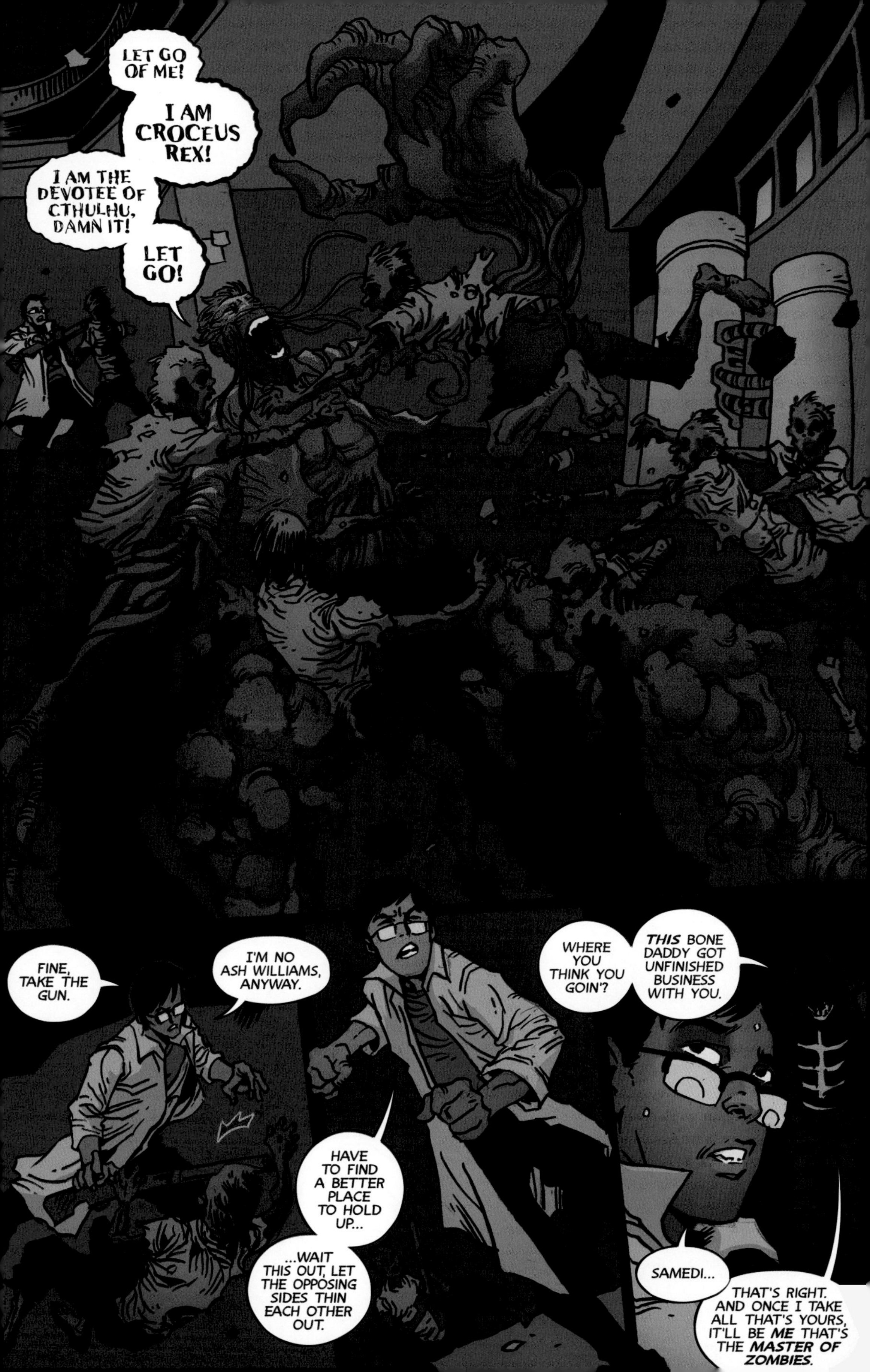
LET GO OF ME!
I AM CROCEUS REX!
I AM THE DEVOTEE OF CTHULHU, DAMN IT!
LET GO!
FINE, TAKE THE GUN.
I'M NO ASH WILLIAMS, ANYWAY.
HAVE TO FIND A BETTER PLACE TO HOLD UP...
...WAIT THIS OUT, LET THE OPPOSING SIDES THIN EACH OTHER OUT.
WHERE YOU THINK YOU GOIN'?
THIS BONE DADDY GOT UNFINISHED BUSINESS WITH YOU.
SAMEDI...
THAT'S RIGHT. AND ONCE I TAKE ALL THAT'S YOURS, IT'LL BE ME THAT'S THE MASTER OF ZOMBIES.

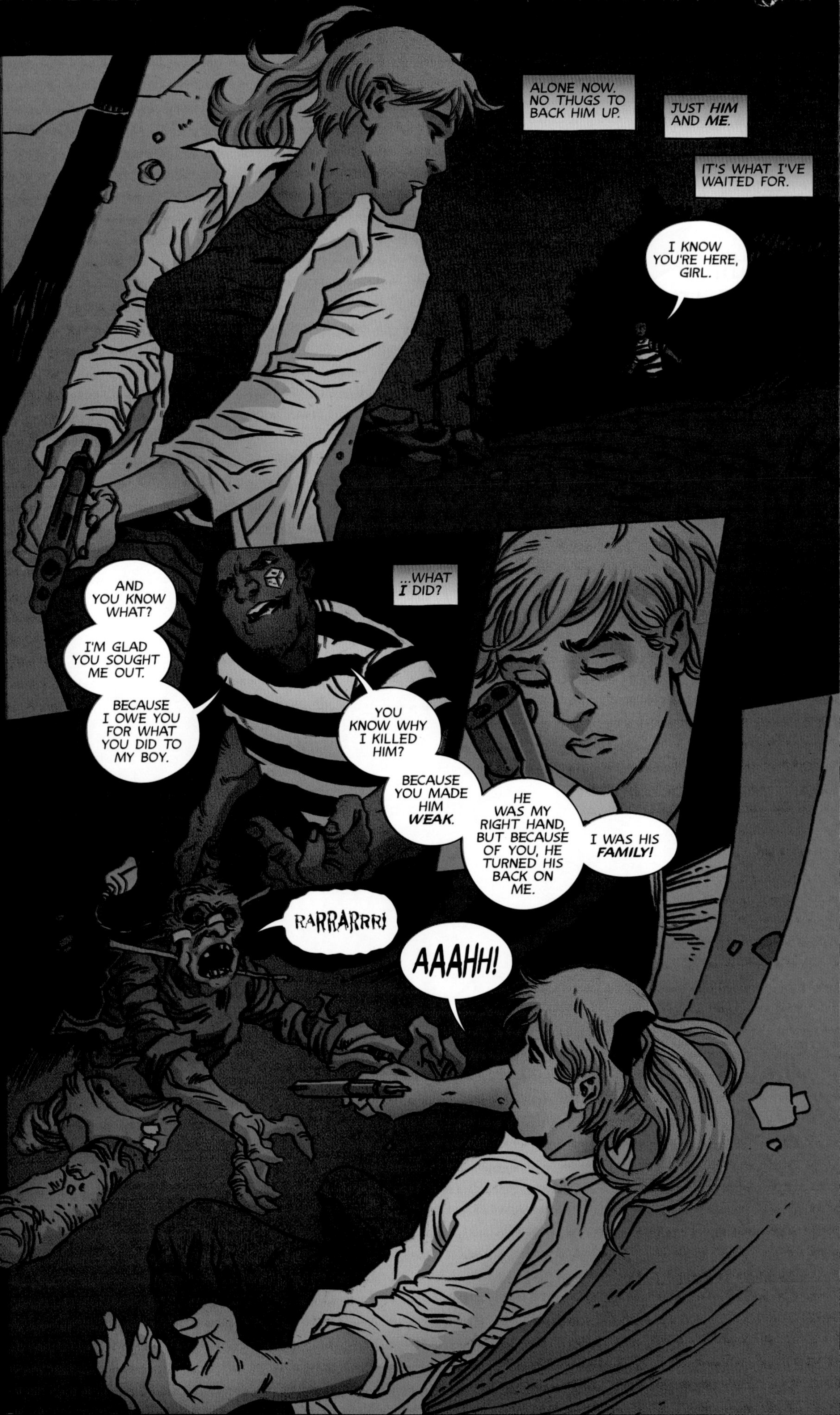
ALONE NOW. NO THUGS TO BACK HIM UP.
JUST HIM AND ME.
IT'S WHAT I'VE WAITED FOR.
I KNOW YOU'RE HERE, GIRL.
AND YOU KNOW WHAT?
I'M GLAD YOU SOUGHT ME OUT.
BECAUSE I OWE YOU FOR WHAT YOU DID TO MY BOY.
...WHAT I DID?
YOU KNOW WHY I KILLED HIM?
BECAUSE YOU MADE HIM WEAK.
HE WAS MY RIGHT HAND, BUT BECAUSE OF YOU, HE TURNED HIS BACK ON ME.
I WAS HIS FAMILY!
RARRARRR!
AAAHH!

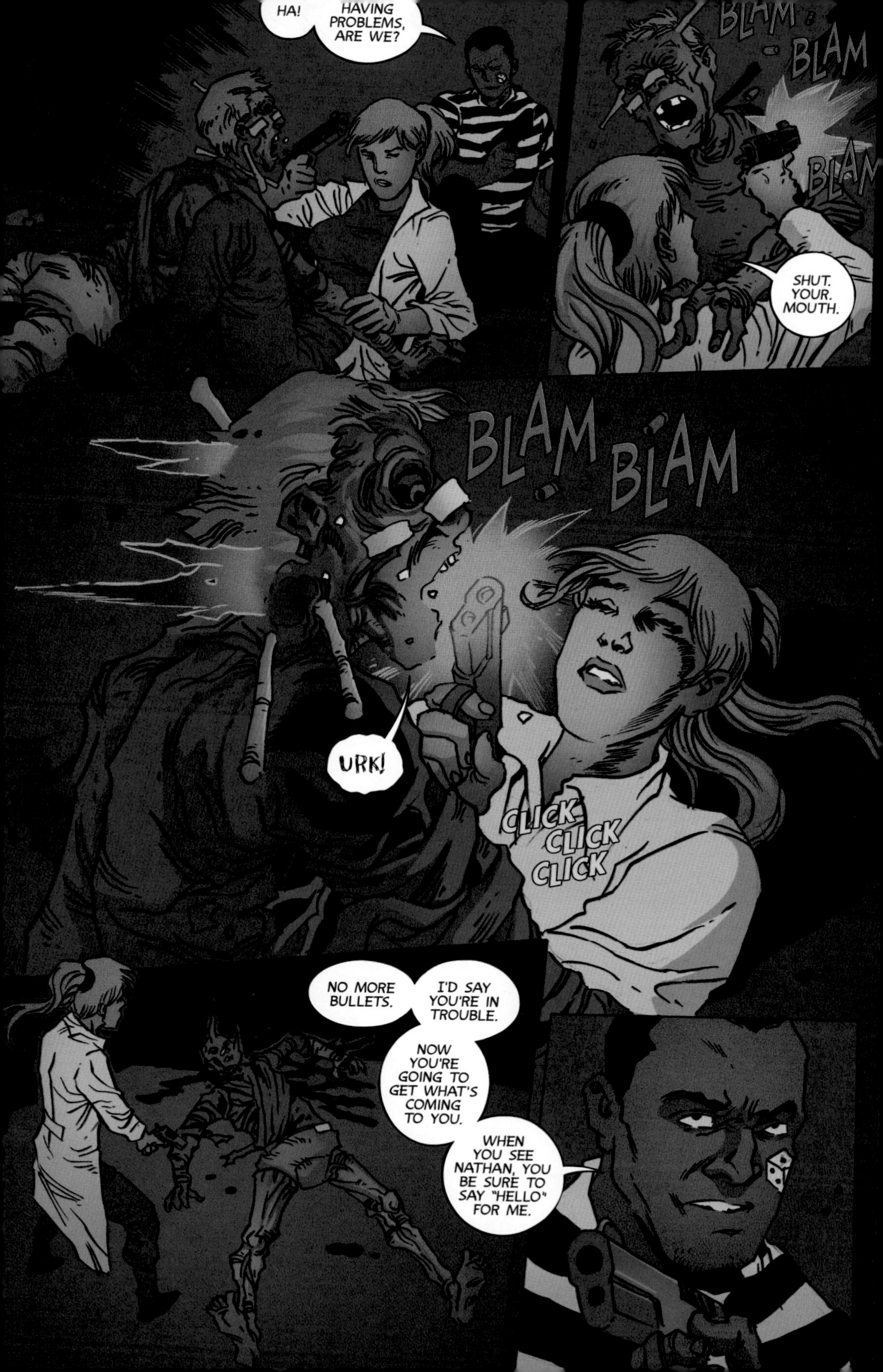
HA!
HAVING PROBLEMS, ARE WE?
BLAM
BLAM
BLAM
SHUT. YOUR. MOUTH.
BLAM
BLAM
URK!
CLICK
CLICK
CLICK
NO MORE BULLETS.
I'D SAY YOU'RE IN TROUBLE.
NOW YOU'RE GOING TO GET WHAT'S COMING TO YOU.
WHEN YOU SEE NATHAN, YOU BE SURE TO SAY "HELLO" FOR ME.

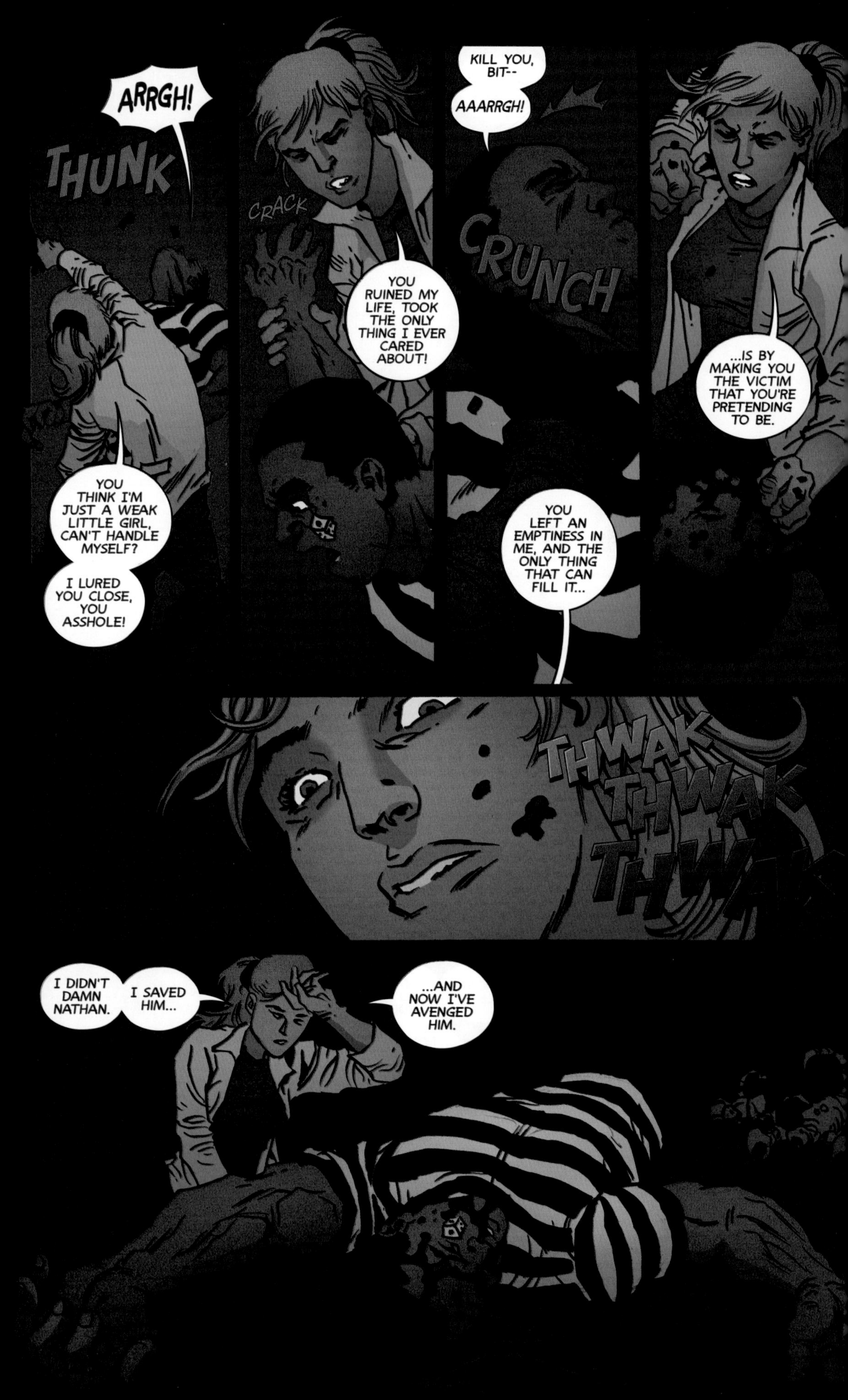

ARRGH!
THUNK
YOU THINK I'M JUST A WEAK LITTLE GIRL, CAN'T HANDLE MYSELF?
I LURED YOU CLOSE, YOU ASSHOLE!
CRACK
YOU RUINED MY LIFE, TOOK THE ONLY THING I EVER CARED ABOUT!
KILL YOU, BIT--
AAARRGH!
CRUNCH
YOU LEFT AN EMPTINESS IN ME, AND THE ONLY THING THAT CAN FILL IT...
...IS BY MAKING YOU THE VICTIM THAT YOU'RE PRETENDING TO BE.
THWAK
THWAK
I DIDN'T DAMN NATHAN.
I SAVED HIM...
...AND NOW I'VE AVENGED HIM.

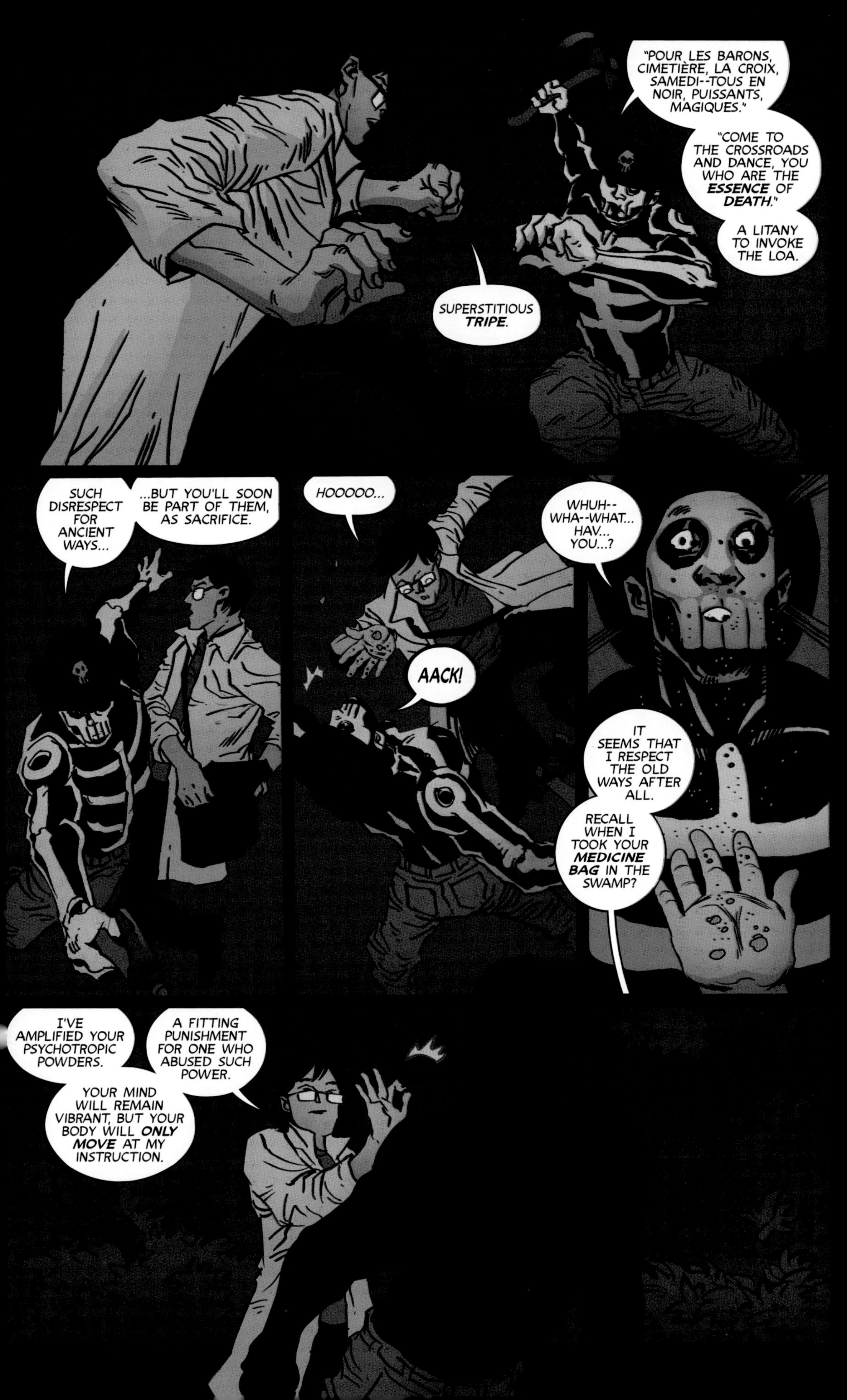
"POUR LES BARONS, CIMETIÈRE, LA CROIX, SAMEDI--TOUS EN NOIR, PUISSANTS, MAGIQUES."
"COME TO THE CROSSROADS AND DANCE, YOU WHO ARE THE ***ESSENCE*** OF ***DEATH***."
A LITANY TO INVOKE THE LOA.
SUPERSTITIOUS ***TRIPE***.
SUCH DISRESPECT FOR ANCIENT WAYS...
...BUT YOU'LL SOON BE PART OF THEM, AS SACRIFICE.
HOOOOO...
AACK!
WHUH-- WHA--WHAT... HAV... YOU...?
IT SEEMS THAT I RESPECT THE OLD WAYS AFTER ALL.
RECALL WHEN I TOOK YOUR ***MEDICINE BAG*** IN THE SWAMP?
I'VE AMPLIFIED YOUR PSYCHOTROPIC POWDERS.
A FITTING PUNISHMENT FOR ONE WHO ABUSED SUCH POWER.
YOUR MIND WILL REMAIN VIBRANT, BUT YOUR BODY WILL ***ONLY MOVE*** AT MY INSTRUCTION.

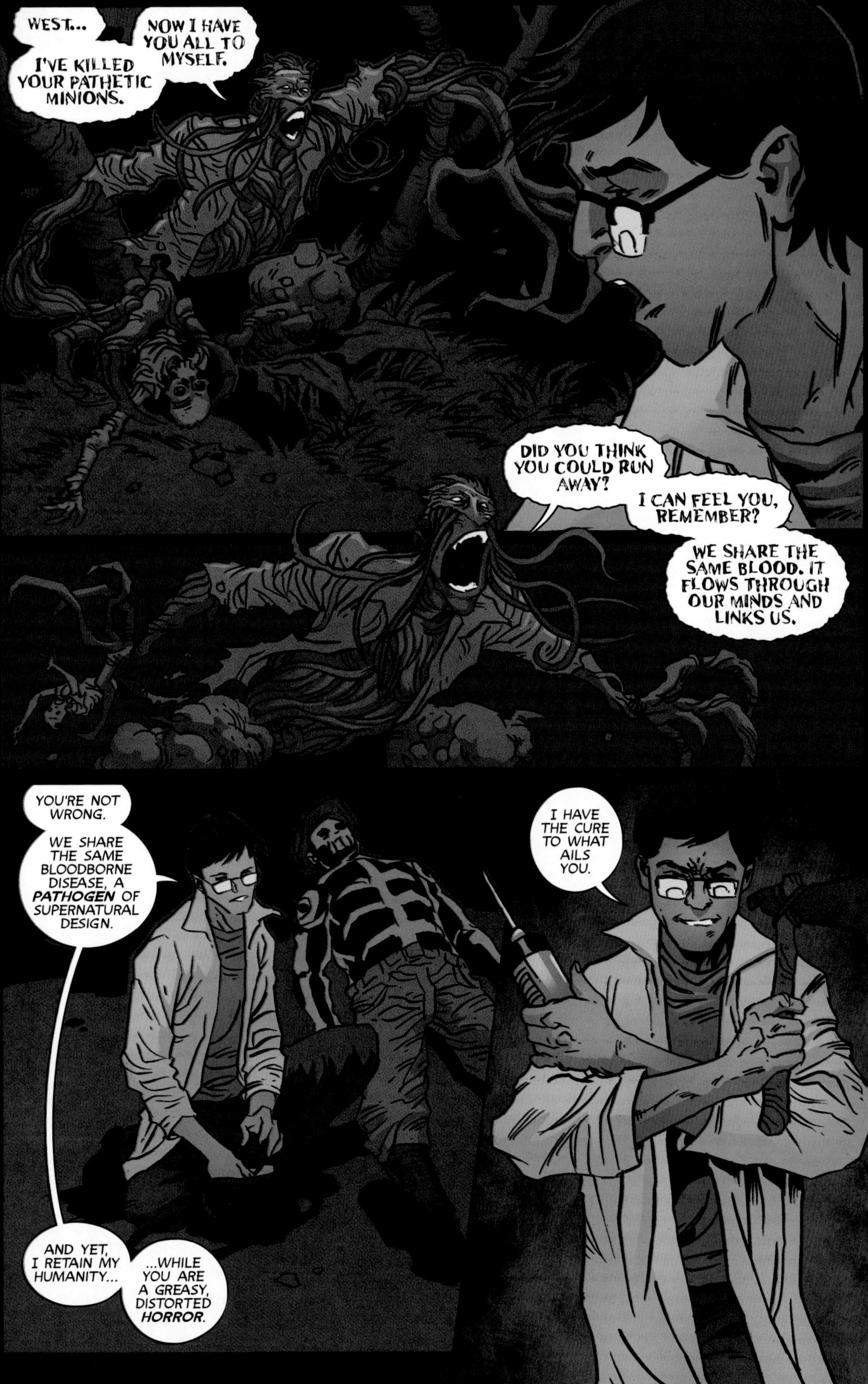
WEST...
I'VE KILLED YOUR PATHETIC MINIONS.
NOW I HAVE YOU ALL TO MYSELF.
DID YOU THINK YOU COULD RUN AWAY?
I CAN FEEL YOU, REMEMBER?
WE SHARE THE SAME BLOOD. IT FLOWS THROUGH OUR MINDS AND LINKS US.
YOU'RE NOT WRONG.
WE SHARE THE SAME BLOODBORNE DISEASE, A PATHOGEN OF SUPERNATURAL DESIGN.
AND YET, I RETAIN MY HUMANITY...
...WHILE YOU ARE A GREASY, DISTORTED HORROR.
I HAVE THE CURE TO WHAT AILS YOU.

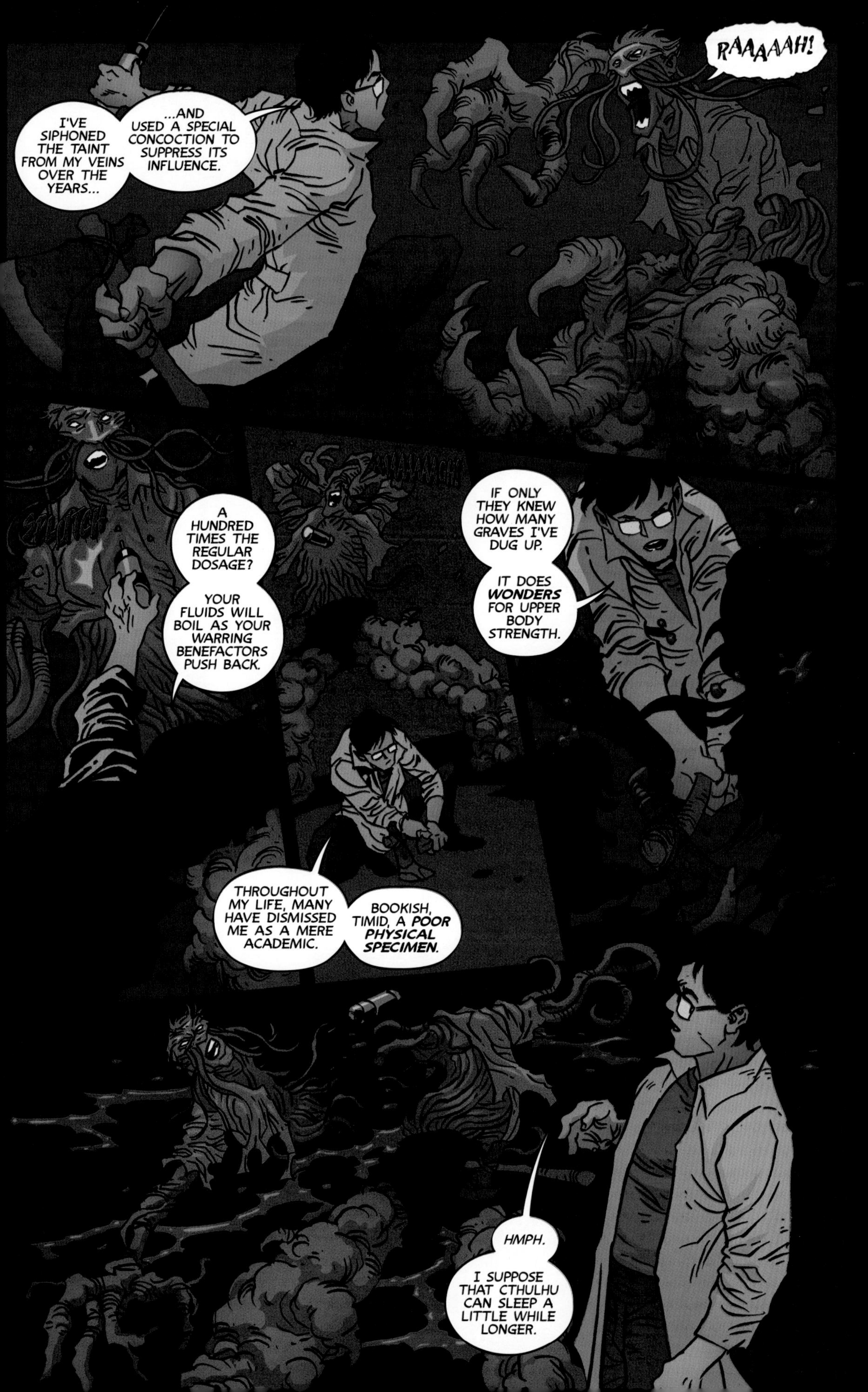
I'VE SIPHONED THE TAINT FROM MY VEINS OVER THE YEARS...
...AND USED A SPECIAL CONCOCTION TO SUPPRESS ITS INFLUENCE.
RAAAAAH!
A HUNDRED TIMES THE REGULAR DOSAGE?
YOUR FLUIDS WILL BOIL AS YOUR WARRING BENEFACTORS PUSH BACK.
THROUGHOUT MY LIFE, MANY HAVE DISMISSED ME AS A MERE ACADEMIC.
BOOKISH, TIMID, A ***POOR PHYSICAL SPECIMEN***.
IF ONLY THEY KNEW HOW MANY GRAVES I'VE DUG UP.
IT DOES ***WONDERS*** FOR UPPER BODY STRENGTH.
HMPH.
I SUPPOSE THAT CTHULHU CAN SLEEP A LITTLE WHILE LONGER.

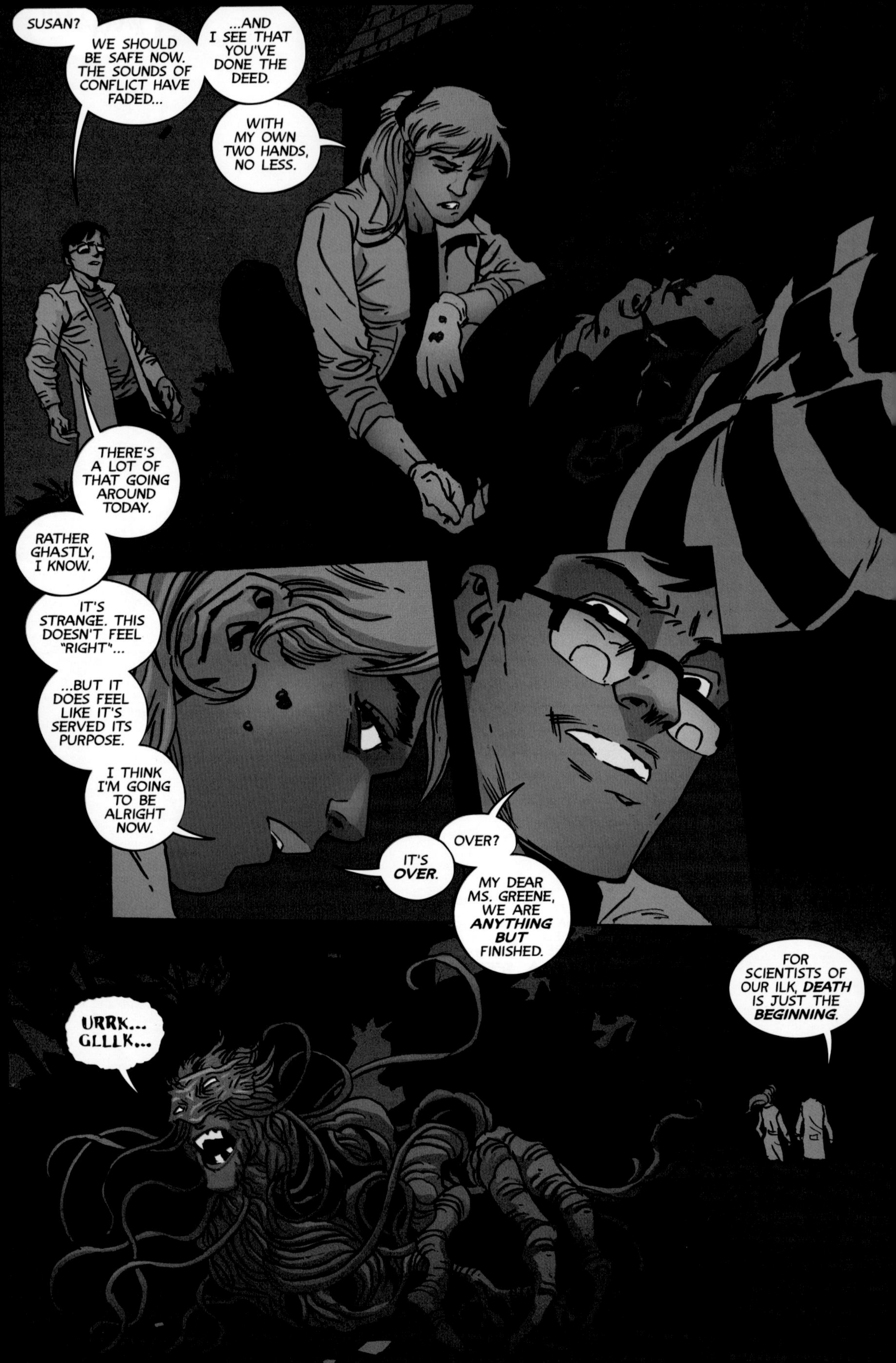
SUSAN?
WE SHOULD BE SAFE NOW. THE SOUNDS OF CONFLICT HAVE FADED...
...AND I SEE THAT YOU'VE DONE THE DEED.
WITH MY OWN TWO HANDS, NO LESS.
THERE'S A LOT OF THAT GOING AROUND TODAY.
RATHER GHASTLY, I KNOW.
IT'S STRANGE. THIS DOESN'T FEEL "RIGHT"...
...BUT IT DOES FEEL LIKE IT'S SERVED ITS PURPOSE.
I THINK I'M GOING TO BE ALRIGHT NOW.
IT'S OVER.
OVER?
MY DEAR MS. GREENE, WE ARE ANYTHING BUT FINISHED.
URRK... GLLLK...
FOR SCIENTISTS OF OUR ILK, DEATH IS JUST THE BEGINNING.

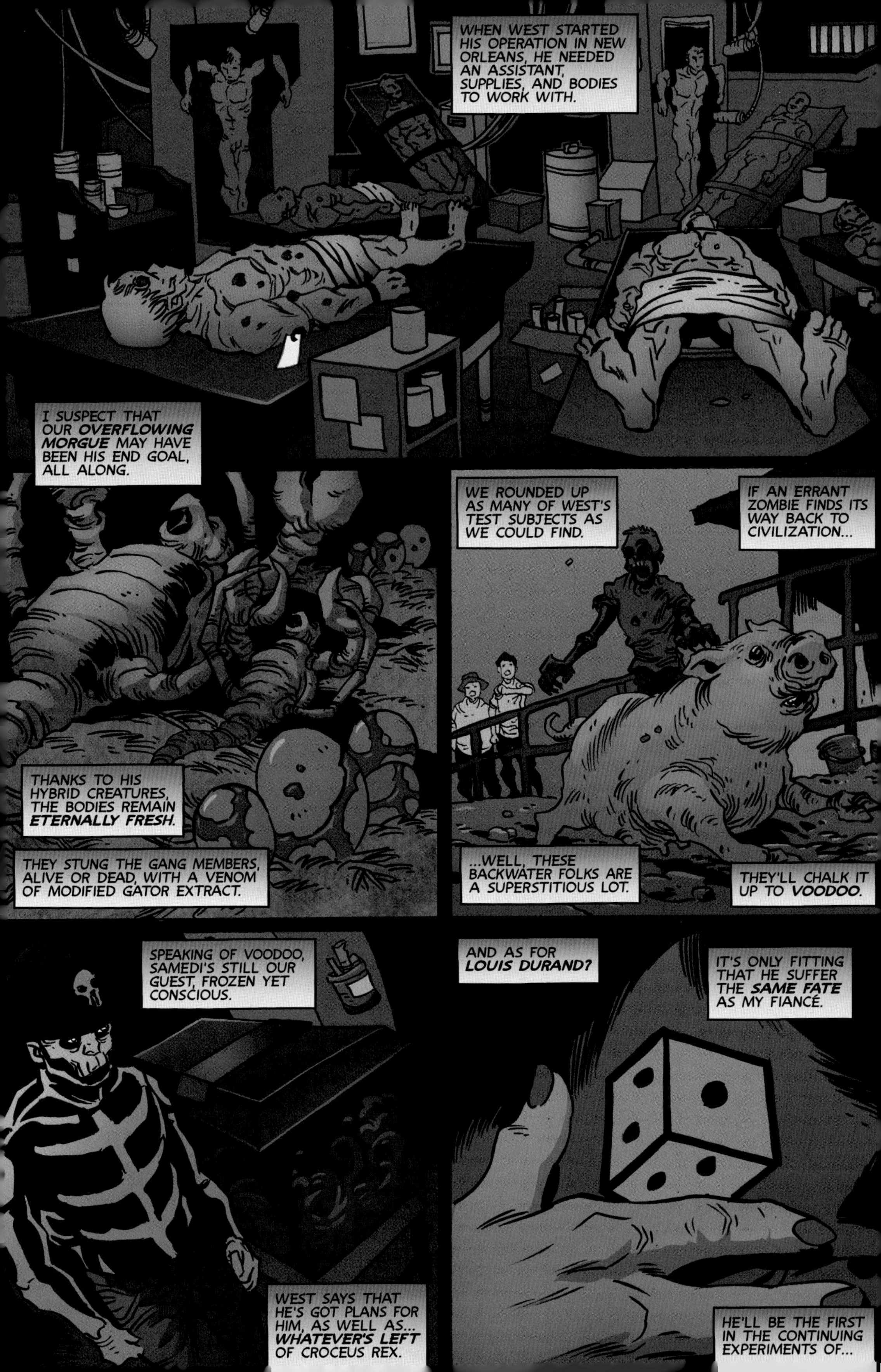

WHEN WEST STARTED HIS OPERATION IN NEW ORLEANS, HE NEEDED AN ASSISTANT, SUPPLIES, AND BODIES TO WORK WITH.
I SUSPECT THAT OUR ***OVERFLOWING MORGUE*** MAY HAVE BEEN HIS END GOAL, ALL ALONG.
THANKS TO HIS HYBRID CREATURES, THE BODIES REMAIN ***ETERNALLY FRESH***.
THEY STUNG THE GANG MEMBERS, ALIVE OR DEAD, WITH A VENOM OF MODIFIED GATOR EXTRACT.
WE ROUNDED UP AS MANY OF WEST'S TEST SUBJECTS AS WE COULD FIND.
IF AN ERRANT ZOMBIE FINDS ITS WAY BACK TO CIVILIZATION...
...WELL, THESE BACKWATER FOLKS ARE A SUPERSTITIOUS LOT.
THEY'LL CHALK IT UP TO ***VOODOO***.
SPEAKING OF VOODOO, SAMEDI'S STILL OUR GUEST, FROZEN YET CONSCIOUS.
WEST SAYS THAT HE'S GOT PLANS FOR HIM, AS WELL AS... ***WHATEVER'S LEFT*** OF CROCEUS REX.
AND AS FOR ***LOUIS DURAND?***
IT'S ONLY FITTING THAT HE SUFFER THE ***SAME FATE*** AS MY FIANCÉ.
HE'LL BE THE FIRST IN THE CONTINUING EXPERIMENTS OF...

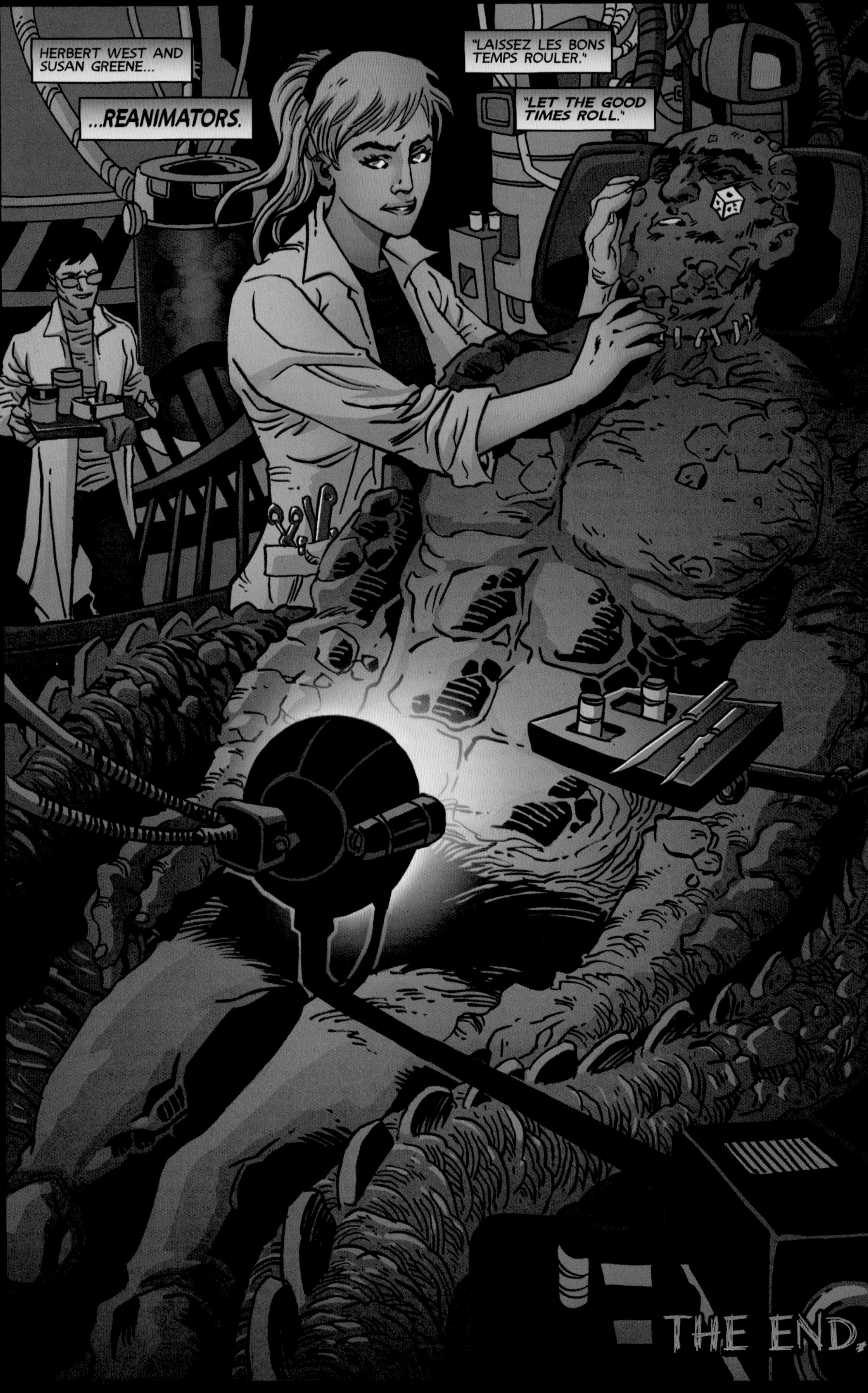
HERBERT WEST AND SUSAN GREENE...
...REANIMATORS.
"LAISSEZ LES BONS TEMPS ROULER."
"LET THE GOOD TIMES ROLL."
THE END.

LOVECRAFT REFERENCES AND WRITER COMMENTARY

by Keith Davidsen

REANIMATOR #1

REANIMATOR #1 Inside Front Cover – Tagline

"Good. Evil. Such storybook notions are beneath Herbert West. He is a man of Science. He is the Reanimator." This tagline was the very first thing I wrote when putting together my *Reanimator* pitch to Dynamite Entertainment. In truth, I obsessed over it – writing it over and over until I'd refined it to what I consider to be the character's implacable outlook on the world. Once defined, Herbert West became a fixed point, and practically every piece of action or dialogue that followed wrote itself."

REANIMATOR #1 Inside Front Cover: "The Wonder and Diabolism"

A reference from H.P. Lovecraft's original *Herbert West – Reanimator* serial, specifically from the first paragraph of *Part I: From the Dark*. "While he was with me, the wonder and diabolism of his experiments fascinated me utterly, and I was his closest companion." The line, as is the entirety of Lovecraft's work, is in the voice of an unnamed narrator, and foreshadows the relationship of Susan Greene and

Herbert West.

REANIMATOR #1 Inside Front Cover – Preamble

Presented here in its entirety: "Once an ambitious student at Miskatonic University, Herbert West harbored radical theories on returning life to the recently dead. At first, the young man was fanatical in pursuing a scientific means to that end... but the Necronomicon, a book of forbidden lore, seduced him to a more unorthodox approach. For a time, West reveled in its arcane teachings; he created legions of walking corpses, challenged power-mad rivals, and even averted an ancient doomsday prophecy. However, West fell victim to the tome's sinister influence. Thrown through time to the early 20th century, torn to pieces and reconstructed by sorcery, he returned to the present day more determined than ever to perfect his reanimation solution and conquer mortality."

REANIMATOR #1 Inside Front Cover – Preamble: "Miskatonic University"

Miskatonic University is a fictional setting found frequently in Lovecraftian works. The school was first referenced in the opening paragraph of the *Reanimator* serial's *From the Dark* chapter: "...when we were in the third year of our course at the Miskatonic University Medical School in Arkham." The school was likely modeled after Brown University in Lovecraft's hometown of Providence, RI. The school harbors a thorough occult library, and its faculty are frequently drawn to events of supernatural horror. Dynamite Entertainment co-opted Miskatonic University into their mythos for Herbert West's debut, *Reanimator* #0 (2005).

REANIMATOR #1 Inside Front Cover – Preamble: "radical theories on returning life to the dead".

Paraphrased from *Herbert West – Reanimator Part II: The Plague Demon*. "In the radical theory of reanimation they saw nothing but the immature vagaries of a youthful enthusiast whose slight form, yellow hair, spectacled blue eyes, and soft voice gave no hint of the supernormal—almost diabolical—power of the cold brain within." West's ideas were not only radical by the standards of his so-called peers, they were verboten.

REANIMATOR #1 Inside Front Cover – Preamble: "Necronomicon"

The Necronomicon is a fictional grimoire created by H.P. Lovecraft, referenced or featured throughout his works, and adopted by his Cthulhu Mythos peers and subsequent horror writers. The creators of the *Evil Dead* film franchise – the extremely popular horror series which includes the sequel *Army of Darkness* (of which Dynamite Entertainment holds the comic book publishing license) – incorporated the Necronomicon into their mythology, calling it "Necronomicon Ex Mortis" (which they "roughly translate" as "The Book of the Dead"). The preamble reference is specific to this version, as the majority of Dynamite's Herbert West appearances have taken place in *Army of Darkness* comics. In the *Army of Darkness vs. Reanimator* storyline (2005) and subsequent appearances (in 2012's *Prophecy* and 2013's *Army of Darkness / Reanimator* one-shot), Herbert West is a student of and eventual authority on the Necronomicon, which differs greatly from Lovecraft's original character – for whom the supernatural never held any allure. From *Part IV: The Scream of the Dead*: "West was a materialist."

Since the 2015 *Reanimator* series was published independently of the *Army of Darkness* line, one of the earliest editorial notes was that we needed to downplay the Necronomicon, limiting its appearances in the narrative and – if absolutely necessary to show – do not show the very specific visual of the *Army of Darkness* version. I was 100% on-board with this rule, as one of my story points was that West had rejected mysticism in favor of his earlier scientific zeal.

REANIMATOR #1 Inside Front Cover – Preamble: "legions of walking corpses"

The word "legion" was chosen to harken back to the title of Lovecraft's *Part VI: The Tomb-Legions*. Specifically, it refers to West's command of zombie hordes in the four-part *Army of Darkness vs. Reanimator* series.

REANIMATOR #1 Inside Front Cover – Preamble: "power-mad rivals"

In *Reanimator* #0 and *Army of Darkness vs. Reanimator*, Herbert West fell victim to the villainous Dr. Whately, identified as the chairman of Miskatonic University and a devotee of the Outer God known as Yog-Sothoth. Whately saw a potential ally in the singularly-focused West, and literally ripped any sense of decency from West's core by supernatural means (i.e. the Necronomicon).

Dr. Whately is Dynamite's incarnation of Lovecraft's own Wilbur Whately, a central figure of *The Dunwich Horror*. Described as a grotesque man of considerable height (nine feet) with a noxious odor, Whately is revealed as the half-human son of Yog-Sothoth. The literary Whately is obsessed with the Necronomicon as well, intent on using it to summon the terrifying Old Ones… and he pays for that fixation with his unnatural life, being mauled to death by a Miskatonic University guard dog.

REANIMATOR #1 Inside Front Cover – Preamble: "ancient doomsday prophecy"

The *Prophecy* comic book series was Dynamite's first-ever attempt at creating a single, cohesive universe for their various company-owned and licensed properties. Featured characters included Herbert West, Ash Williams (of *Army of Darkness*), Red Sonja, Vampirella, Eva, Dracula, Athena, and Pantha, to name a few. In the earliest chapters, West – whom I should reinforce is a character set in modern times, according to Dynamite continuity – discovered evidence in the Necronomicon that the world would end in 2012, corresponding to a real-world eschatological belief. Popularly known as the Mayan Doomsday Prophecy (and variations thereof), the prediction that the world would end in December 2012 stems from interpretations of the Mesoamerican Long Count calendar.

REANIMATOR #1 Inside Front Cover – Preamble: "thrown through time to the early 20th century"

In the *Army of Darkness / Reanimator* one-shot, Herbert West had experimented with the Necronomicon and been hurled back in time to 1906. The trip through time unhinged his mind and damaged his memory. Personality-wise, West shifted from a more comical and manic character (as seen in the earlier *Army of Darkness vs. Reanimator* and *Prophecy* storylines, and reminiscent to the vibe of the unaffiliated *Re-Animator* film series) to a serious, dark villain. As a bit of a Lovecraft traditionalist, I greatly appreciated this shift, as it created the opportunity for me to tell a story more attuned to the source material. Furthermore, the events of this one-shot comic adapted – to a large degree – Lovecraft's original tale. West attended the early 20th century Miskatonic University and completed his studies, earning his doctorate nearly a century before he originally enrolled at the school.

REANIMATOR #1 Inside Front Cover – Preamble: "torn to pieces and reconstructed by sorcery"

At the conclusion of *Army of Darkness / Reanimator*, West was ripped apart by a horde of his failed experiments, mirroring the events of Lovecraft's *Part VI: The Tomb-Legions*. While the phrase "torn to pieces" and everything else in the preamble summarized the events of previous Dynamite comics, the phrase "reconstructed by sorcery" offered something new. With Herbert West effectively killed in his last previous appearance (not to mention stranded still in 1922), I needed to bring him back to life and the modern era. With comic book deaths being notoriously temporary, plus the character's history with scientific resurrection and Necronomicon spell-casting, this simple explanation is all that's really necessary to move the plot forward.

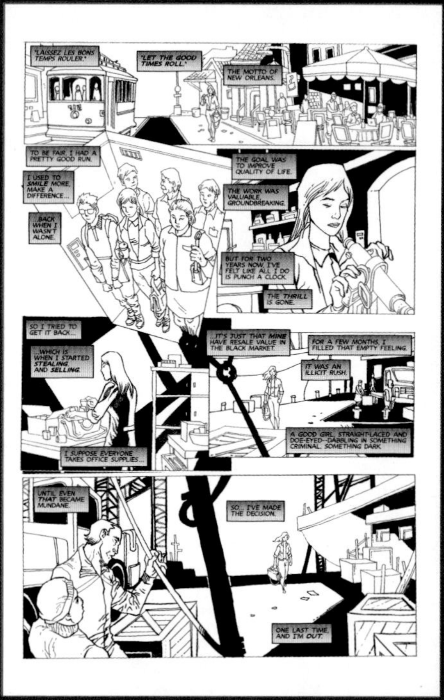
"LAISSEZ LES BONS TEMPS ROULER."
"LET THE GOOD TIMES ROLL."
THE MOTTO OF NEW ORLEANS.
TO BE FAIR, I HAD A PRETTY GOOD RUN.
I USED TO SMILE MORE, MAKE A DIFFERENCE...
...BACK WHEN I WASN'T ALONE.
THE GOAL WAS TO IMPROVE QUALITY OF LIFE.
THE WORK WAS VALUABLE, GROUNDBREAKING.
BUT FOR TWO YEARS NOW, I'VE FELT LIKE ALL I DO IS PUNCH A CLOCK.
THE THRILL IS GONE.
SO I TRIED TO GET IT BACK...
...WHICH IS WHEN I STARTED STEALING, AND SELLING.
I SUPPOSE EVERYONE TAKES OFFICE SUPPLIES...
...IT'S JUST THAT MINE HAVE RESALE VALUE IN THE BLACK MARKET.
FOR A FEW MONTHS, I FILLED THAT EMPTY FEELING.
IT WAS AN ILLICIT RUSH.
A GOOD GIRL, STRAIGHT-LACED AND DOE-EYED--DABBLING IN SOMETHING CRIMINAL. SOMETHING DARK.
UNTIL EVEN THAT BECAME MUNDANE.
SO... I'VE MADE THE DECISION.
ONE LAST TIME, AND I'M OUT.
Issue 1 page 1 original line art by Randy Vallente

REANIMATOR #1, Page 1: "New Orleans"

Lovecraft's writings are predominantly located in New England, where he spent the majority of his life. New Orleans, however, factors greatly into the author's work, *The Call of Cthulhu*, specifically *Part II: The Tale of Inspector Legrasse*. That narrative reveals the presence of a Cthulhu cult in the darkest wilderness south of the city.

The determination to set *Reanimator* in New Orleans stemmed from an original "comic book event" pitch that I proposed to Dynamite publisher Nick Barrucci. In anticipation of Mardi Gras 2015, I recommended that Dynamite release weekly one-shot comics to run through the month of February, each set in New Orleans and focusing on a different Dynamite horror property, namely *Vampirella*, *Army of Darkness*, *Eva* (the Daughter of Dracula), and *Reanimator*. New villains would be introduced (including Cthulhu), with a common thread to connect them. As Dynamite already had plans for *Vampirella* and *AOD* projects underway, Barrucci recommended that I expand the *Reanimator* tale into its own series.

REANIMATOR #1, Page 1: Narration

Like so many of Lovecraft's tales, the original *Herbert West – Reanimator* was presented as a first-person account. The Narrator of the classic tale is West's unnamed assistant. As such, the only person in this comic book series whose inner workings are shared with the audience (Herbert West's lengthy monologue in issue #3 notwithstanding) is Susan Greene, the woman who would become his new assistant.

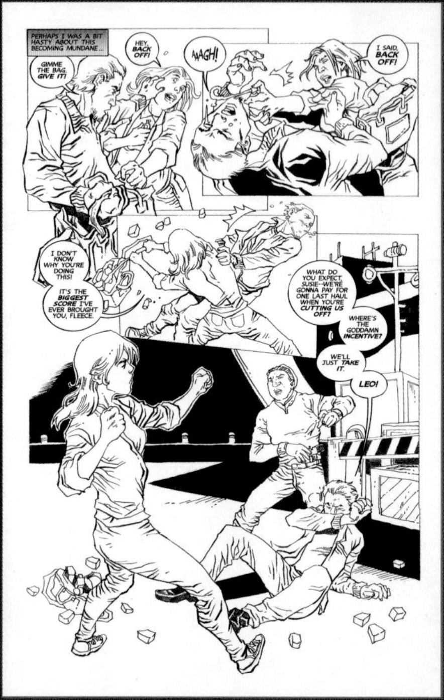

PERHAPS I WAS A BIT HASTY ABOUT THIS BECOMING MUNDANE...
GIMME THE BAG. GIVE IT!
HEY, BACK OFF!
AAAGH!
I SAID, BACK OFF!
I DON'T KNOW WHY YOU'RE DOING THIS!
IT'S THE BIGGEST SCORE I'VE EVER BROUGHT YOU, FLEECE.
WHAT DO YOU EXPECT, SUSIE--WE'RE GONNA PAY FOR ONE LAST HAUL WHEN YOU'RE CUTTING US OFF?
WHERE'S THE GODDAMN INCENTIVE?
WE'LL JUST TAKE IT.
LEO!

Issue 1 page 2 original line art by Randy Valiente

REANIMATOR #1, Page 2: Fleece

The name "Fleece" is a nod to *Poison Elves*, the gothic fantasy comic book series created by the late Drew Hayes. During my time as an editor at Sirius Entertainment, I was fortunate enough to write several spin-off series. Fleece was a supporting character in *Poison Elves*, and the lead in a one-shot story that never saw the light of day.

REANIMATOR #1, Page 4: Herbert West's appearance

Lovecraft described an elder Herbert West in *Part VI: The Tomb-Legions* as "cold, slight, and yellow-haired, with spectacled blue eyes and a general aspect of youth which years and fears seemed never to change." Dynamite had already solidified their incarnation of the character as having brown hair. I had hoped to model the new series' main character after the appearance of actor Joseph Gordon-Levitt, whom I felt looked eternally youthful as Lovecraft described. However, as the talented Randy Valiente had already defined the look of the character with his work on *Army of Darkness / Reanimator*, we decided to maintain that appearance for the sake of consistency.

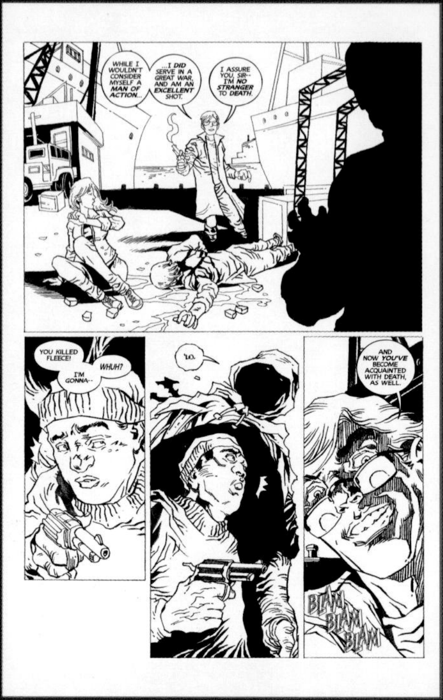

WHILE I WOULDN'T CONSIDER MYSELF A MAN OF ACTION...
...I DID SERVE IN A GREAT WAR, AND AM AN EXCELLENT SHOT.
I ASSURE YOU, SIR-- I'M NO STRANGER TO DEATH.
YOU KILLED FLEECE!
I'M GONNA--
WHUH?
'LO.
AND NOW YOU'VE BECOME ACQUAINTED WITH DEATH, AS WELL.
BLAM BLAM BLAM

Issue 1 page 4 original line art by Randy Valiente

REANIMATOR #1, Page 4: "great war"

As indicated in Lovecraft's *Herbert West – Reanimator Part V: The Horror from the Shadows*, "Dr. West had been avid for a chance to serve as surgeon in a great war". The Reanimator joined a Canadian regiment in 1915 for access to the bodies of World War I's fallen. Dynamite had incorporated West's experiences in the Great War into their mythology in the events of *Army of Darkness / Reanimator*, as the doctor had been thrown through time to the early 20th century.

REANIMATOR #1, Page 4: "excellent shot"

Herbert West uses a revolver several times in the classic prose, most notably in *Part III: Six Shots by Moonlight*. As best summarized in *Part VI: The Tomb-Legions*, "he usually finished his experiments with a revolver".

REANIMATOR #1, Page 5: "Susan Greene"

The majority of female characters in Lovecraft's works are peripheral. Creating the character of Susan Greene was my attempt not only to fill this void, but to honor the two women who arguably most influenced Lovecraft's life. The given name "Susan" is a reference to Sarah Susan Phillips Lovecraft, his infamously overbearing mother. The surname "Greene" comes from Sonia Greene, the woman whom he married in 1924; scholars would agree that, despite a marriage that ended in 1929, she was a positive influence on his worldview.

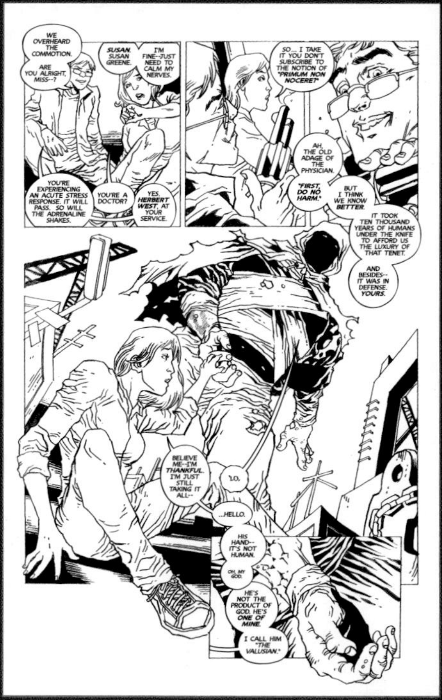
WE OVERHEARD THE COMMOTION.
ARE YOU ALRIGHT, MISS--?
SUSAN. SUSAN GREENE.
I'M FINE--JUST NEED TO CALM MY NERVES.
YOU'RE EXPERIENCING AN ACUTE STRESS RESPONSE. IT WILL PASS. SO WILL THE ADRENALINE SHAKES.
YOU'RE A DOCTOR?
YES. HERBERT WEST, AT YOUR SERVICE.
SO... I TAKE IT YOU DON'T SUBSCRIBE TO THE NOTION OF "PRIMUM NON NOCERE?"
AH, THE OLD ADAGE OF THE PHYSICIAN.
"FIRST, DO NO HARM."
BUT I THINK WE KNOW BETTER.
IT TOOK TEN THOUSAND YEARS OF HUMANS UNDER THE KNIFE TO AFFORD US THE LUXURY OF THAT TENET.
AND BESIDES-- IT WAS IN DEFENSE. YOURS.
BELIEVE ME--I'M THANKFUL. I'M JUST STILL TAKING IT ALL--
'LO.
...HELLO.
HIS HAND-- IT'S NOT HUMAN.
OH, MY GOD.
HE'S NOT THE PRODUCT OF GOD. HE'S ONE OF MINE.
I CALL HIM "THE VALUSIAN."

issue 1 page 5 original line art by Randy Valiente

REANIMATOR #1, Page 5: "Valusian"

In *The Haunter of the Dark*, Lovecraft refers to "the serpent-men of Valusia", itself a reference to a kingdom invented for Robert E. Howard's *Kull* mythos. The two authors were friends, and each honored the other by seeding their works with borrowed concepts. Howard would contribute numerous tales to the Cthulhu Mythos, as well.

REANIMATOR #1, Page 6: "weird fiction"

Weird fiction constitutes a subgenre of fantasy and horror that deals with the macabre. H.P. Lovecraft is perhaps the author most identified with the subgenre, alongside such notable authors as Edgar Allan Poe, Lord Dunsany, and Clark Ashton Smith. The majority of Lovecraft's published work appeared in the pulp magazine entitled *Weird Tales*. This is a meta moment, meant to indicate that Herbert West at one point read Lovecraft, therefore giving a nod to his own creator.

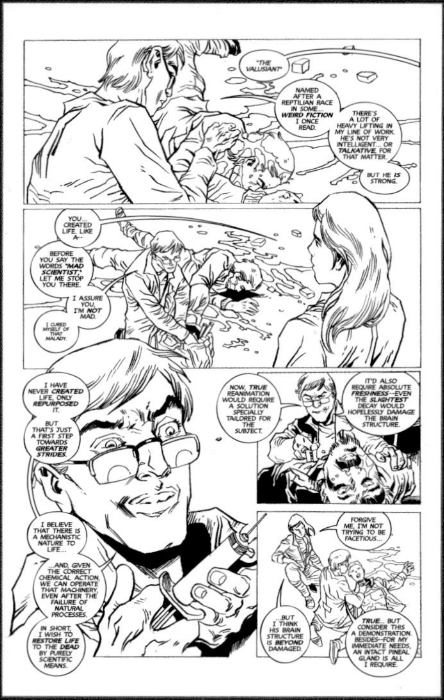
"THE VALUSIAN?"
NAMED AFTER A REPTILIAN RACE IN SOME... WEIRD FICTION I ONCE READ.
THERE'S A LOT OF HEAVY LIFTING IN MY LINE OF WORK. HE'S NOT VERY INTELLIGENT... OR TALKATIVE, FOR THAT MATTER.
BUT HE IS STRONG.
YOU... CREATED LIFE. LIKE A--
BEFORE YOU SAY THE WORDS "MAD SCIENTIST," LET ME STOP YOU THERE.
I ASSURE YOU, I'M NOT MAD.
I CURED MYSELF OF THAT MALADY.
I HAVE NEVER CREATED LIFE, ONLY REPURPOSED IT.
BUT THAT'S JUST A FIRST STEP TOWARDS GREATER STRIDES.
NOW, TRUE REANIMATION WOULD REQUIRE A SOLUTION SPECIALLY TAILORED FOR THE SUBJECT.
IT'D ALSO REQUIRE ABSOLUTE FRESHNESS--EVEN THE SLIGHTEST DECAY WOULD HOPELESSLY DAMAGE THE BRAIN STRUCTURE.
I BELIEVE THAT THERE IS A MECHANISTIC NATURE TO LIFE...
...AND, GIVEN THE CORRECT CHEMICAL ACTION, WE CAN OPERATE THAT MACHINERY, EVEN AFTER THE FAILURE OF NATURAL PROCESSES.
IN SHORT, I WISH TO RESTORE LIFE TO THE DEAD BY PURELY SCIENTIFIC MEANS.
FORGIVE ME, I'M NOT TRYING TO BE FACETIOUS...
...BUT I THINK HIS BRAIN STRUCTURE IS BEYOND DAMAGED.
TRUE... BUT CONSIDER THIS A DEMONSTRATION. BESIDES--FOR MY IMMEDIATE NEEDS, AN INTACT PINEAL GLAND IS ALL I REQUIRE.

issue 1 page 6 original line art by Randy Valiente

REANIMATOR #1, Page 6: "cured myself of that malady"

In the comic book *Army of Darkness / Reanimator*, Herbert West's jaunt through time to the early 20th century unhinges his mental state. This reflects Lovecraft's original character, who – by the events of *Part V: The Horror from the Shadows* – had begun to sink into a morally unsound state of mind. "It dawned on me that his once normal scientific zeal for prolonging life had subtly degenerated into a mere morbid and ghoulish curiosity and secret sense of charnel picturesqueness. His interest became a hellish and perverse addiction to the repellently and fiendishly abnormal; he gloated calmly over artificial monstrosities which would make most healthy men drop dead from fright and disgust."

REANIMATOR #1, Page 6: "mechanistic nature to life"

This phrase and the majority of the following word balloon are taken almost verbatim from Lovecraft's *Part I: From the Dark*: "His views... hinged on the essentially mechanistic nature of life; and concerned means for operating the organic machinery of mankind by calculated chemical action after the failure of natural processes."

REANIMATOR #1, Page 6: "slightest decay would hopelessly damage"

Lifted from *Herbert West – Reanimator Part IV: The Scream of the Dead*: "...even the least decay hopelessly damaged the brain structure".

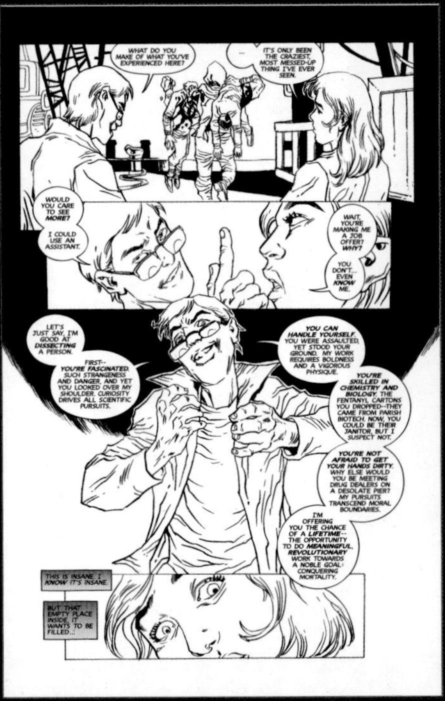
WHAT DO YOU MAKE OF WHAT YOU'VE EXPERIENCED HERE?
...
IT'S ONLY BEEN THE CRAZIEST, MOST MESSED-UP THING I'VE EVER SEEN.
WOULD YOU CARE TO SEE MORE?
I COULD USE AN ASSISTANT.
WAIT, YOU'RE MAKING ME A JOB OFFER? WHY?
YOU DON'T... EVEN KNOW ME.
LET'S JUST SAY, I'M GOOD AT DISSECTING A PERSON.
FIRST-- YOU'RE FASCINATED. SUCH STRANGENESS AND DANGER, AND YET YOU LOOKED OVER MY SHOULDER. CURIOSITY DRIVES ALL SCIENTIFIC PURSUITS.
YOU CAN HANDLE YOURSELF. YOU WERE ASSAULTED, YET STOOD YOUR GROUND. MY WORK REQUIRES BOLDNESS AND A VIGOROUS PHYSIQUE.
YOU'RE SKILLED IN CHEMISTRY AND BIOLOGY. THE FENTANYL CARTONS YOU DROPPED--THEY CAME FROM PARISH BIOTECH. NOW, YOU COULD BE THEIR JANITOR, BUT I SUSPECT NOT.
YOU'RE NOT AFRAID TO GET YOUR HANDS DIRTY. WHY ELSE WOULD YOU BE MEETING DRUG DEALERS ON A DESOLATE PIER? MY PURSUITS TRANSCEND MORAL BOUNDARIES.
I'M OFFERING YOU THE CHANCE OF A LIFETIME-- THE OPPORTUNITY TO DO MEANINGFUL, REVOLUTIONARY WORK TOWARDS A NOBLE GOAL: CONQUERING MORTALITY.
THIS IS INSANE. I KNOW IT'S INSANE.
BUT THAT EMPTY PLACE INSIDE, IT WANTS TO BE FILLED...

issue 1 page 8 original line art by Randy Valiente

REANIMATOR #1, Page 8: "I could use an assistant"

The invention of Susan Greene as Herbert West's assistant was to introduce a relatable "everywoman" character. As I mentioned in Dynamite's original press release, "I think it's a fun twist on the premise from *Doctor Who*, that the Doctor needs a grounded Companion to serve as his moral compass... but in the case of *Reanimator*, we see that Susan feels the seduction of casting her ethics aside."

REANIMATOR #1, Page 8: "vigorous physique"

In *Part VI: The Tomb-Legions*, West is described as having "a hardened eye which sometimes glanced with a kind of hideous and calculating appraisal at men of especially sensitive brain and especially vigorous physique".

REANIMATOR #1, Page 9: "Hamilton House"

In H.P. Lovecraft's hometown of Providence, Rhode Island, there stands a building called Hamilton House at 276 Angell Street, referenced in *The Shunned House* as a "sumptuous but hideous French-roofed mansion". This building is a featured destination for Lovecraftian walking tours of the city.

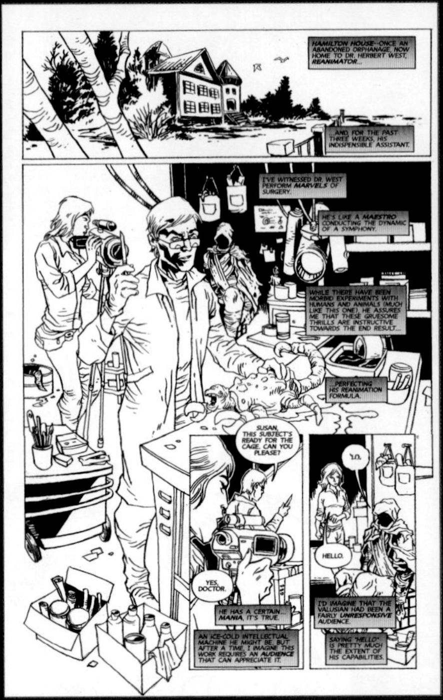
HAMILTON HOUSE--ONCE AN ABANDONED ORPHANAGE, NOW HOME TO DR. HERBERT WEST, REANIMATOR...
...AND, FOR THE PAST THREE WEEKS, HIS INDISPENSIBLE ASSISTANT.
I'VE WITNESSED DR. WEST PERFORM MARVELS OF SURGERY.
HE'S LIKE A MAESTRO CONDUCTING THE DYNAMIC OF A SYMPHONY.
WHILE THERE HAVE BEEN MORBID EXPERIMENTS WITH HUMANS AND ANIMALS (MUCH LIKE THIS ONE), HE ASSURES ME THAT THESE GRUESOME THRILLS ARE INSTRUCTIVE TOWARDS THE END RESULT...
...PERFECTING HIS REANIMATION FORMULA.
SUSAN, THIS SUBJECT'S READY FOR THE CAGE. CAN YOU PLEASE?
YES, DOCTOR.
HE HAS A CERTAIN... MANIA, IT'S TRUE.
AN ICE-COLD INTELLECTUAL MACHINE HE MIGHT BE, BUT AFTER A TIME, I IMAGINE THIS WORK REQUIRES AN AUDIENCE THAT CAN APPRECIATE IT.
HELLO.
I'D IMAGINE THAT THE VALUSIAN HAD BEEN A FAIRLY UNRESPONSIVE AUDIENCE.
SAYING "HELLO" IS PRETTY MUCH THE EXTENT OF HIS CAPABILITIES.

issue 1 page 9 original line art by Randy Valiente

REANIMATOR #1, Page 9: "Herbert West, Reanimator"

Name-dropping the official title of Lovecraft's original work, of course.

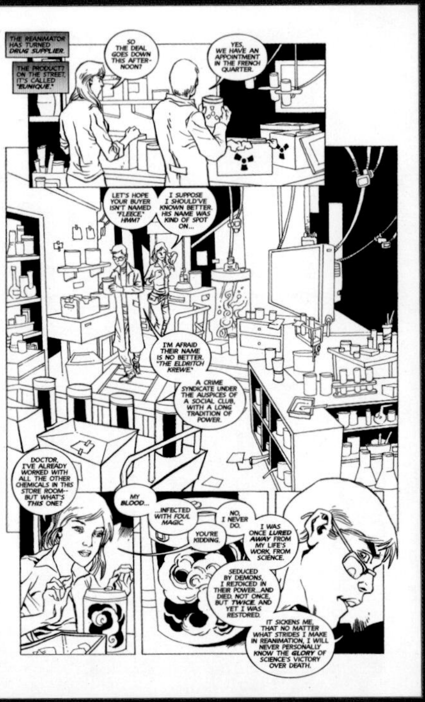
THE REANIMATOR HAS TURNED DRUG SUPPLIER.
THE PRODUCT? ON THE STREET, IT'S CALLED "EUNIQUE."
SO THE DEAL GOES DOWN THIS AFTER-NOON?
YES, WE HAVE AN APPOINTMENT IN THE FRENCH QUARTER.
LET'S HOPE YOUR BUYER ISN'T NAMED "FLEECE," HMM?
I SUPPOSE I SHOULD'VE KNOWN BETTER. HIS NAME WAS KIND OF SPOT ON...
I'M AFRAID THEIR NAME IS NO BETTER. "THE ELDRITCH KREWE."
A CRIME SYNDICATE UNDER THE AUSPICES OF A SOCIAL CLUB, WITH A LONG TRADITION OF POWER.
DOCTOR, I'VE ALREADY WORKED WITH ALL THE OTHER CHEMICALS IN THIS STORE ROOM-- BUT WHAT'S THIS ONE?
MY BLOOD...
...INFECTED WITH FOUL MAGIC.
YOU'RE KIDDING.
NO, I NEVER DO.
I WAS ONCE LURED AWAY FROM MY LIFE'S WORK, FROM SCIENCE.
SEDUCED BY DEMONS, I REJOICED IN THEIR POWER...AND DIED. NOT ONCE, BUT TWICE. AND YET I WAS RESTORED.
IT SICKENS ME, THAT NO MATTER WHAT STRIDES I MAKE IN REANIMATION, I WILL NEVER PERSONALLY KNOW THE GLORY OF SCIENCE'S VICTORY OVER DEATH.

issue 1 page 11 original line art by Randy Valiente

REANIMATOR #1, Page 11: "Eunique"

In coming up with the name "Eunique" as Herbert West's designer drug, I wanted something as flashy as the street drug "Euphoria" (4-Methylaminorex), also known as "Ice" – which members of my generation may remember as the drug of choice of bad girl Emily Valentine (played by Christine Elise), Brandon Walsh's one-time girlfriend on *Beverly Hills 90210*.

REANIMATOR #1, Page 11: "Eldritch Krewe"

The term "Eldritch" is a word notoriously prevalent throughout Lovecraft's fiction, meaning "otherworldly" or "weird". To quote author and Lovecraft enthusiast Neil Gaiman from the thoroughly enjoyable *Lovecraft: Fear of the Unknown – A Wyrd Documentary*: "He will pick a few words and overuse them appallingly," lovingly citing "eldritch" as the prime example. Despite this infamy, the term only appears once in the entirety of *The Call of Cthulhu*, and never rears its so-ugly-it's-beautiful head in *Herbert West – Reanimator*.

The term "Krewe" is believed to originate from Ye Mystic Krewe of Comus, one of the longest-serving organizations responsible for hosting Mardi Gras celebrations in New Orleans. This particular organization, named for the Greek God of festivity, was inspired by an Alabama-based mystic society, and was known for having secret membership. The term became colloquial, so that any organization that hosts a Mardi Gras parade or celebration is called a "krewe", and the colorful history and rivalries of these groups make for very fascinating reads. As mentioned previously, the concept for the *Reanimator* comic series sprung out of a comic book event proposal. The original thread that united the *Vampirella*, *Army of Darkness*, *Eva*, and *Reanimator* one-shots would have been a power struggle between various krewes, each with its own sinister agenda; therefore, the Eldritch Krewe is a holdover from that original germ.

REANIMATOR #1, Page 11: "seduced by demons"

A reference to Yog-Sothoth and the Deadites from Herbert West's unfortunate adventures in *Reanimator* #0 and *Army of Darkness vs. Reanimator*.

REANIMATOR #1, Page 11: "Not once, but twice"

Herbert West was killed twice in Dynamite comics… or, depending on your definition, three times. The first time was questionable; in *Reanimator* #0, his physical body was torn asunder and misshapen by a spell from the Necronomicon, and his consciousness was sent to a dimension of exile. When the story concluded, his body and mind were placed back together. In *Prophecy*, he was skewered by the storm god Chaac, and Ash Williams administered the reanimation formula to revive him. Finally, in *Army of Darkness / Reanimator*, he was ripped to pieces by zombies.

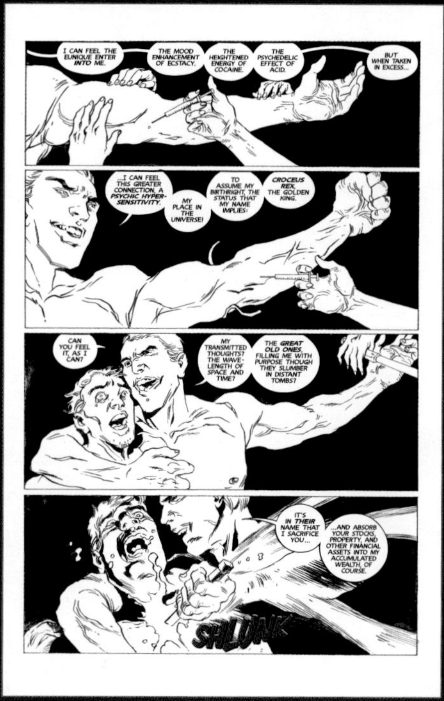

I CAN FEEL THE EUNIQUE ENTER *INTO* ME.
THE MOOD ENHANCEMENT OF ECSTACY.
THE HEIGHTENED ENERGY OF COCAINE.
THE PSYCHEDELIC EFFECT OF ACID.
BUT WHEN TAKEN IN EXCESS...
...I CAN FEEL THIS GREATER CONNECTION, A *PSYCHIC HYPER-SENSITIVITY*.
MY PLACE IN THE UNIVERSE!
TO ASSUME MY BIRTHRIGHT, THE STATUS THAT MY NAME IMPLIES:
CROCEUS REX, THE GOLDEN KING.
CAN YOU FEEL IT, AS I CAN?
MY TRANSMITTED THOUGHTS? THE WAVE-LENGTH OF SPACE AND TIME?
THE *GREAT OLD ONES*, FILLING ME WITH PURPOSE THOUGH THEY SLUMBER IN DISTANT TOMBS?
IT'S IN *THEIR* NAME THAT I SACRIFICE YOU...
...AND ABSORB YOUR STOCKS, PROPERTY, AND OTHER FINANCIAL ASSETS INTO MY ACCUMULATED WEALTH, OF COURSE.
SHLUNK

issue 1 page 13 original line art by Randy Valiente

REANIMATOR #1, Page 13: "psychic hypersensitivity"

In *The Call of Cthulhu*, an artist character named Henry Anthony Wilcox is the unwitting recipient of psychic signals from Cthulhu. He "had from childhood excited attention through the strange stories and odd dreams he was in the habit of relating. He called himself 'psychically hypersensitive'".

REANIMATOR #1, Page 13: "Croceus Rex, the Golden King"

One of the New Orleans carnival krewes is called "Rex", and each year, they choose one individual to serve as their parade's figurehead "King Rex", a century-old tradition.

While I would love to claim that the "Golden King" was a namesake of *The King in Yellow*, a short story collection by author Robert W. Chambers that Lovecraft frequently referenced in his writings. I only came to learn of this work after writing the *Reanimator* comic series. The focus on the color gold was another holdover from the original proposal, wherein each of the three rival krewes plaguing Vampirella, Ash Williams, Eva, and Herbert West would be dedicated to a different color associated with the traditional colors of New Orleans' Mardi Gras. Purple represented Justice, green represented Faith, and gold represented Power. As West points out later in the series, Croceus Rex may claim to be a man of faith (to Cthulhu), but ultimately, his end goal is the acquisition of power.

REANIMATOR #1, Page 13: "Great Old Ones"

The Great Old Ones were the multitude of vastly powerful entities that featured so prominently in Lovecraft's works, and included Cthulhu among their number. To quote *The Call of Cthulhu*: "The Great Old Ones... lived ages before there were any men, and... came to the young world out of the sky. These Old Ones were gone now, inside the earth and under the sea; but their dead bodies had told their secrets in dreams to the first men, who formed a cult which had never died."

REANIMATOR #1, Page 13: "distant tombs"

The Great Old Ones slumbered in the submerged necropolis of R'lyeh, as indicated in *The Call of Cthulhu*. "But although They no longer lived, They would never really die. They all lay in stone houses in Their great city of R'lyeh, preserved by the spells of mighty Cthulhu for a glorious resurrection."

REANIMATOR #1, Page 14: "That is not dead which can eternal lie..."

According to Lovecraft's *The Call of Cthulhu Part II: The Tale of Inspector Legrasse*, the Mad Arab Abdul Alhazred composed this "much-discussed couplet" in the Necronomicon, copied here verbatim. The Great Old Ones are beyond life and death, and will return.

REANIMATOR #1, Page 14: "Cthulhu fhtagn"

First mentioned in the ramblings of Henry Anthony Wilcox in *The Call of Cthulhu Part I: The Horror in Clay* ("he attempted to render by the almost unpronounceable jumble of letters, 'Cthulhu fhtagn'"), the phrase can be alternately translated as "Cthulhu waits" or "Cthulhu dreams". It remains perhaps one of the most popular phrases in Lovecraftian literature.

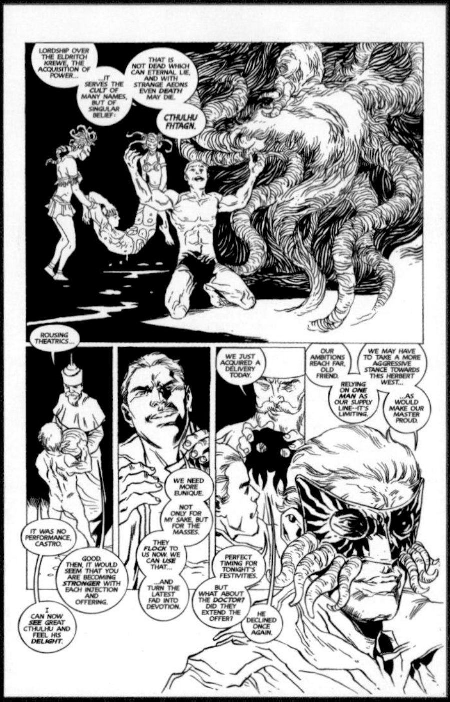
LORDSHIP OVER THE ELDRITCH KREWE, THE ACQUISITION OF POWER...
...IT SERVES THE CULT OF MANY NAMES, BUT OF SINGULAR BELIEF:
THAT IS NOT DEAD WHICH CAN ETERNAL LIE, AND WITH STRANGE AEONS EVEN DEATH MAY DIE.
CTHULHU FHTAGN.
ROUSING THEATRICS...
WE JUST ACQUIRED A DELIVERY TODAY.
OUR AMBITIONS REACH FAR, OLD FRIEND.
WE MAY HAVE TO TAKE A MORE AGGRESSIVE STANCE TOWARDS THIS HERBERT WEST...
RELYING ON ONE MAN AS OUR SUPPLY LINE--IT'S LIMITING.
...AS WOULD MAKE OUR MASTER PROUD.
WE NEED MORE EUNIQUE.
NOT ONLY FOR MY SAKE, BUT FOR THE MASSES.
THEY FLOCK TO US NOW. WE CAN USE THAT...
...AND TURN THE LATEST FAD INTO DEVOTION.
IT WAS NO PERFORMANCE, CASTRO.
GOOD. THEN, IT WOULD SEEM THAT YOU ARE BECOMING STRONGER WITH EACH INJECTION AND OFFERING.
I CAN NOW SEE GREAT CTHULHU AND FEEL HIS DELIGHT.
PERFECT TIMING FOR TONIGHT'S FESTIVITIES.
BUT WHAT ABOUT THE DOCTOR? DID THEY EXTEND THE OFFER?
HE DECLINED ONCE AGAIN.
issue 1 page 14 original line art by Randy Valiente

REANIMATOR #1, Page 14: "Castro"

Croceus Rex's majordomo, Castro, is an important character introduced in *The Call of Cthulhu*. In the prose, he is "an immensely aged mestizo... who claimed to have sailed to strange ports and talked with undying leaders of the cult in the mountains of China". Part of the murderous Louisiana-based Cthulhu cult, Castro is captured by Inspector John Raymond Legrasse and interrogated, revealing many secrets of their faith's history before dying. The Dynamite version is less aged and hardier.

REANIMATOR #1, Page 16: "Gris-Gris"

"Gris-gris" is an amulet from Vodou tradition, meant to ward off evil spirits or intent, or bring luck.

REANIMATOR #1, Page 17: "Samedi"

Baron Samedi, the skull-faced namesake of this *Reanimator* character, is a prominent figure in Haitian Vodou. Perhaps most famously popularized in Western culture due to the appearance of a similarly-named villain in the Roger Moore *James Bond* film, *Live and Let Die*, the traditional figure is a Loa, or spirit, of the dead – a mischievous being responsible for escorting souls to the realm of the dead. This new Dynamite incarnation of the character is a human hitman who uses Vodou psychotropic powders to dominate the minds of enslaved women. He's meant to bank on the Loa's reputation by lingering in cemeteries and wearing a skull on his cowboy hat.

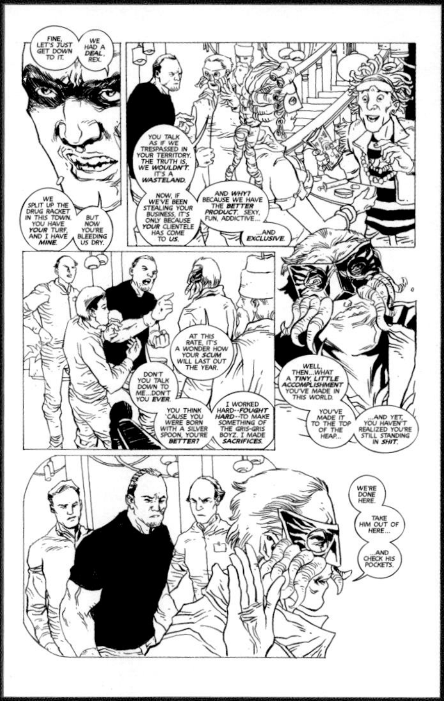
FINE, LET'S JUST GET DOWN TO IT.
WE HAD A DEAL, REX.
WE SPLIT UP THE DRUG RACKET IN THIS TOWN. YOU HAVE YOUR TURF, AND I HAVE MINE.
BUT NOW YOU'RE BLEEDING US DRY.
YOU TALK AS IF WE TRESPASSED IN YOUR TERRITORY. THE TRUTH IS, WE WOULDN'T. IT'S A WASTELAND.
NOW, IF WE'VE BEEN STEALING YOUR BUSINESS, IT'S ONLY BECAUSE YOUR CLIENTELE HAS COME TO US.
AND WHY? BECAUSE WE HAVE THE BETTER PRODUCT. SEXY, FUN, ADDICTIVE...
...AND EXCLUSIVE.
AT THIS RATE, IT'S A WONDER HOW YOUR SCUM WILL LAST OUT THE YEAR.
DON'T YOU TALK DOWN TO ME...DON'T YOU EVER.
YOU THINK 'CAUSE YOU WERE BORN WITH A SILVER SPOON, YOU'RE BETTER?
I WORKED HARD--FOUGHT HARD--TO MAKE SOMETHING OF THE GRIS-GRIS BOYZ. I MADE SACRIFICES.
WELL, THEN...WHAT A TINY, LITTLE ACCOMPLISHMENT YOU'VE MADE IN THIS WORLD.
YOU'VE MADE IT TO THE TOP OF THE HEAP...
...AND YET, YOU HAVEN'T REALIZED YOU'RE STILL STANDING IN SHIT.
WE'RE DONE HERE.
TAKE HIM OUT OF HERE...
...AND CHECK HIS POCKETS.

issue 1 page 16 original line art by Randy Vallente

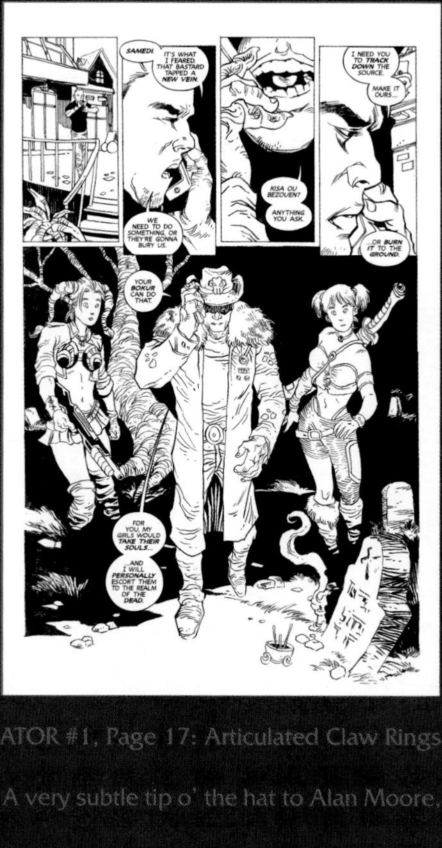
SAMEDI.
IT'S WHAT I FEARED. THAT BASTARD TAPPED A NEW VEIN.
WE NEED TO DO SOMETHING, OR THEY'RE GONNA BURY US.
KISA OU BEZOUEN?
ANYTHING YOU ASK.
I NEED YOU TO TRACK DOWN THE SOURCE.
MAKE IT OURS...
...OR BURN IT TO THE GROUND.
YOUR BOKUR CAN DO THAT.
FOR YOU, MY GIRLS WOULD TAKE THEIR SOULS...
...AND I WILL PERSONALLY ESCORT THEM TO THE REALM OF THE DEAD.

issue 1 page 17 original line art by Randy Vallente

REANIMATOR #1, Page 17: Articulated Claw Rings

A very subtle tip o' the hat to Alan Moore, the master graphic novelist and Lovecraftian expert, who has been known to wear such rings.

REANIMATOR #1, Page 17: "Kisa ou bezouen?"

Translated from Creole, "What do you need?"

REANIMATOR #1, Page 17: "Bokur"

A "Bokur" or "Bokor" is a black magician in Haitian Vodou culture, sometimes available for hire.

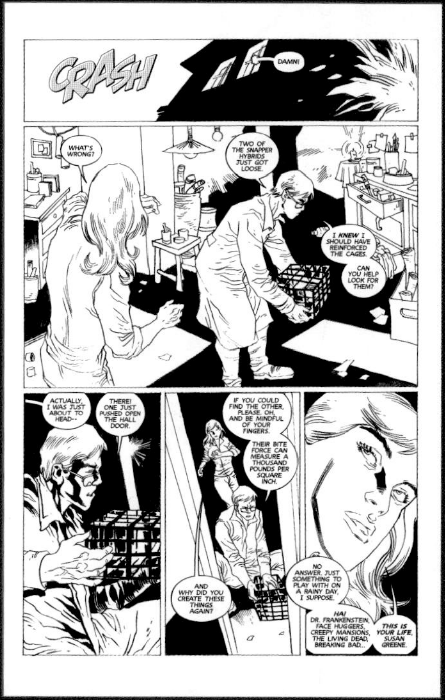
CRASH
DAMN!
WHAT'S WRONG?
TWO OF THE SNAPPER HYBRIDS JUST GOT LOOSE.
I KNEW I SHOULD HAVE REINFORCED THE CAGES.
CAN YOU HELP LOOK FOR THEM?
ACTUALLY, I WAS JUST ABOUT TO HEAD--
THERE! ONE JUST PUSHED OPEN THE HALL DOOR.
IF YOU COULD FIND THE OTHER, PLEASE. OH, AND BE MINDFUL OF YOUR FINGERS.
THEIR BITE FORCE CAN MEASURE A THOUSAND POUNDS PER SQUARE INCH.
AND WHY DID YOU CREATE THESE THINGS AGAIN?
NO ANSWER. JUST SOMETHING TO PLAY WITH ON A RAINY DAY, I SUPPOSE.
HA! DR. FRANKENSTEIN, FACE HUGGERS, CREEPY MANSIONS, THE LIVING DEAD, BREAKING BAD...
THIS IS YOUR LIFE, SUSAN GREENE.

issue 1 page 18 original line art by Randy Vallente

REANIMATOR #1, Page 18: "Dr. Frankenstein"

Naturally, this is a reference to the mad scientist of Mary Shelley's *Frankenstein*. Two notes: first, Frankenstein's Monster does exist in the Dynamite universe, never having interacted with Herbert West, but having crossed paths with the Reanimator's *Prophecy* fellows Vampirella, Eva, and Ash Williams. Second, in the aforementioned *Lovecraft: Fear of the Unknown – A Wyrd Documentary*, biographer S.T. Joshi makes an interesting argument that Frankenstein's drive to create life from component parts and West's desire to revive a whole deceased person are almost at cross purposes. Had Dynamite's West heard Susan Greene's comparison, he may have not taken it lightly.

REANIMATOR #1, Page 18: "The living dead"

George A. Romero's 1968 horror classic, *Night of the Living Dead*, is credited as the originator of the flesh-eating zombie trope – at least in film. Lovecraft's *Part III: Six Shots by Moonlight* establishes that the reanimated boxer Buck Robinson had eaten a child.

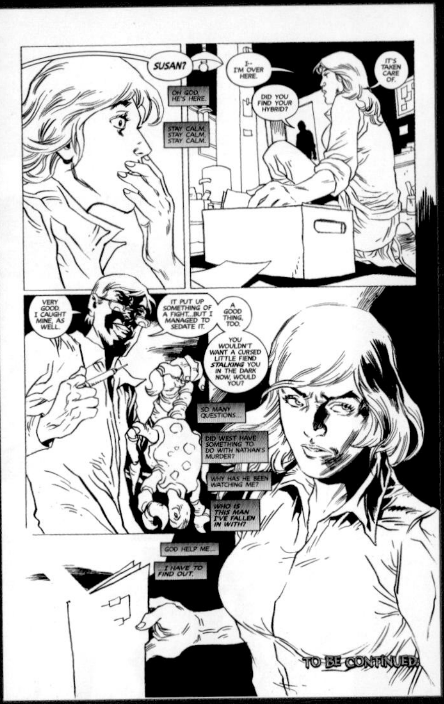

SUSAN?
I-- I'M OVER HERE.
OH GOD, HE'S HERE.
STAY CALM, STAY CALM, STAY CALM.
DID YOU FIND YOUR HYBRID?
IT'S TAKEN CARE OF.
VERY GOOD. I CAUGHT MINE, AS WELL.
IT PUT UP SOMETHING OF A FIGHT...BUT I MANAGED TO SEDATE IT.
A GOOD THING, TOO.
YOU WOULDN'T WANT A CURSED LITTLE FIEND STALKING YOU IN THE DARK NOW, WOULD YOU?
SO MANY QUESTIONS...
DID WEST HAVE SOMETHING TO DO WITH NATHAN'S MURDER?
WHY HAS HE BEEN WATCHING ME?
WHO IS THIS MAN I'VE FALLEN IN WITH?
GOD HELP ME...
...I HAVE TO FIND OUT.
TO BE CONTINUED!

issue 1 page 22 original line art by Randy Valiente

REANIMATOR #1, Page 22: "cursed little fiend"

Drawn from the final line of Lovecraft's *Part IV: The Scream of the Dead*: "Help! Keep off, you cursed little tow-head fiend — keep that damned needle away from me!" This moment in the original *Herbert West – Reanimator* narrative shifts everything, as the unnamed narrator discovered that a revived subject was actually murdered by West prior to experimentation. The narrator becomes more fearful and suspicious in West's presence, a situation that parallels Susan Greene's discovery in these last few pages.

REANIMATOR #2

REANIMATOR #2 Inside Front Cover: "Making Mad"

The only issue title not originating from Lovecraftian history, "Making Mad" is a reference to the acclaimed AMC television program, *Breaking Bad*. The program's protagonist, Walter White (played by Bryan Cranston), is a high school chemistry teacher who – suffering from cancer and hoping to attain financial security for his family – begins producing and selling methamphetamines. As the series progresses, he increasingly delves into darkness. The phrase "breaking bad" is a Southern colloquialism that means "raise hell".

Originally, "Making Mad" was to be the subtitle for the entire series, rhyming with "Breaking Bad" and alluding to Lovecraft's penchant for driving his characters insane (the narrator in *Herbert West – Reanimator* is an example, as the story's ending is ambiguous as he is considered mad). The themes that the Reanimator turns to drug manufacture, that Susan will become increasingly fascinated with the darkness of his work, that Croceus Rex seeks to raise Cthulhu… they all reflect at least surface elements from *Breaking Bad.*

REANIMATOR #2 Inside Front Cover – Preamble

"Setting up a laboratory in New Orleans, Dr. Herbert West recruits Susan Greene, a young pharmacologist, to assist in his experiments. Still numb from her fiancée's murder the year before, Susan hopes that her new employer's fascinating (yet macabre) work can fill the emptiness in her life. She's unfazed by his undead patients, patchwork creatures, and his hulking reptilian manservant, the Valusian. She even accepts West's means of funding his research: selling zombie brain fluid as a narcotic called "Eunique" to the Eldritch Krewe, the city's reigning cartel. However, her job satisfaction takes a frightening turn when she discovers that West was present at her fiancée's crime scene. She suspects foul play.

"Meanwhile, the crime lord Croceus Rex has been abusing the psychoactive drug... and gleefully communing with the fearsome Elder God known as Cthulhu. And the Gris-Gris Boyz, a rival gang headed by "Dice" Durand and threatened by the city's new drug of choice, is determined to hunt down whomever is supplying the Eunique. Namely, the Reanimator!"

REANIMATOR #2, Page 2: "massacre in Massachusetts"

In *Army of Darkness vs. Reanimator*, the Arkham mental institution (named for the fictional city from Lovecraft's works, mentioned in the opening paragraph of

Herbert West – Reanimator), became a slaughterhouse as Dr. Whately and the possessed Herbert West turned patients and medical students into medical and demonic abominations… and Ash Williams killed them by the droves. As established in *Prophecy*, West became the scapegoat for the massacre.

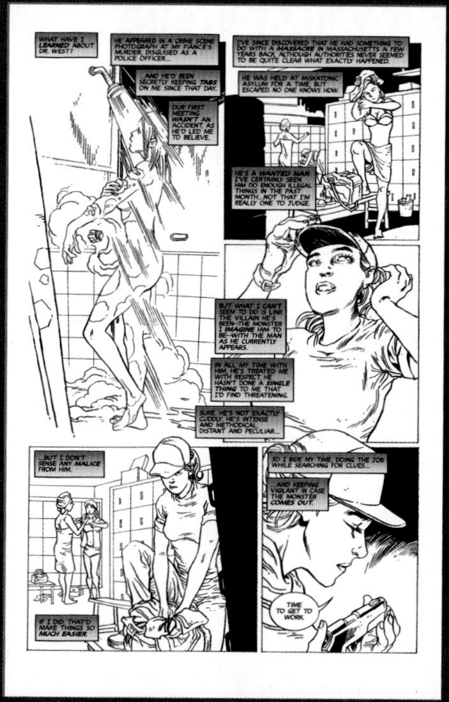

WHAT HAVE I LEARNED ABOUT DR. WEST?
HE APPEARED IN A CRIME SCENE PHOTOGRAPH AT MY FIANCE'S MURDER, DISGUISED AS A POLICE OFFICER...
...AND HE'D BEEN SECRETLY KEEPING TABS ON ME SINCE THAT DAY.
OUR FIRST MEETING WASN'T AN ACCIDENT, AS HE'D LED ME TO BELIEVE.
I'VE SINCE DISCOVERED THAT HE HAD SOMETHING TO DO WITH A MASSACRE IN MASSACHUSETTS A FEW YEARS BACK, ALTHOUGH AUTHORITIES NEVER SEEMED TO BE QUITE CLEAR WHAT EXACTLY HAPPENED.
HE WAS HELD AT MISKATONIC ASYLUM FOR A TIME, BUT ESCAPED. NO ONE KNOWS HOW.
HE'S A WANTED MAN. I'VE CERTAINLY SEEN HIM DO ENOUGH ILLEGAL THINGS IN THE PAST MONTH...NOT THAT I'M REALLY ONE TO JUDGE.
BUT WHAT I CAN'T SEEM TO DO IS LINK THE VILLAIN HE'S BEEN--THE MONSTER I IMAGINE HIM TO BE--WITH THE MAN AS HE CURRENTLY APPEARS.
IN ALL MY TIME WITH HIM, HE'S TREATED ME WITH RESPECT. HE HASN'T DONE A SINGLE THING TO ME THAT I'D FIND THREATENING.
SURE, HE'S NOT EXACTLY CUDDLY. HE'S INTENSE AND METHODICAL, DISTANT AND PECULIAR...
...BUT I DON'T SENSE ANY MALICE FROM HIM.
IF I DID, THAT'D MAKE THINGS SO MUCH EASIER.
SO I BIDE MY TIME, DOING THE JOB WHILE SEARCHING FOR CLUES...
...AND KEEPING VIGILANT IN CASE THE MONSTER COMES OUT.
TIME TO GET TO WORK.

issue 2 page 2 original line art by Randy Valiente

REANIMATOR #2, Page 2: "Miskatonic Asylum"

Also in *Prophecy*, it's established that there's a Miskatonic Asylum in Essex, Massachusetts (named for Lovecraft's fictional Miskatonic University, prevalent throughout his works, and specifically in the opening paragraph of *Part I: From the Dark*). West is incarcerated there after his arrest for the murders at Arkham.

REANIMATOR #2, Page 2: "escaped"

West disappeared from his cell at Miskatonic Asylum in *Prophecy #2*. He claimed to have "secret knowledge" about the impending Mayan doomsday, and "no choice" but to take action to prevent it. Presumably, he used the arcane knowledge of the Necronomicon to affect his escape.

REANIMATOR #2, Page 4: "Homer"

A quick note – I named Homer not after the beloved oaf of *The Simpsons*, but rather after the false, backwoods identity that Michael Westen assumes in the episode "Unpaid Debts" of the television series *Burn Notice*.

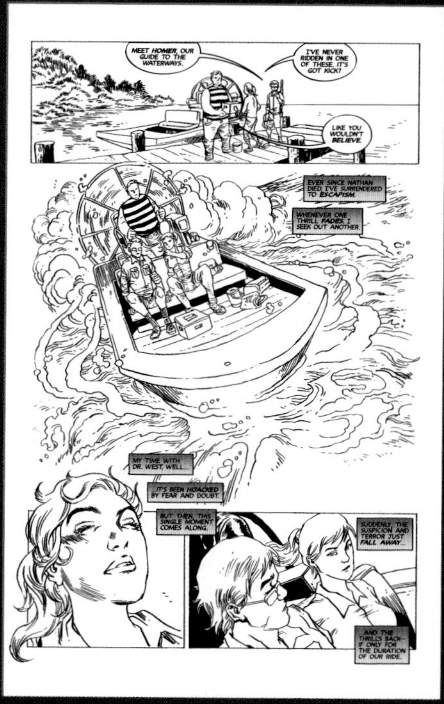

MEET HOMER, OUR GUIDE TO THE WATERWAYS.
I'VE NEVER RIDDEN IN ONE OF THESE. IT'S GOT KICK?
LIKE YOU WOULDN'T BELIEVE.
EVER SINCE NATHAN DIED, I'VE SURRENDERED TO ESCAPISM.
WHENEVER ONE THRILL FADES, I SEEK OUT ANOTHER.
MY TIME WITH DR. WEST, WELL...
...IT'S BEEN HIJACKED BY FEAR AND DOUBT.
BUT THEN, THIS SINGLE MOMENT COMES ALONG.
SUDDENLY, THE SUSPICION AND TERROR JUST FALL AWAY...
...AND THE THRILL'S BACK--IF ONLY FOR THE DURATION OF OUR RIDE.

issue 2 page 4 original line art by Randy Valiente

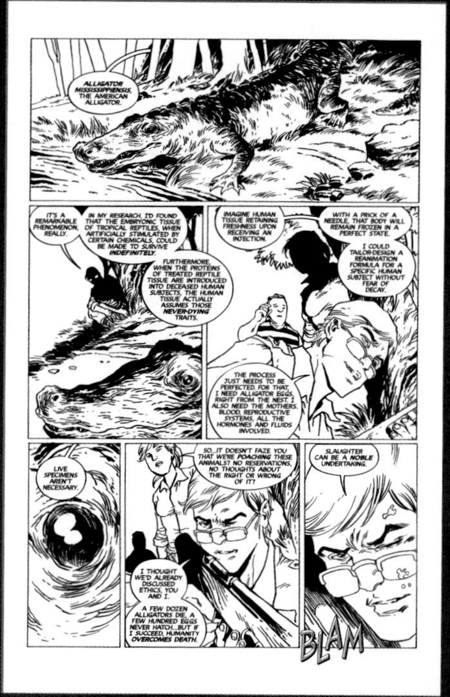

ALLIGATOR MISSISSIPPIENSIS, THE AMERICAN ALLIGATOR.
IT'S A REMARKABLE PHENOMENON, REALLY.
IN MY RESEARCH, I'D FOUND THAT THE EMBRYONIC TISSUE OF TROPICAL REPTILES, WHEN ARTIFICIALLY STIMULATED BY CERTAIN CHEMICALS, COULD BE MADE TO SURVIVE INDEFINITELY.
FURTHERMORE, WHEN THE PROTEINS OF TREATED REPTILE TISSUE ARE INTRODUCED INTO DECEASED HUMAN SUBJECTS, THE HUMAN TISSUE ACTUALLY ASSUMES THOSE NEVER-DYING TRAITS.
IMAGINE HUMAN TISSUE RETAINING FRESHNESS UPON RECEIVING AN INJECTION.
WITH A PRICK OF A NEEDLE, THAT BODY WILL REMAIN FROZEN IN A PERFECT STATE.
I COULD TAILOR-DESIGN A REANIMATION FORMULA FOR A SPECIFIC HUMAN SUBJECT WITHOUT FEAR OF DECAY.
THE PROCESS JUST NEEDS TO BE PERFECTED. FOR THAT, I NEED ALLIGATOR EGGS, RIGHT FROM THE NEST. I ALSO NEED THE MOTHERS. BLOOD, REPRODUCTIVE SYSTEMS, ALL THE HORMONES AND FLUIDS INVOLVED.
LIVE SPECIMENS AREN'T NECESSARY.
SO...IT DOESN'T FAZE YOU THAT WE'RE POACHING THESE ANIMALS? NO RESERVATIONS, NO THOUGHTS ABOUT THE RIGHT OR WRONG OF IT?
I THOUGHT WE'D ALREADY DISCUSSED ETHICS, YOU AND I.
A FEW DOZEN ALLIGATORS DIE, A FEW HUNDRED EGGS NEVER HATCH...BUT IF I SUCCEED, HUMANITY OVERCOMES DEATH.
SLAUGHTER CAN BE A NOBLE UNDERTAKING.
BLAM

issue 2 page 5 original line art by Randy Valiente

REANIMATOR #2, Page 5: "embryonic tissue"

In Lovecraft's *Part V: The Horror from the Shadows*, West is described as having utilized "never-dying, artificially nourished tissue obtained from the nearly hatched eggs of an indescribable tropical reptile", and kept "a large covered vat full of this reptilian cell-matter; which multiplied and grew puffily and hideously". To prevent atrophy, West would place limbs and even severed heads into the vat.

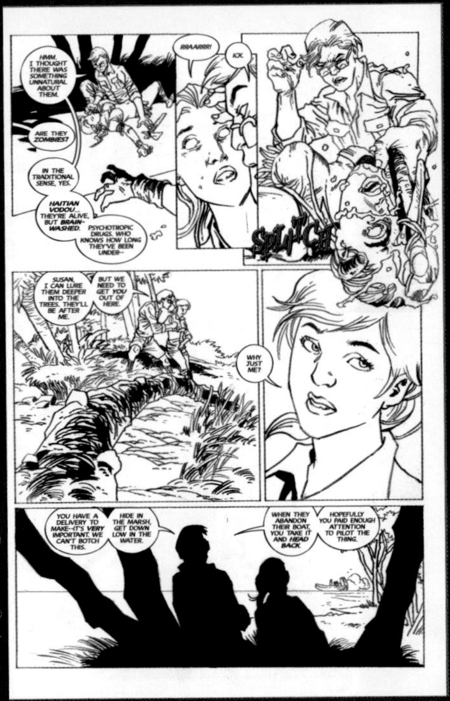
HMM. I THOUGHT THERE WAS SOMETHING UNNATURAL ABOUT THEM.
ARE THEY ZOMBIES?
IN THE TRADITIONAL SENSE, YES.
HAITIAN VODOU... THEY'RE ALIVE, BUT BRAIN-WASHED.
PSYCHOTROPIC DRUGS. WHO KNOWS HOW LONG THEY'VE BEEN UNDER--
RRAARRR!
ICK.
SPLITCH
SUSAN, I CAN LURE THEM DEEPER INTO THE TREES. THEY'LL BE AFTER ME.
BUT WE NEED TO GET YOU OUT OF HERE.
WHY JUST ME?
YOU HAVE A DELIVERY TO MAKE--IT'S VERY IMPORTANT. WE CAN'T BOTCH THIS.
HIDE IN THE MARSH, GET DOWN LOW IN THE WATER.
WHEN THEY ABANDON THEIR BOAT, YOU TAKE IT AND HEAD BACK.
HOPEFULLY YOU PAID ENOUGH ATTENTION TO PILOT THE THING.

issue 2 page 11 original line art by Randy Valiente

REANIMATOR #2, Page 11: "zombies"

This *Reanimator* series features the animated dead (popularized by *Night of the Living Dead*, albeit in our case, not necessarily flesh-eaters), as well as the more traditional Haitian Vodou model (meaning alive but entranced, a kind that first appeared on film in 1932's *White Zombie*, starring Bela Lugosi). A "war of the zombies" based on differing means or philosophies held quite an appeal to me.

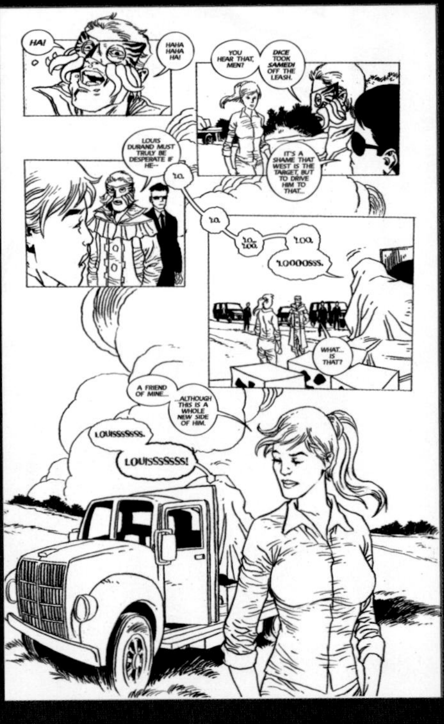
HA!
HAHA HAHA HA!
YOU HEAR THAT, MEN?
DICE TOOK SAMEDI OFF THE LEASH.
IT'S A SHAME THAT WEST IS THE TARGET, BUT TO DRIVE HIM TO THAT...
LOUIS DURAND MUST TRULY BE DESPERATE IF HE--
'LO.
'LO.
'LO... 'LOO.
'LOO.
'LOOOOSSS.
WHAT... IS THAT?
A FRIEND OF MINE...
...ALTHOUGH THIS IS A WHOLE NEW SIDE OF HIM.
LOUISSSSSSS.
LOUISSSSSSS!

issue 2 page 19 original line art by Randy Valiente

REANIMATOR #2, Page 19: "Louis Durand"

The name "Louis" was a conscious nod to *Poison Elves*, the series I'd written ten years prior. The protagonist of the fantasy series was Lusiphur Malaché, frequently called "Luse" for short, an Elvin assassin and thief.

REANIMATOR #3

REANIMATOR #3 Inside Front Cover: "Grewsome Tales"

In January of 1922, the humor magazine *Home Brew* published the first chapter of *Herbert West – Reanimator* under the banner of "Grewsome Tales", later to be renamed.

REANIMATOR #3 Inside Front Cover – Preamble

"Susan Greene, still haunted after two years by the unsolved murder of her fiancé, sought to fill the void in her life by working as Dr. Herbert West's assistant. West, the infamous Reanimator, is obsessed with overcoming death by chemical means, a process that requires costly resources. His solution to the financial burden? He sells zombie brain fluid as a narcotic to the Eldritch Krewe, whose leader Croceus Rex has abused the mind-altering drug, and can now commune with the sleeping Elder God, Cthulhu. While Herbert West survives an attempted assassination by Samedi, a Voodoo hitman employed by a rival drug cartel, Susan gets caught in a double-cross, as the Eldritch Krewe capture her as leverage against West. Witnessing the death of The Valusian, a half-human, half-alligator hybrid created as the Reanimator's loyal servant, Susan discovers the weird creature's true identity: none other than her own beloved Nathan Davis, raised from the dead. Captured by Croceus Rex, Susan is overwhelmed by the belief that Herbert West killed the love of her life."

REANIMATOR #3, Page 1: "wheelchair"

Castro appears in a wheelchair here, which is an error that – had this series been released by another publisher about thirty years ago – would've been great fodder for a No Prize. During The Valusian's rampage in issue #2, Castro was supposed to be crippled, but due to an oversight on the parts of everyone involved (myself included), the scene was left out, creating a disconnect for his appearance here in the chair.

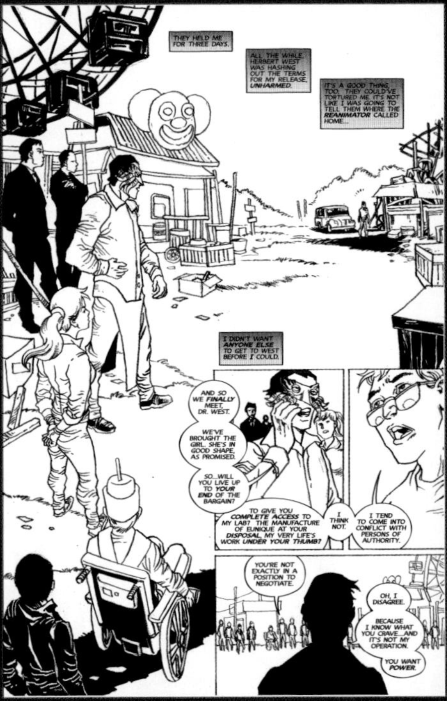

THEY HELD ME FOR THREE DAYS.
ALL THE WHILE, HERBERT WEST WAS HASHING OUT THE TERMS FOR MY RELEASE, UNHARMED.
IT'S A GOOD THING, TOO. THEY COULD'VE TORTURED ME. IT'S NOT LIKE I WAS GOING TO TELL THEM WHERE THE REANIMATOR CALLED HOME...
I DIDN'T WANT ANYONE ELSE TO GET TO WEST BEFORE I COULD.
AND SO WE FINALLY MEET, DR. WEST.
WE'VE BROUGHT THE GIRL. SHE'S IN GOOD SHAPE, AS PROMISED.
SO...WILL YOU LIVE UP TO YOUR END OF THE BARGAIN?
TO GIVE YOU COMPLETE ACCESS TO MY LAB? THE MANUFACTURE OF EUNIQUE AT YOUR DISPOSAL, MY VERY LIFE'S WORK UNDER YOUR THUMB?
I THINK NOT.
I TEND TO COME INTO CONFLICT WITH PERSONS OF AUTHORITY.
YOU'RE NOT EXACTLY IN A POSITION TO NEGOTIATE.
OH, I DISAGREE.
BECAUSE I KNOW WHAT YOU CRAVE...AND IT'S NOT MY OPERATION.
YOU WANT POWER.

issue 3 page 1 original line art by Randy Valiente

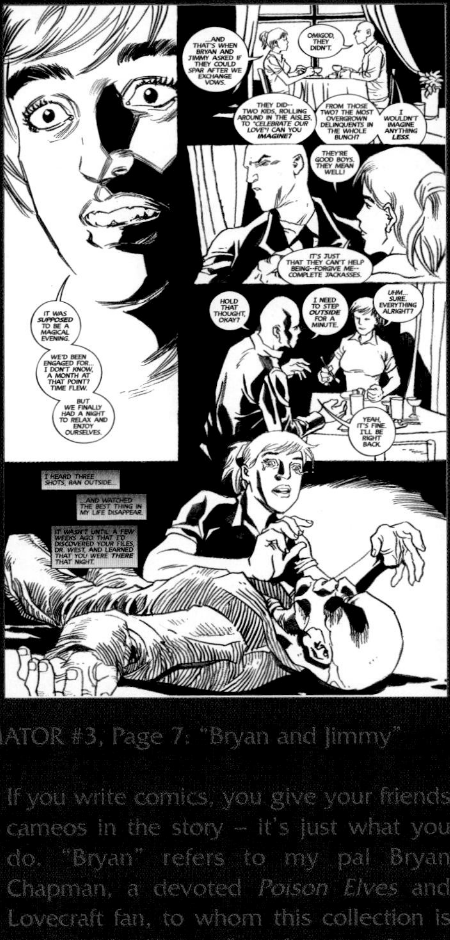

...AND THAT'S WHEN BRYAN AND JIMMY ASKED IF THEY COULD SPAR AFTER WE EXCHANGE VOWS.
OMIGOD, THEY DIDN'T.
THEY DID-- TWO KIDS, ROLLING AROUND IN THE AISLES, TO "CELEBRATE OUR LOVE"! CAN YOU IMAGINE?
FROM THOSE TWO? THE MOST OVERGROWN DELINQUENTS IN THE WHOLE BUNCH?
I WOULDN'T IMAGINE ANYTHING LESS.
THEY'RE GOOD BOYS. THEY MEAN WELL!
IT'S JUST THAT THEY CAN'T HELP BEING--FORGIVE ME-- COMPLETE JACKASSES.
IT WAS SUPPOSED TO BE A MAGICAL EVENING.
WE'D BEEN ENGAGED FOR... I DON'T KNOW, A MONTH AT THAT POINT? TIME FLEW.
BUT WE FINALLY HAD A NIGHT TO RELAX AND ENJOY OURSELVES.
HOLD THAT THOUGHT, OKAY?
I NEED TO STEP OUTSIDE FOR A MINUTE.
UHM... SURE. EVERYTHING ALRIGHT?
YEAH, IT'S FINE. I'LL BE RIGHT BACK.
I HEARD THREE SHOTS, RAN OUTSIDE...
...AND WATCHED THE BEST THING IN MY LIFE DISAPPEAR.
IT WASN'T UNTIL A FEW WEEKS AGO THAT I'D DISCOVERED YOUR FILES, DR. WEST, AND LEARNED THAT YOU WERE THERE THAT NIGHT.

issue 3 page 7 original line art by Randy Valiente

REANIMATOR #3, Page 7: "Bryan and Jimmy"

If you write comics, you give your friends cameos in the story – it's just what you do. "Bryan" refers to my pal Bryan Chapman, a devoted *Poison Elves* and Lovecraft fan, to whom this collection is dedicated. "Jimmy" refers to James Kuhoric, the writer of numerous Dynamite titles (*Army of Darkness, Six Million Dollar Man, Dead Irons, Legendary Talespinners*) and my boss at two previous places of employment. I delightfully called them "overgrown delinquents" during this scene of small talk.

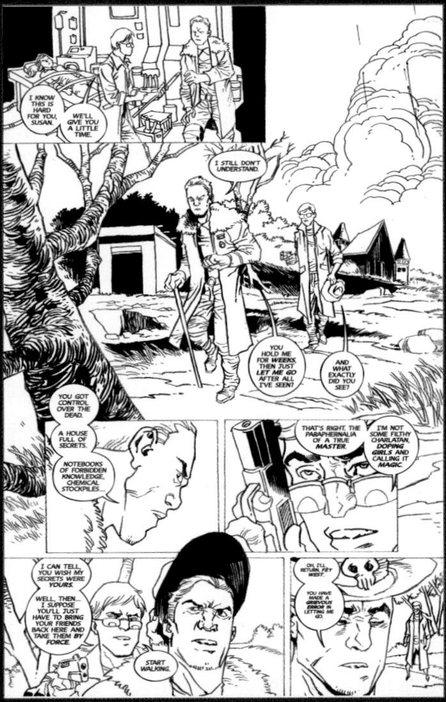

I KNOW THIS IS HARD FOR YOU, SUSAN.
WE'LL GIVE YOU A LITTLE TIME.
I STILL DON'T UNDERSTAND.
YOU HOLD ME FOR WEEKS, THEN JUST LET ME GO AFTER ALL I'VE SEEN?
AND WHAT EXACTLY DID YOU SEE?
YOU GOT CONTROL OVER THE DEAD.
A HOUSE FULL OF SECRETS.
NOTEBOOKS OF FORBIDDEN KNOWLEDGE, CHEMICAL STOCKPILES...
THAT'S RIGHT. THE PARAPHERNALIA OF A TRUE MASTER.
I'M NOT SOME FILTHY CHARLATAN, DOPING GIRLS AND CALLING IT MAGIC.
I CAN TELL, YOU WISH MY SECRETS WERE YOURS.
WELL, THEN... I SUPPOSE YOU'LL JUST HAVE TO BRING YOUR FRIENDS BACK HERE AND TAKE THEM BY FORCE.
START WALKING.
OH, I'LL RETURN, FEY WEST.
YOU HAVE MADE A GRIEVOUS ERROR IN LETTING ME GO.

issue 3 page 11 original line art by Randy Valiente

REANIMATOR #3, Page 11: "fey"

While "fey" means "leaf" in Creole, "dokte fey" means "witch doctor", referring to their usage of herbs and powders.

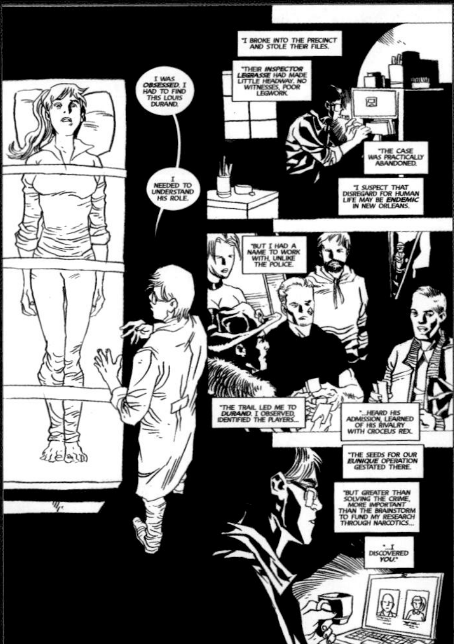

"I BROKE INTO THE PRECINCT AND STOLE THEIR FILES.
"THEIR INSPECTOR LEGRASSE HAD MADE LITTLE HEADWAY. NO WITNESSES, POOR LEGWORK.
I WAS OBSESSED. I HAD TO FIND THIS LOUIS DURAND.
I NEEDED TO UNDERSTAND HIS ROLE.
"THE CASE WAS PRACTICALLY ABANDONED.
"I SUSPECT THAT DISREGARD FOR HUMAN LIFE MAY BE ENDEMIC IN NEW ORLEANS.
"BUT I HAD A NAME TO WORK WITH, UNLIKE THE POLICE.
"THE TRAIL LED ME TO DURAND. I OBSERVED, IDENTIFIED THE PLAYERS...
"...HEARD HIS ADMISSION, LEARNED OF HIS RIVALRY WITH CROCEUS REX.
"THE SEEDS FOR OUR EUNIQUE OPERATION GESTATED THERE.
"BUT GREATER THAN SOLVING THE CRIME, MORE IMPORTANT THAN THE BRAINSTORM TO FUND MY RESEARCH THROUGH NARCOTICS...
"...I DISCOVERED YOU."

issue 3 page 14 original line art by Randy Valiente

REANIMATOR #3, Page 14: "Inspector Legrasse"

Inspector John Raymond Legrasse from *The Call of Cthulhu* is name-dropped here. Originally, I'd intended Legrasse to have a more prominent role in *Reanimator*. During his investigation into the murder of Nathan Davis, he'd discover a link between Susan Greene and Herbert West. Susan's discovery of the police file at the end of issue #1 was originally an appearance by Legrasse, but in trimming the series from a proposed five issue length down to four, the inspector was written out of the script.

REANIMATOR #3, Page 14: "disregard for human life may be endemic"

Hurricane Katrina devastated New Orleans in August 2005, resulting in the deaths of almost 1,500 Louisianans. In its wake, members of the public and media made accusations – many of them racially charged – regarding how authorities responded to the emergency… or didn't, to be more accurate. I felt that the investigation into Davis' murder having "poor legwork" and being "practically abandoned" is a commentary on the climate evident in New Orleans at the time.

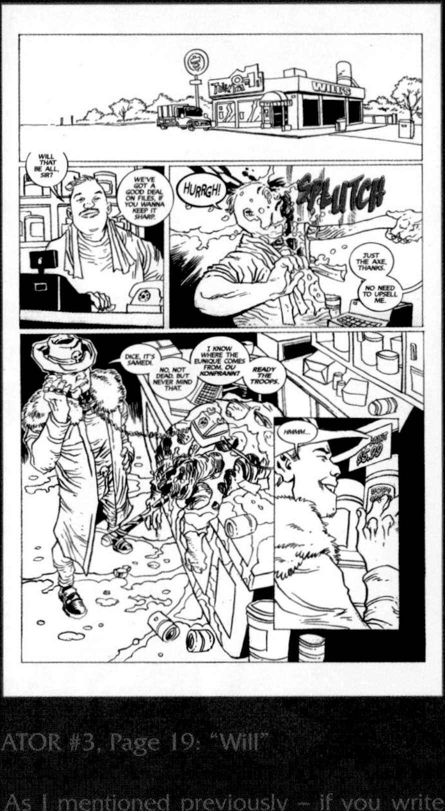
WILL THAT BE ALL, SIR?
WE'VE GOT A GOOD DEAL ON FILES, IF YOU WANNA KEEP IT SHARP.
HURRGH!
SPLUTCH
JUST THE AXE, THANKS.
NO NEED TO UPSELL ME.
DICE, IT'S SAMEDI.
NO, NOT DEAD, BUT NEVER MIND THAT.
I KNOW WHERE THE EUNIQUE COMES FROM. OU KONPRANN?
READY THE TROOPS.
HMMM...

issue 3 page 19 original line art by Randy Valiente

REANIMATOR #3, Page 19: "Will"

As I mentioned previously – if you write comics, you give your friends cameos in the story. However, if the bonds of friendship are particularly strong, then you kill 'em off in comics. "Will" is a reference to my buddy Will West, who – aside from sharing a namesake with the main character of *Reanimator* – worked with me for a time at Diamond Comics.

REANIMATOR #3, Page 19: "Ou konprann?"

Translated from Creole, a phrase meaning, "You understand?"

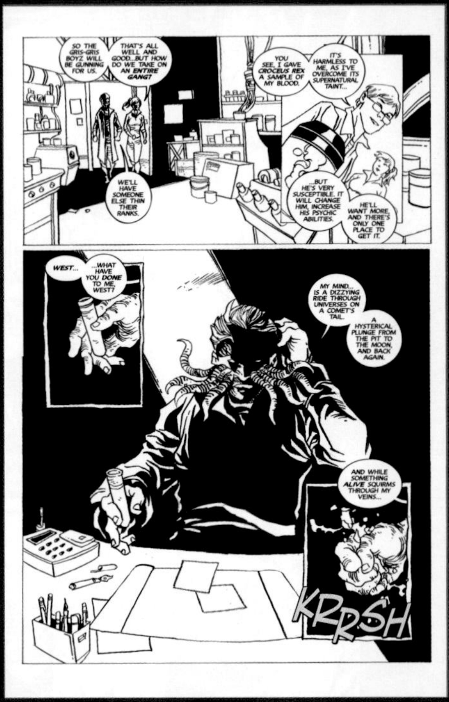
SO THE GRIS-GRIS BOYZ WILL BE GUNNING FOR US.
THAT'S ALL WELL AND GOOD...BUT HOW DO WE TAKE ON AN ENTIRE GANG?
WE'LL HAVE SOMEONE ELSE THIN THEIR RANKS.
YOU SEE, I GAVE CROCEUS REX A SAMPLE OF MY BLOOD.
IT'S HARMLESS TO ME, AS I'VE OVERCOME ITS SUPERNATURAL TAINT...
...BUT HE'S VERY SUSCEPTIBLE. IT WILL CHANGE HIM, INCREASE HIS PSYCHIC ABILITIES.
HE'LL WANT MORE, AND THERE'S ONLY ONE PLACE TO GET IT.
WEST...
...WHAT HAVE YOU DONE TO ME, WEST?
MY MIND... IS A DIZZYING RIDE THROUGH UNIVERSES ON A COMET'S TAIL.
A HYSTERICAL PLUNGE FROM THE PIT TO THE MOON, AND BACK AGAIN.
AND WHILE SOMETHING ALIVE SQUIRMS THROUGH MY VEINS...
KRRSH

issue 3 page 20 original line art by Randy Valiente

REANIMATOR #3, Page 20: "dizzying ride through universes on a comet's tail"

In *The Call of Cthulhu Part III: The Madness from the Sea*, the brave Norwegian sailor Gustaf Johansen is the sole survivor of a run-in with Cthulhu, the entity waking briefly from its slumber to menace the crew of the freighter Vigilant before sinking once more into the depths of the ocean. After the encounter, Johansen is left to ponder the nighmarish incident, and his reflections are described by narrator Francis Wayland Thurston as, "There is a sense of spectral whirling through liquid gulfs of infinity, of dizzying rides through reeling universes on a comets tail, and of hysterical plunges from the pit to the moon and from the moon back again to the pit, all livened by a cachinnating chorus of the distorted, hilarious elder gods and the green, bat-winged mocking imps of Tartarus."

REANIMATOR #3, Page 21: "great priest of R'lyeh"

In *The Call of Cthulhu*, the cosmic deity is

referred to as "the great priest Cthulhu, from his dark house in the mighty city of R'lyeh under the waters." He is also referred to in other Mythos fiction as the "high priest of the Great Old Ones."

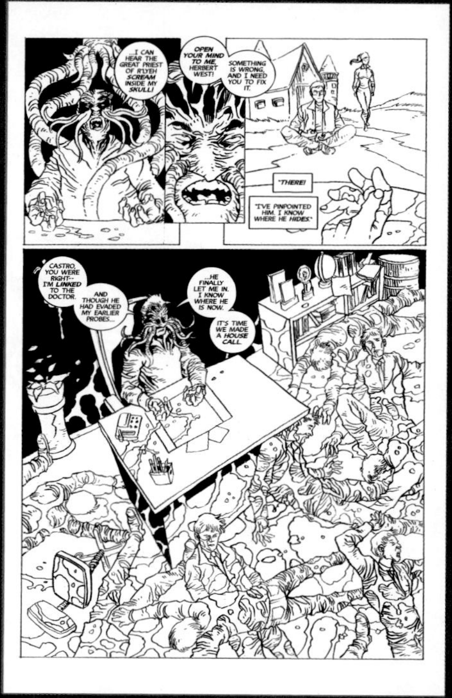

...I CAN HEAR THE GREAT PRIEST OF R'LYEH SCREAM INSIDE MY SKULL!
OPEN YOUR MIND TO ME, HERBERT WEST!
SOMETHING IS WRONG, AND I NEED YOU TO FIX IT.
"THERE!
"I'VE PINPOINTED HIM. I KNOW WHERE HE HIDES."
CASTRO, YOU WERE RIGHT-- I'M LINKED TO THE DOCTOR.
AND THOUGH HE HAD EVADED MY EARLIER PROBES...
...HE FINALLY LET ME IN. I KNOW WHERE HE IS NOW.
IT'S TIME WE MADE A HOUSE CALL.

issue 3 page 21 original line art by Randy Valiente

REANIMATOR #4

REANIMATOR #4 Inside Front Cover: "Beyond Good and Evil"

In *The Call of Cthulhu*, Castro relates the effects of the entity's return to life: "mankind would have become as the Great Old Ones; free and wild and beyond good and evil, with laws and morals thrown aside and all men shouting and killing and reveling in joy." While relatable to Croceus Rex's transformation over the course of the series, the phrase also evokes the tagline for the series: "Good. Evil. Such storybook notions are beneath Herbert West. He is a man of Science."

REANIMATOR #4 Inside Front Cover – Preamble

"Dr. Herbert West, the Reanimator, has made peace with his assistant, Susan Greene. She had suspected his involvement in the murder of her fiancée, and although it was true that he had transformed Nathan Davis' corpse into a zombie hybrid servant called The Valusian, he had no part in the homicide. In fact, he had identified the murderer as Louis "Dice" Durand, leader of the Gris-Gris Boyz, and orchestrated their gang war with the Eldritch Krewe simply to present Susan with the opportunity to enact justice for her lost love. She chose to follow through on the Reanimator's plan – to confront Dice in person at ground zero of the coming battle. But will West's defenses at Hamilton House withstand the powerful forces he's lured to the fight? Can he survive the wrath of Voodoo hitman Samedi, whom he humiliated for weeks as a captive? Or the worst threat of all: Croceus Rex, the Eldritch Krewe leader whose blood he infested with the supernatural taint of an Elder God?"

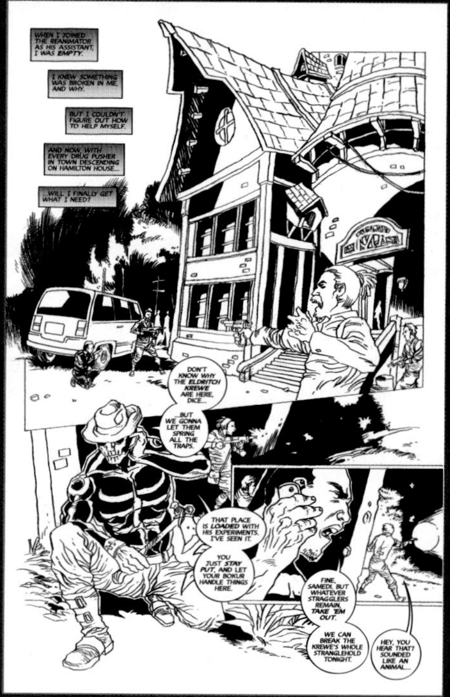

WHEN I JOINED THE REANIMATOR AS HIS ASSISTANT, I WAS EMPTY.
I KNEW SOMETHING WAS BROKEN IN ME, AND WHY.
BUT I COULDN'T FIGURE OUT HOW TO HELP MYSELF.
AND NOW, WITH EVERY DRUG PUSHER IN TOWN DESCENDING ON HAMILTON HOUSE...
...WILL I FINALLY GET WHAT I NEED?
DON'T KNOW WHY THE ELDRITCH KREWE ARE HERE, DICE...
...BUT WE GONNA LET THEM SPRING ALL THE TRAPS.
THAT PLACE IS LOADED WITH HIS EXPERIMENTS. I'VE SEEN IT.
YOU JUST STAY PUT, AND LET YOUR BOKUR HANDLE THINGS HERE.
FINE, SAMEDI. BUT WHATEVER STRAGGLERS REMAIN, TAKE 'EM OUT.
WE CAN BREAK THE KREWE'S WHOLE STRANGLEHOLD TONIGHT.
HEY, YOU HEAR THAT? SOUNDED LIKE AN ANIMAL...

issue 4 page 1 original line art by Randy Valiente

REANIMATOR #4, Page 1 – Samedi's war paint

Samedi, having discovered body paint at Big Will's convenience store in Chapter Three, apparently covers his body in a skeletal design more in tune with Baron Samedi, his namesake. As we see later this issue, he now covets West''s ability to actually reanimate the dead... which appeals to the hitman's identification with Vodou's Loa of the Dead.

REANIMATOR #4, Page 6 – "agony"

It's a subtle change, but when Croceus Rex says, "This... is... agony", there's a font switch for that last word. Throughout the remainder of the issue, all of his dialogue reflects the new font, a visual cue to the character's continuing physical changes. He's still transforming into something inhuman, inside and out.

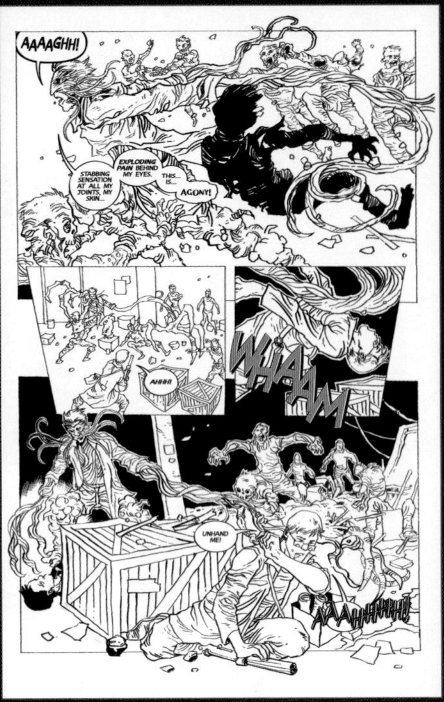
AAAAGHH!
STABBING SENSATION AT ALL MY JOINTS, MY SKIN...
EXPLODING PAIN BEHIND MY EYES.
THIS... IS...
AGONY!
WHAAM
AHHH!
UNHAND ME!

issue 4 page 6 original line art by Randy Valiente

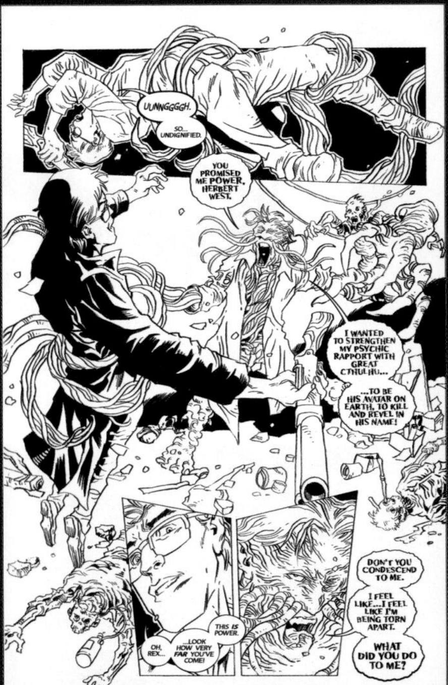
UUNNGGGH.
SO... UNDIGNIFIED.
YOU PROMISED ME POWER, HERBERT WEST.
I WANTED TO STRENGTHEN MY PSYCHIC RAPPORT WITH GREAT CTHULHU...
...TO BE HIS AVATAR ON EARTH, TO KILL AND REVEL IN HIS NAME!
DON'T YOU CONDESCEND TO ME.
I FEEL LIKE... I FEEL LIKE I'M BEING TORN APART.
THIS IS POWER.
OH, REX...
...LOOK HOW VERY FAR YOU'VE COME!
WHAT DID YOU DO TO ME?

issue 4 page 10 original line art by Randy Valiente

REANIMATOR #4, Page 10 – "kill and revel"

Like the phrase "beyond good and evil" from the title to this chapter, "kill and revel" refers to *The Call of Cthulhu* and Castro's promise of the deity's effects on humanity, which continues, "Then the liberated Old Ones would teach them new ways to shout and kill and revel and enjoy themselves, and all the earth would flame with a holocaust of ecstasy and freedom."

REANIMATOR #4, Page 11 – "evil still lurks in my veins"

In *Army of Darkness vs. Reanimator*, Herbert West's body was possessed by a demon tied to Dr. Whately's Yog-Sothoth worship, while his consciousness was locked away in the Mirror Prison. While West expunged the demonic entity, the exposure changed his physiology.

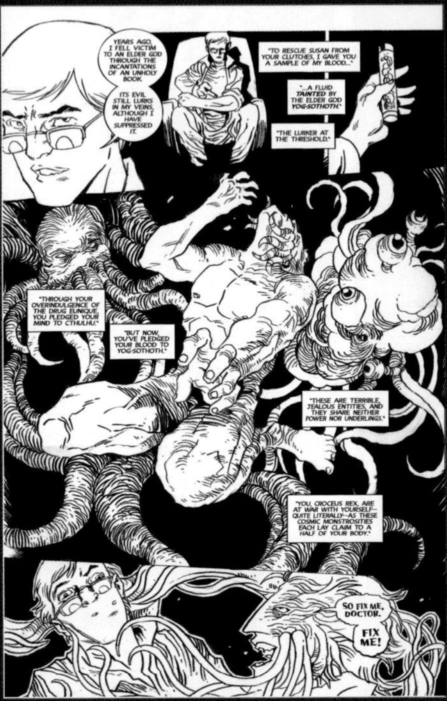
YEARS AGO, I FELL VICTIM TO AN ELDER GOD THROUGH THE INCANTATIONS OF AN UNHOLY BOOK.
ITS EVIL STILL LURKS IN MY VEINS, ALTHOUGH I HAVE SUPPRESSED IT.
"TO RESCUE SUSAN FROM YOUR CLUTCHES, I GAVE YOU A SAMPLE OF MY BLOOD..."
"...A FLUID TAINTED BY THE ELDER GOD YOG-SOTHOTH."
"THE LURKER AT THE THRESHOLD."
"THROUGH YOUR OVERINDULGENCE OF THE DRUG EUNIQUE, YOU PLEDGED YOUR MIND TO CTHULHU."
"BUT NOW, YOU'VE PLEDGED YOUR BLOOD TO YOG-SOTHOTH."
"THESE ARE TERRIBLE, JEALOUS ENTITIES, AND THEY SHARE NEITHER POWER NOR UNDERLINGS."
"YOU, CROCEUS REX, ARE AT WAR WITH YOURSELF--QUITE LITERALLY--AS THESE COSMIC MONSTROSITIES EACH LAY CLAIM TO A HALF OF YOUR BODY."
SO FIX ME, DOCTOR.
FIX ME!

issue 4 page 11 original line art by Randy Valiente

REANIMATOR #4, Page 11 – "lurker at the threshold"

The Lurker at the Threshold is a 1945 novel by August Derleth set within the Cthulhu Mythos, published eight years after Lovecraft's death (although the latter had collaborated with Derleth on part of the story prior to his death). The idea that Yog-Sothoth is associated with a door comes from Lovecraft's *The Dunwich Horror*: "Yog-Sothoth knows the gate. Yog-Sothoth is the gate. Yog-Sothoth is the key and guardian of the gate."

REANIMATOR #4, Page 13 – "I'm no Ash Williams"

The only in-story reference to Ashley J. Williams, the Chosen One and protagonist of *Army of Darkness*. It's also important to note that Herbert West gives credit where credit's due. Williams is a Man of Action, while West is a Man of Science. While West has success with violence in the preceding pages, his coming confrontations with Samedi and Rex are won by employing superior intellect.

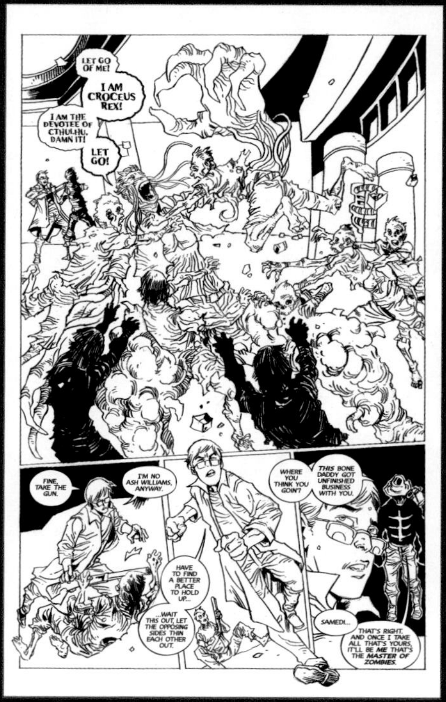

LET GO OF ME!
I AM CROCEUS REX!
I AM THE DEVOTEE OF CTHULHU, DAMN IT!
LET GO!
FINE, TAKE THE GUN.
I'M NO ASH WILLIAMS, ANYWAY.
HAVE TO FIND A BETTER PLACE TO HOLD UP...
...WAIT THIS OUT, LET THE OPPOSING SIDES THIN EACH OTHER OUT.
WHERE YOU THINK YOU GOIN'?
THIS BONE DADDY GOT UNFINISHED BUSINESS WITH YOU.
SAMEDI...
THAT'S RIGHT. AND ONCE I TAKE ALL THAT'S YOURS, IT'LL BE ME THAT'S THE MASTER OF ZOMBIES.

issue 4 page 13 original line art by Randy Vallente

REANIMATOR #4, Page 13 – "bone daddy"

A nod to *The Nightmare Before Christmas*, wherein the zombie band saxophonist James compliments Jack Skellington, the Pumpkin King: "Nice work, bone daddy."

REANIMATOR #4, Page 15 – "hello"

As established in the preceding chapter, West used hypnosis to curb The Valusian's rampaging instability, as well as his involuntary need to repeat the name "Louis Durand." All that remained was his ability to say "'Lo" in Susan's presence, mistaken by the lab assistant as short for "hello". In telling her to say "hello" to Nathan, Dice unconsciously touches that sore spot... and spurs her vicious attack.

REANIMATOR #4, Page 17 – "litany to invoke the loa"

In reading Sallie Ann Glassman's book *Vodou Visions: An Encounter with Divine Mystery*, I came across this litany dedicated to The Bawon — the Loa of sex, death, and regeneration, of which Baron Samedi is considered the leader. Although French and not Creole, the two languages are intertwined in Haiti, where Samedi hails from.

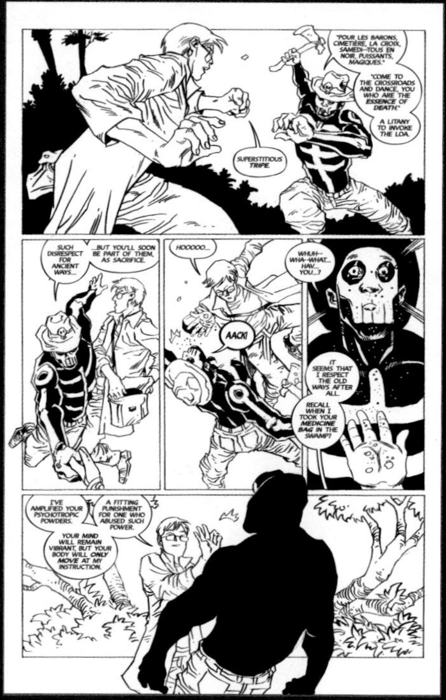

"POUR LES BARONS, CIMETIÈRE, LA CROIX, SAMEDI--TOUS EN NOIR, PUISSANTS, MAGIQUES."
"COME TO THE CROSSROADS AND DANCE, YOU WHO ARE THE ESSENCE OF DEATH."
A LITANY TO INVOKE THE LOA.
SUPERSTITIOUS TRIPE.
SUCH DISRESPECT FOR ANCIENT WAYS...
...BUT YOU'LL SOON BE PART OF THEM, AS SACRIFICE.
HOOOOO...
AACK!
WHUH-- WHA--WHAT... HAV... YOU...?
IT SEEMS THAT I RESPECT THE OLD WAYS AFTER ALL.
RECALL WHEN I TOOK YOUR MEDICINE BAG IN THE SWAMP?
I'VE AMPLIFIED YOUR PSYCHOTROPIC POWDERS.
A FITTING PUNISHMENT FOR ONE WHO ABUSED SUCH POWER.
YOUR MIND WILL REMAIN VIBRANT, BUT YOUR BODY WILL ONLY MOVE AT MY INSTRUCTION.

issue 4 page 17 original line art by Randy Vallente

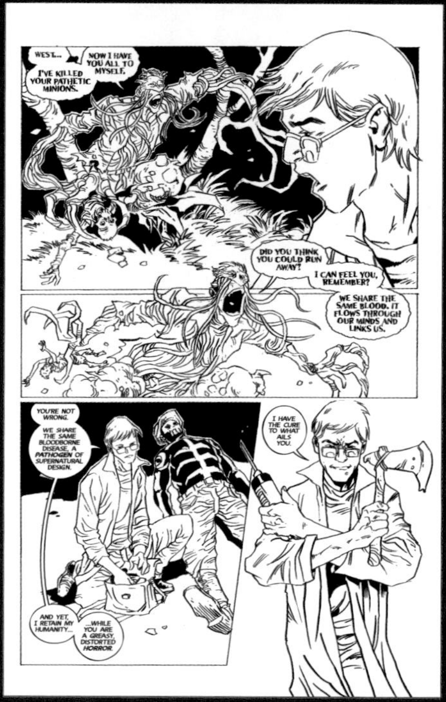

WEST...
NOW I HAVE YOU ALL TO MYSELF.
I'VE KILLED YOUR PATHETIC MINIONS.
DID YOU THINK YOU COULD RUN AWAY?
I CAN FEEL YOU, REMEMBER?
WE SHARE THE SAME BLOOD. IT FLOWS THROUGH OUR MINDS AND LINKS US.
YOU'RE NOT WRONG.
WE SHARE THE SAME BLOODBORNE DISEASE, A PATHOGEN OF SUPERNATURAL DESIGN.
AND YET, I RETAIN MY HUMANITY...
...WHILE YOU ARE A GREASY, DISTORTED HORROR.
I HAVE THE CURE TO WHAT AILS YOU.

issue 4 page 18 original line art by Randy Vallente

REANIMATOR #4, Page 18 – "greasy"

A fitting description for someone physically transforming into a Great Old One's avatar. As described in *The Call of Cthulhu*, "great Cthulhu slid greasily into the water." ■

SKETCHES, PIN-UPS AND ORIGINAL PENCILS

by Randy Valiente

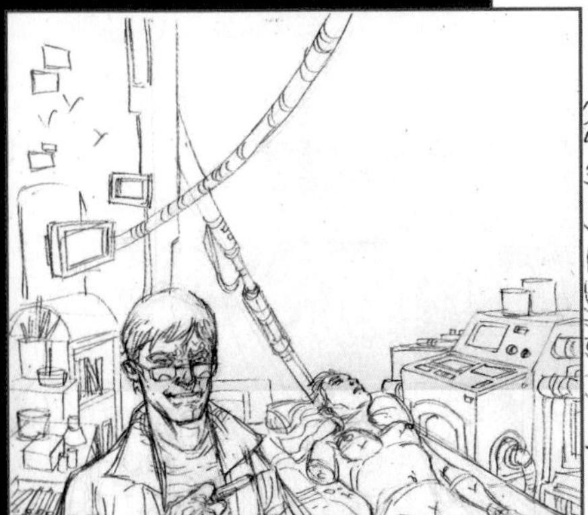
BOX OF
DREAD

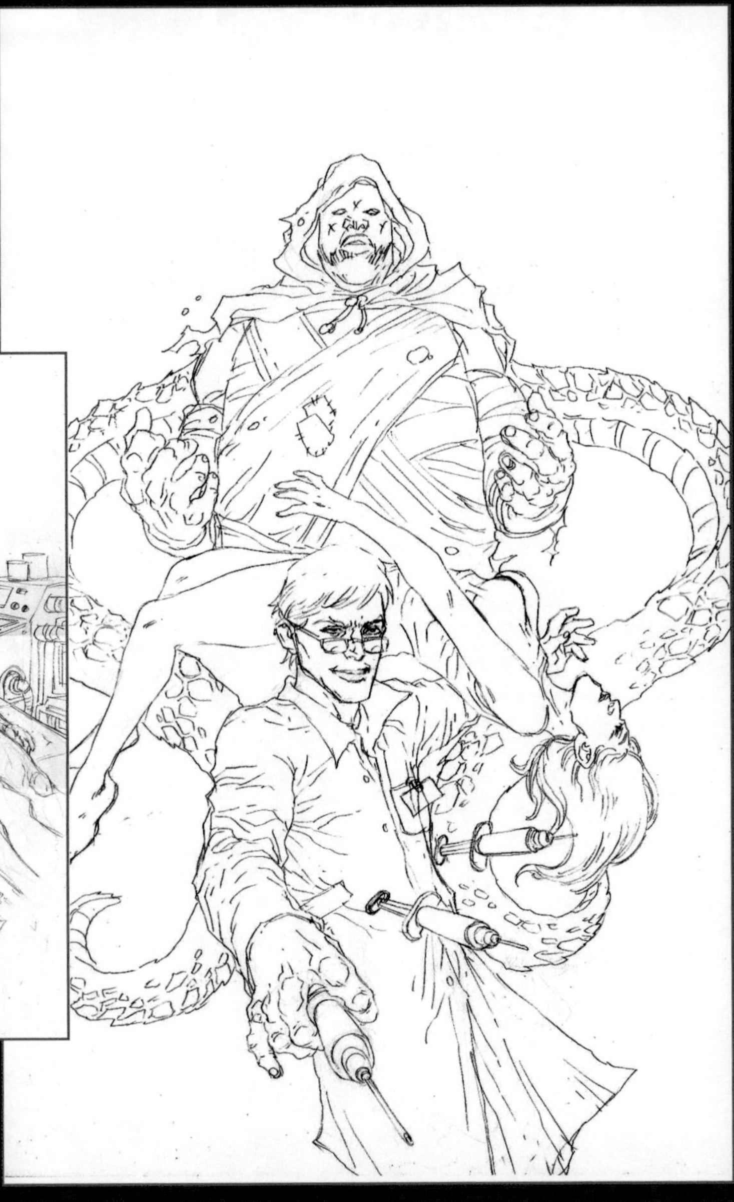

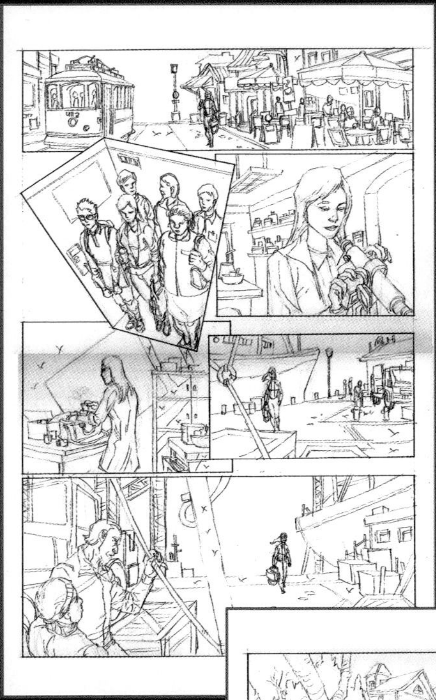

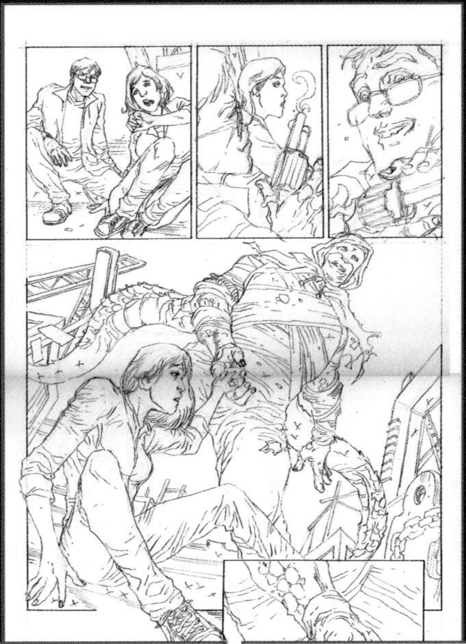

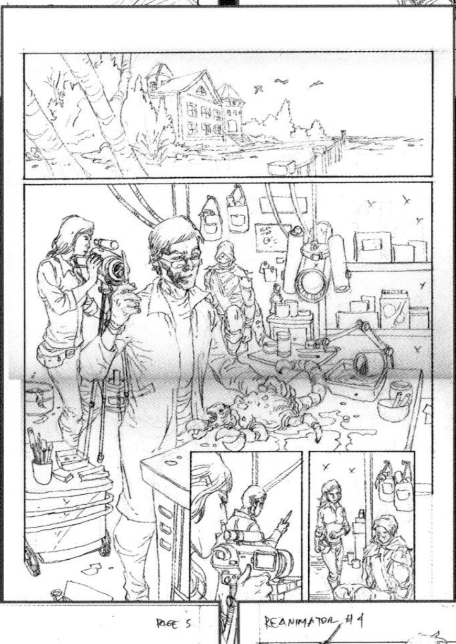

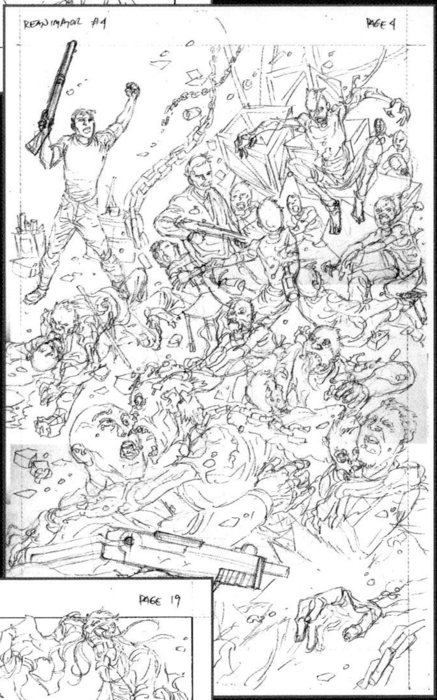
REANIMATOR #4
PAGE 4

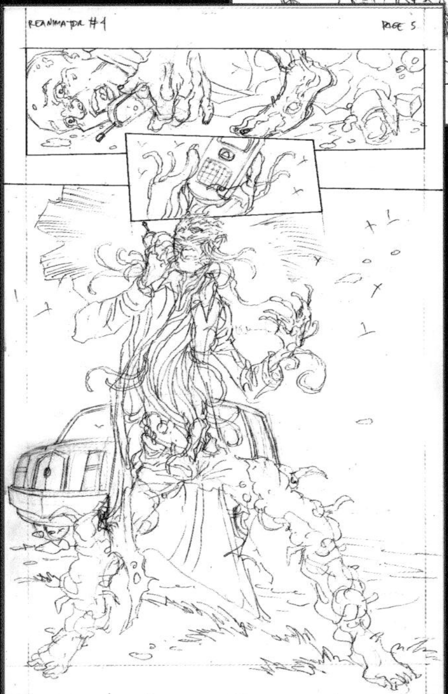
REANIMATOR #4
PAGE 5

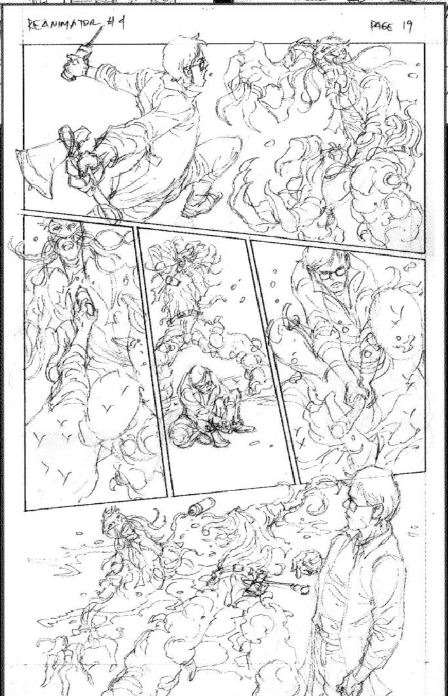
REANIMATOR #4
PAGE 19

COMPLETE COVER GALLERY

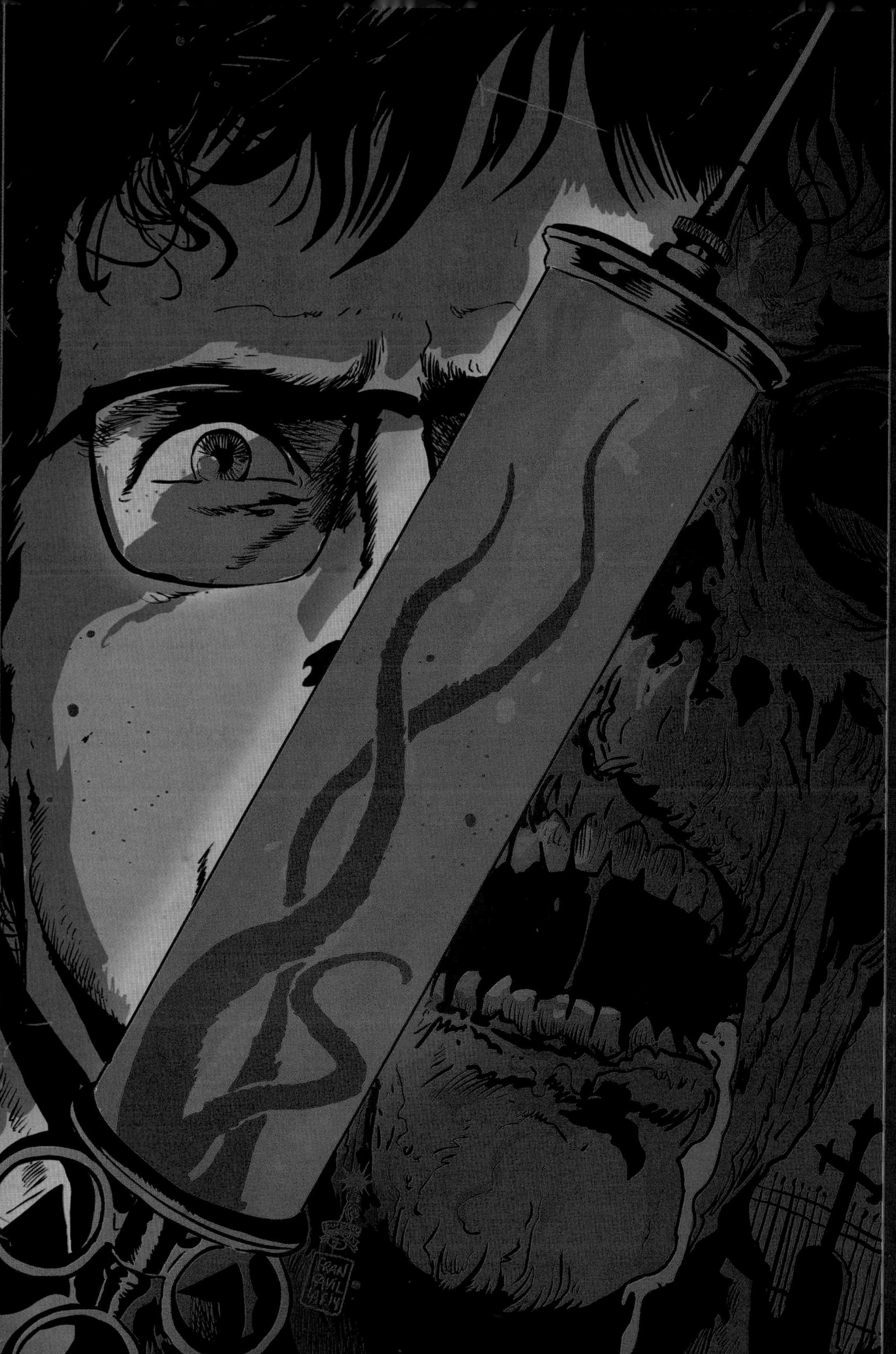

Issue #1 cover by FRANCESCO FRANCAVILLA

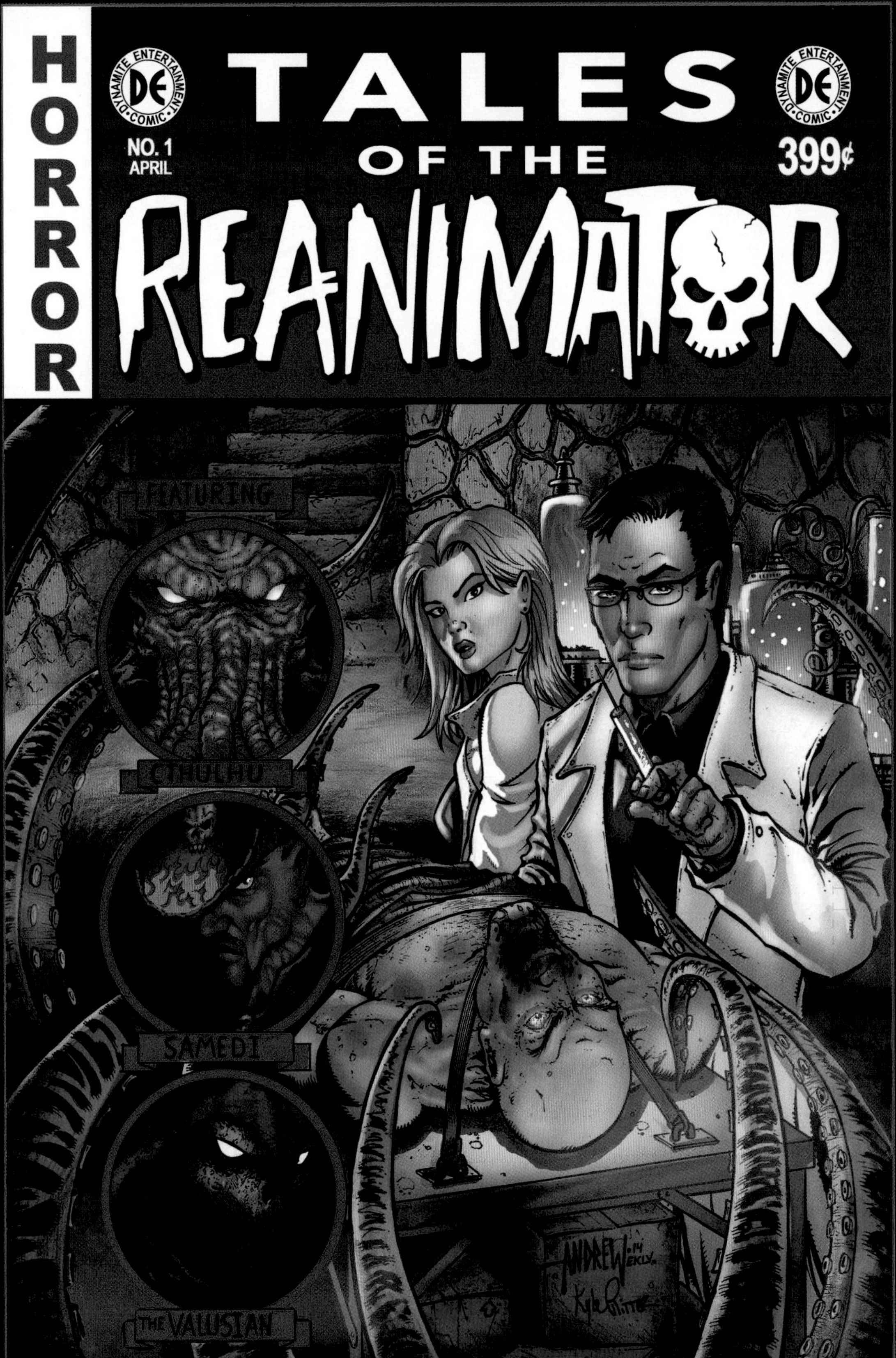
HORROR
TALES OF THE REANIMATOR
NO. 1
APRIL
399¢
DYNAMITE ENTERTAINMENT COMIC
FEATURING
CTHULHU
SAMEDI
THE VALUSIAN

Issue #1 cover by ANDREW MANGUM
Colors by KYLE RITTER

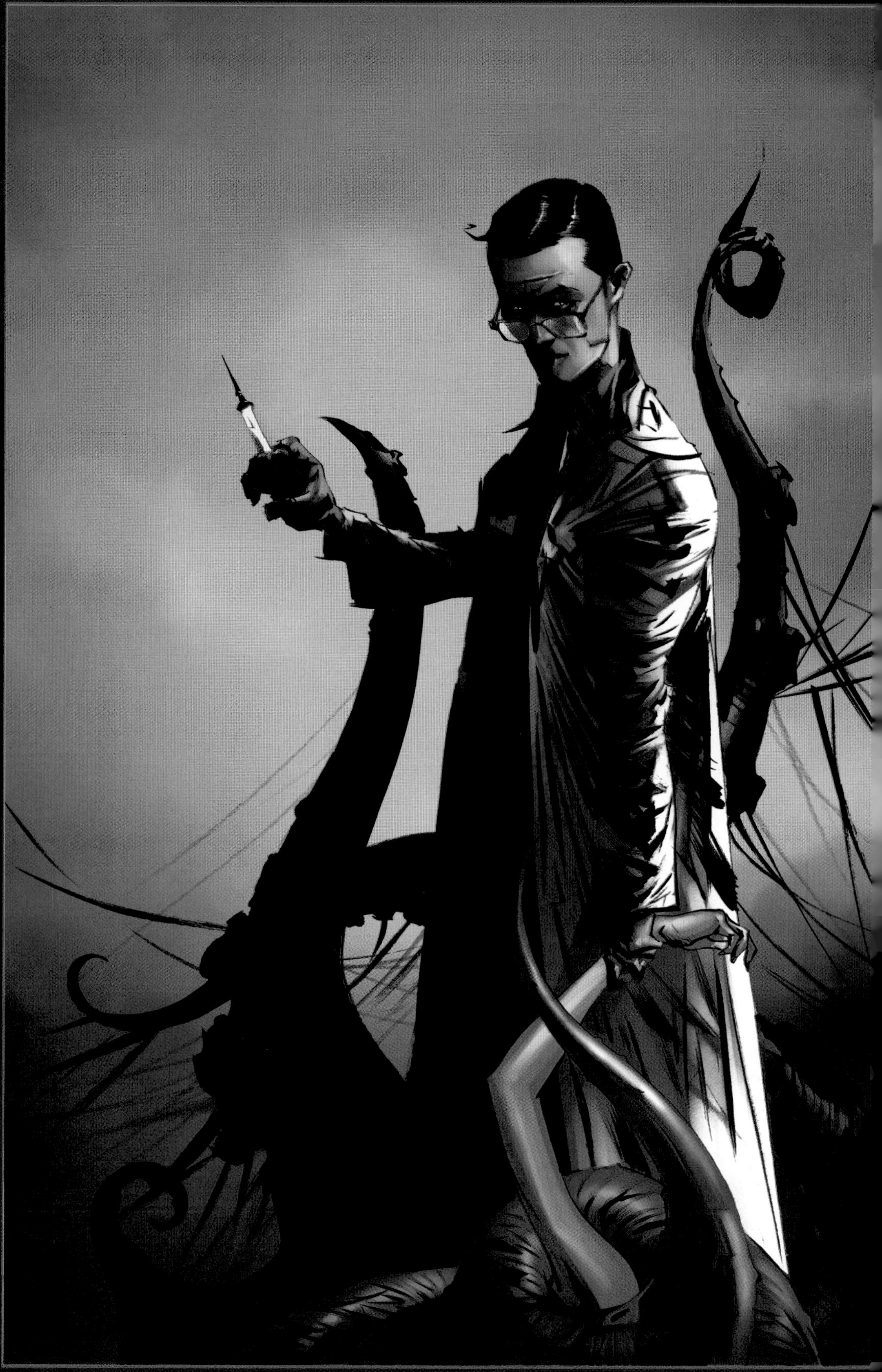

Issue #1 cover by JAE LEE
Colors by IVAN NUNES

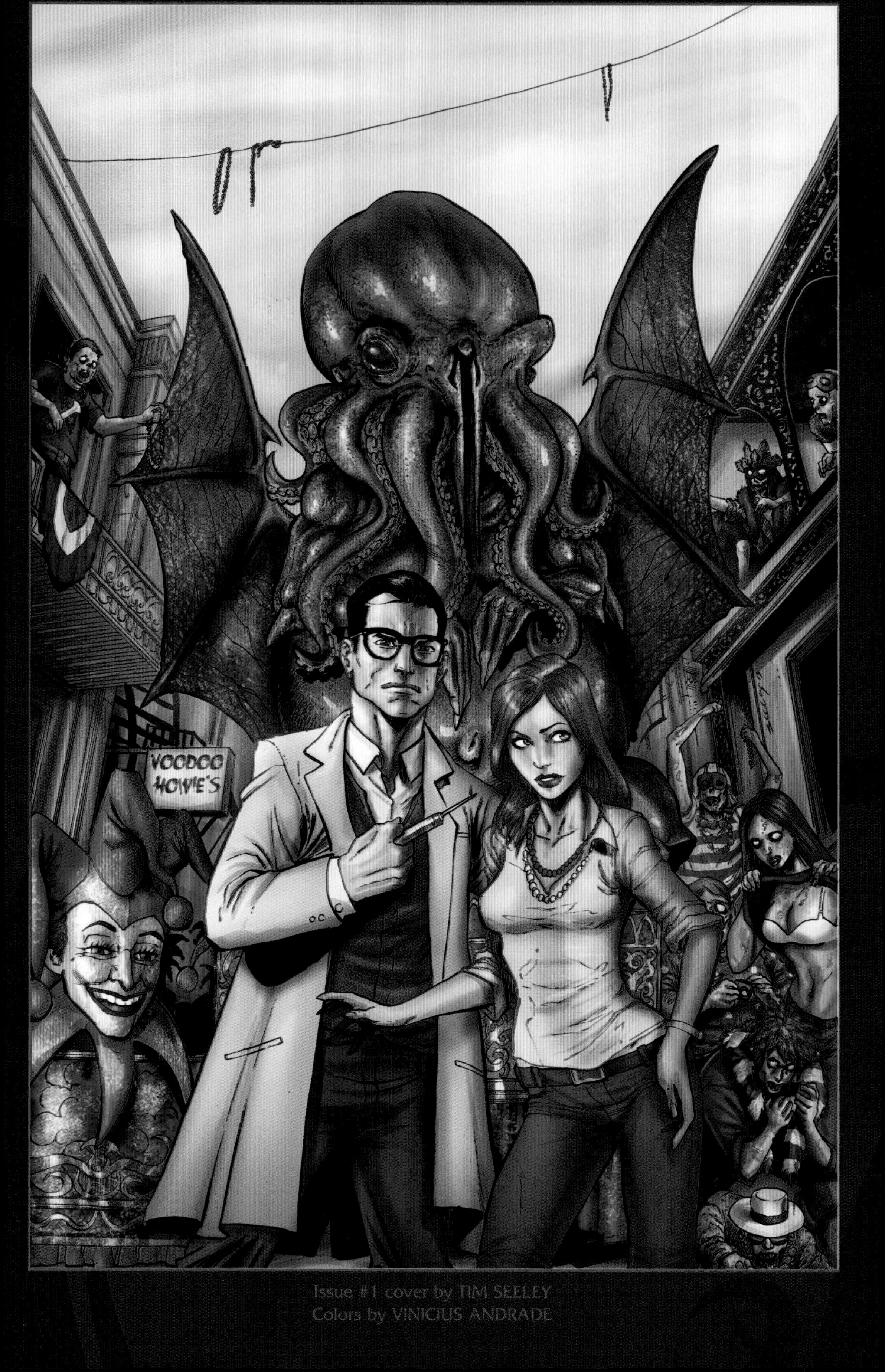
VOODOO HOWIE'S

Issue #1 cover by TIM SEELEY
Colors by VINICIUS ANDRADE

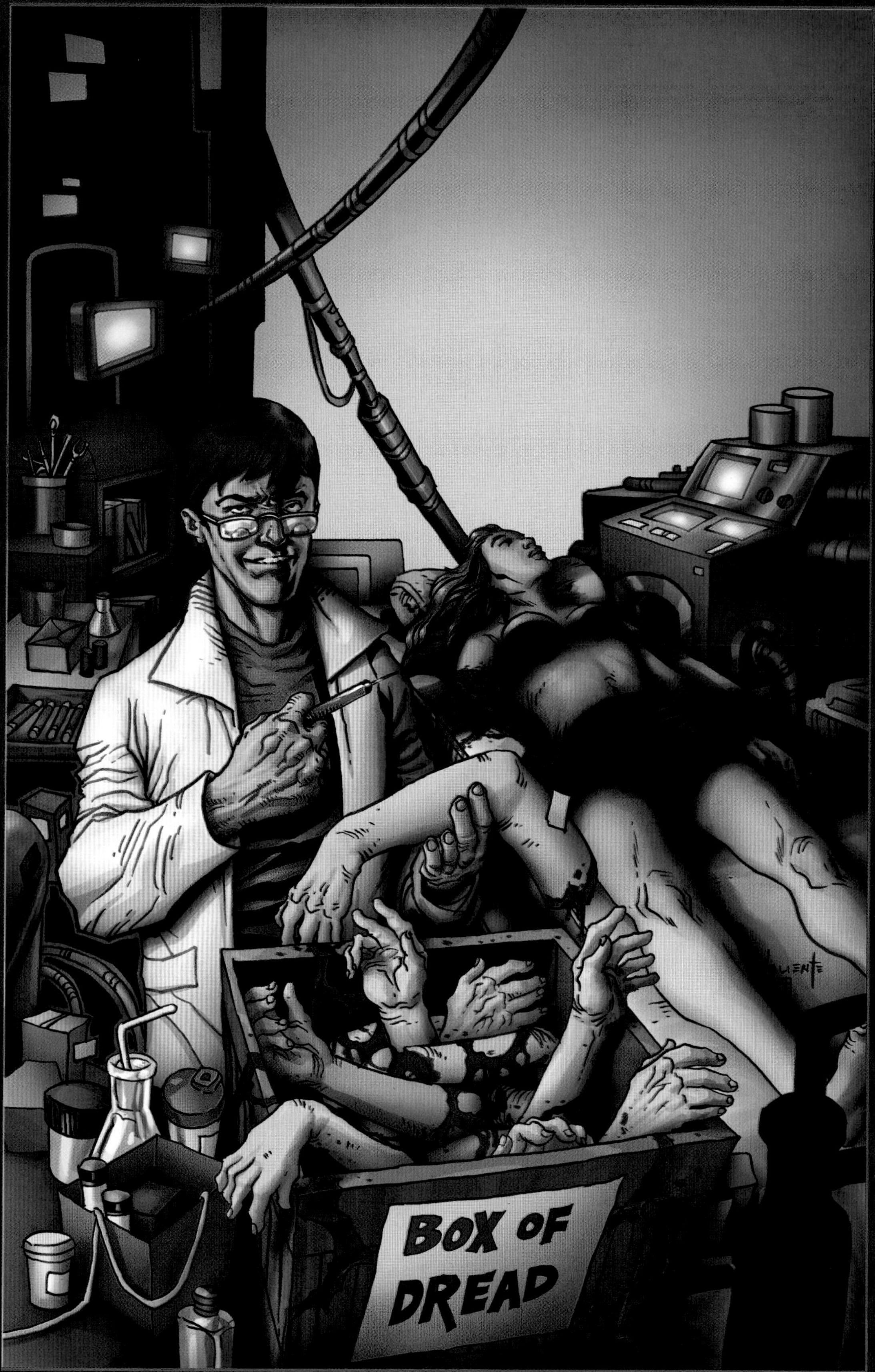
VALIENTE
BOX OF DREAD

Issue #1 Box Of Dread exclusive cover by RANDY VALIENTE
Colors by VINICIUS ANDRADE

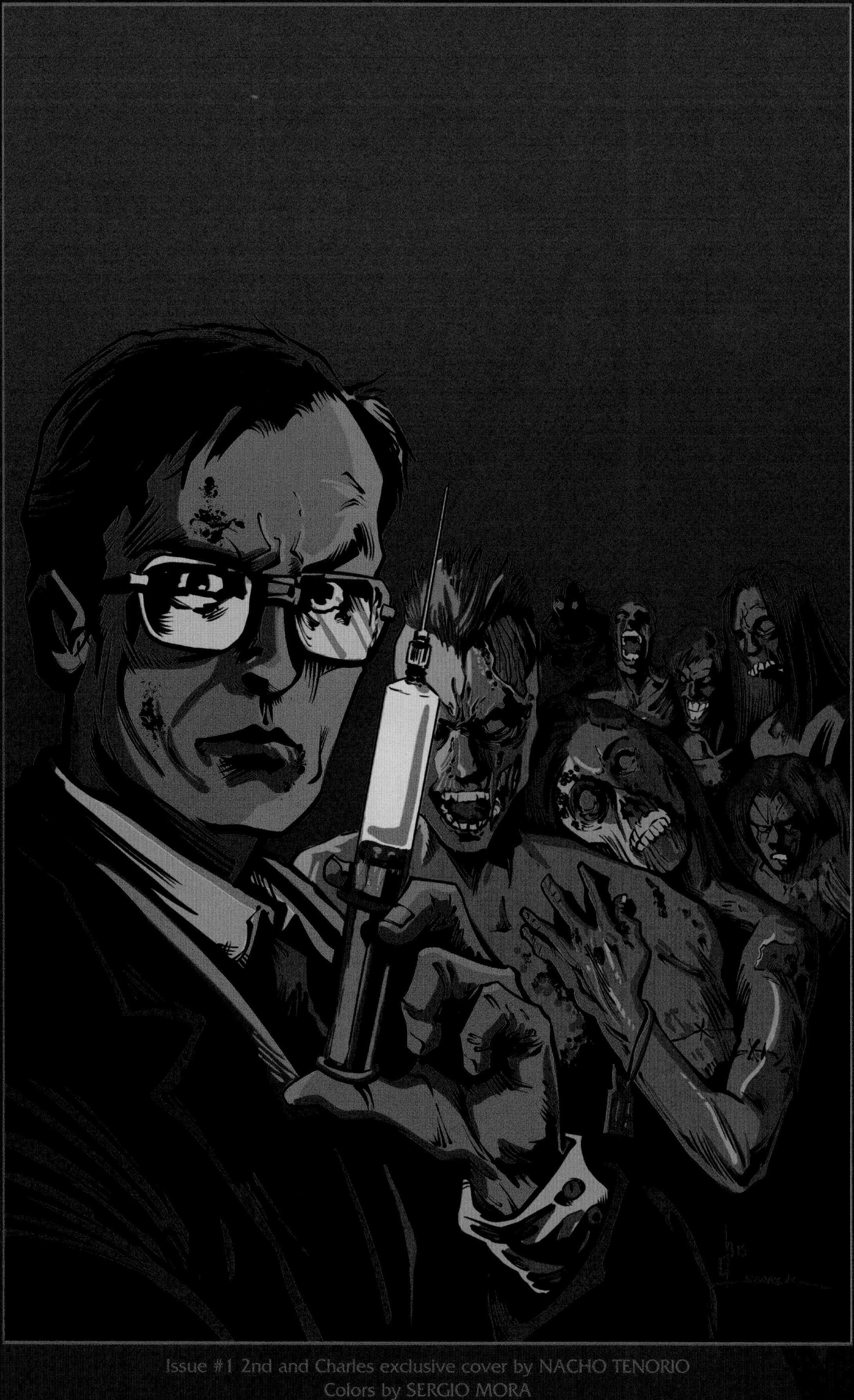

Issue #1 2nd and Charles exclusive cover by NACHO TENORIO
Colors by SERGIO MORA

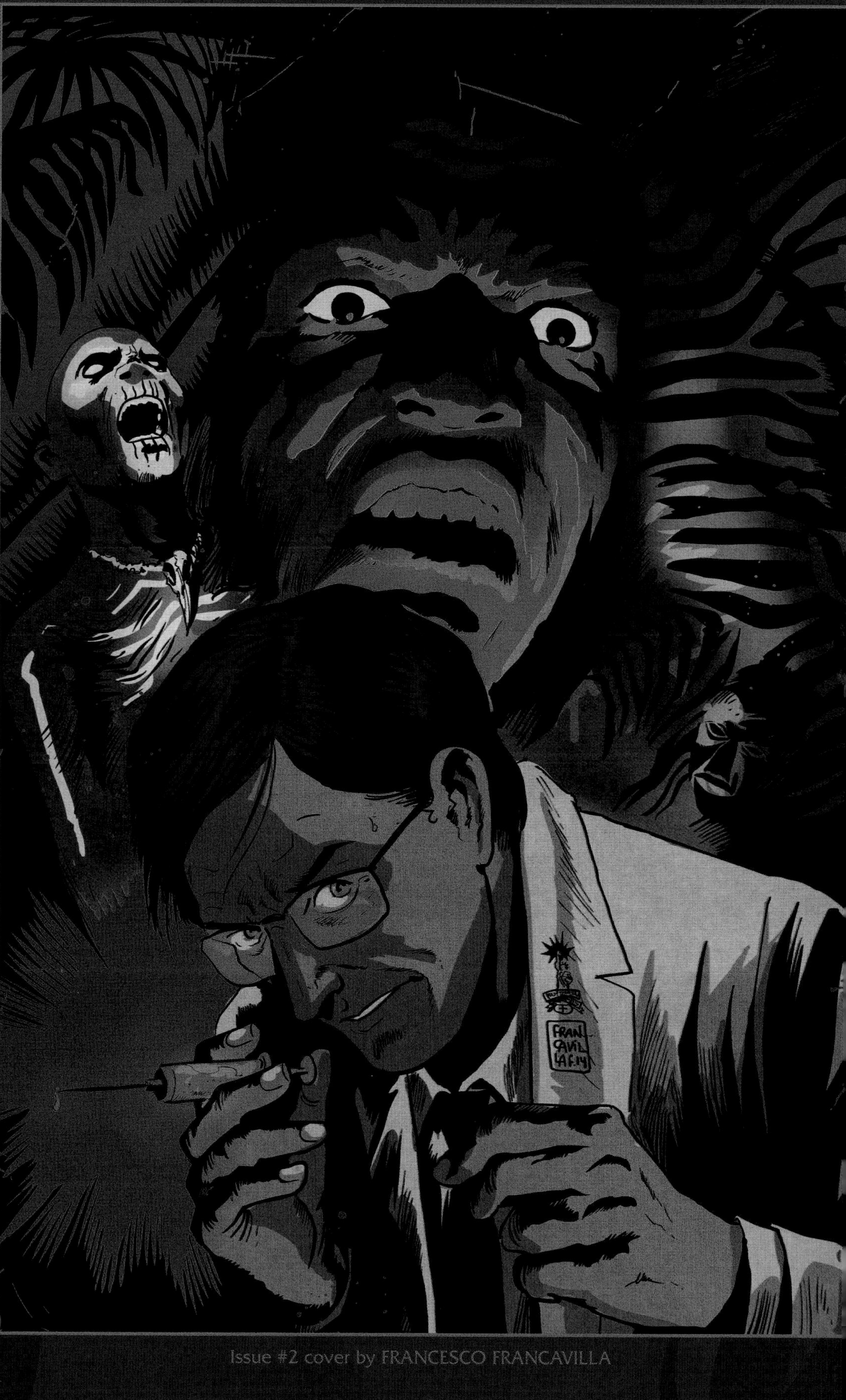

Issue #2 cover by FRANCESCO FRANCAVILLA

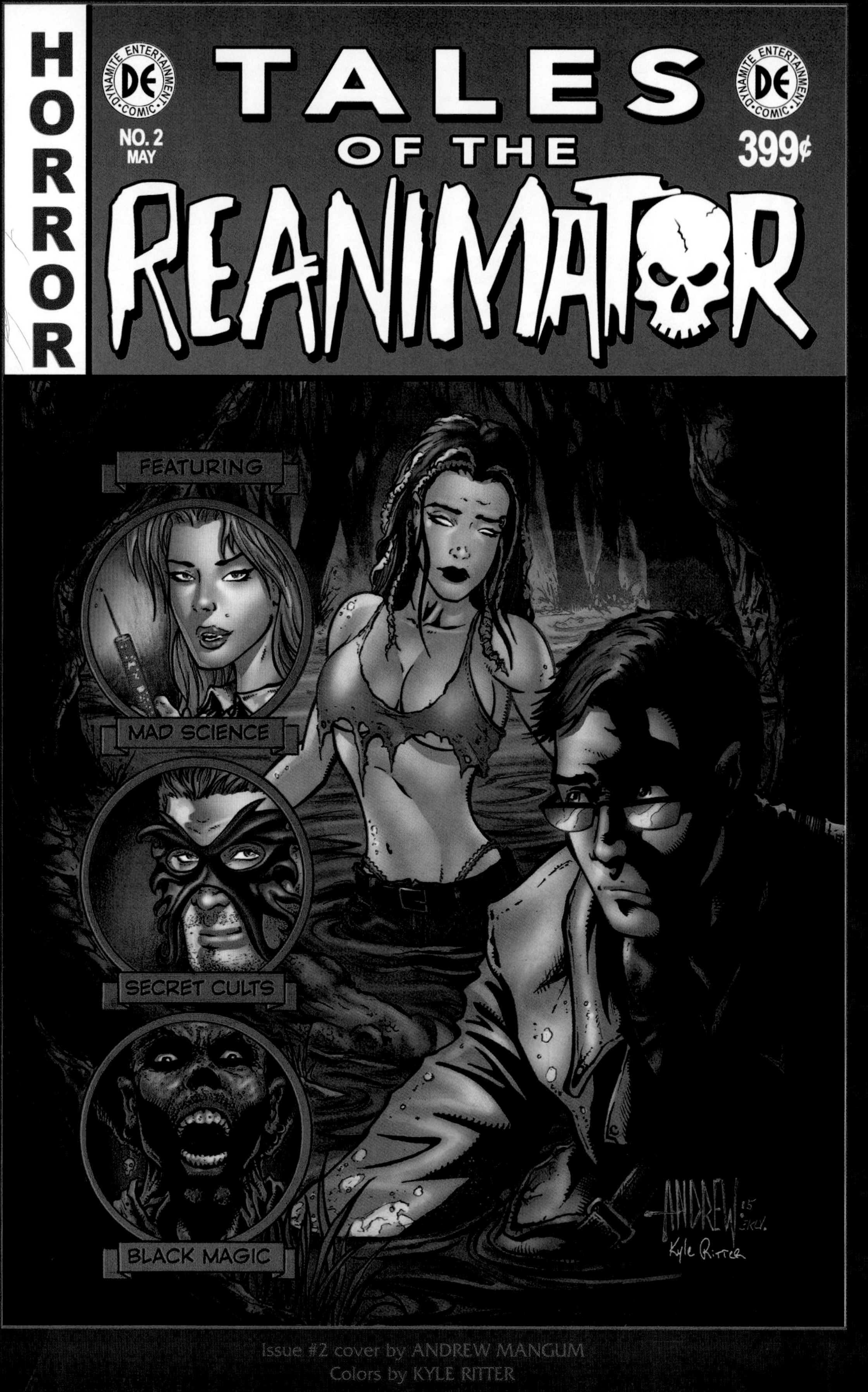
HORROR
DYNAMITE ENTERTAINMENT
DE
COMIC
TALES
OF THE
REANIMATOR
NO. 2
MAY
399¢
FEATURING
MAD SCIENCE
SECRET CULTS
BLACK MAGIC
ANDREW '15
Kyle Ritter

Issue #2 cover by ANDREW MANGUM
Colors by KYLE RITTER

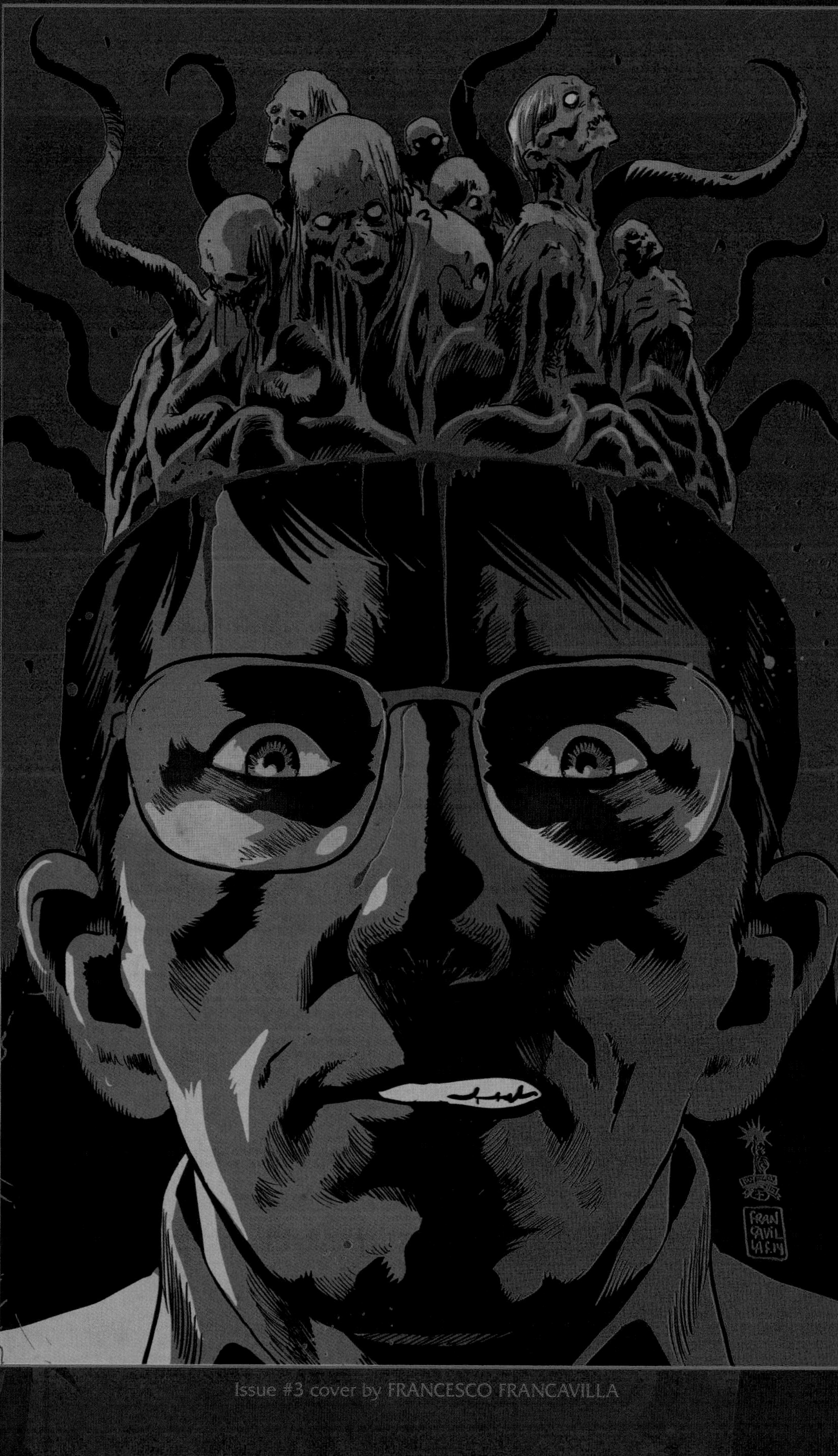

Issue #3 cover by FRANCESCO FRANCAVILLA

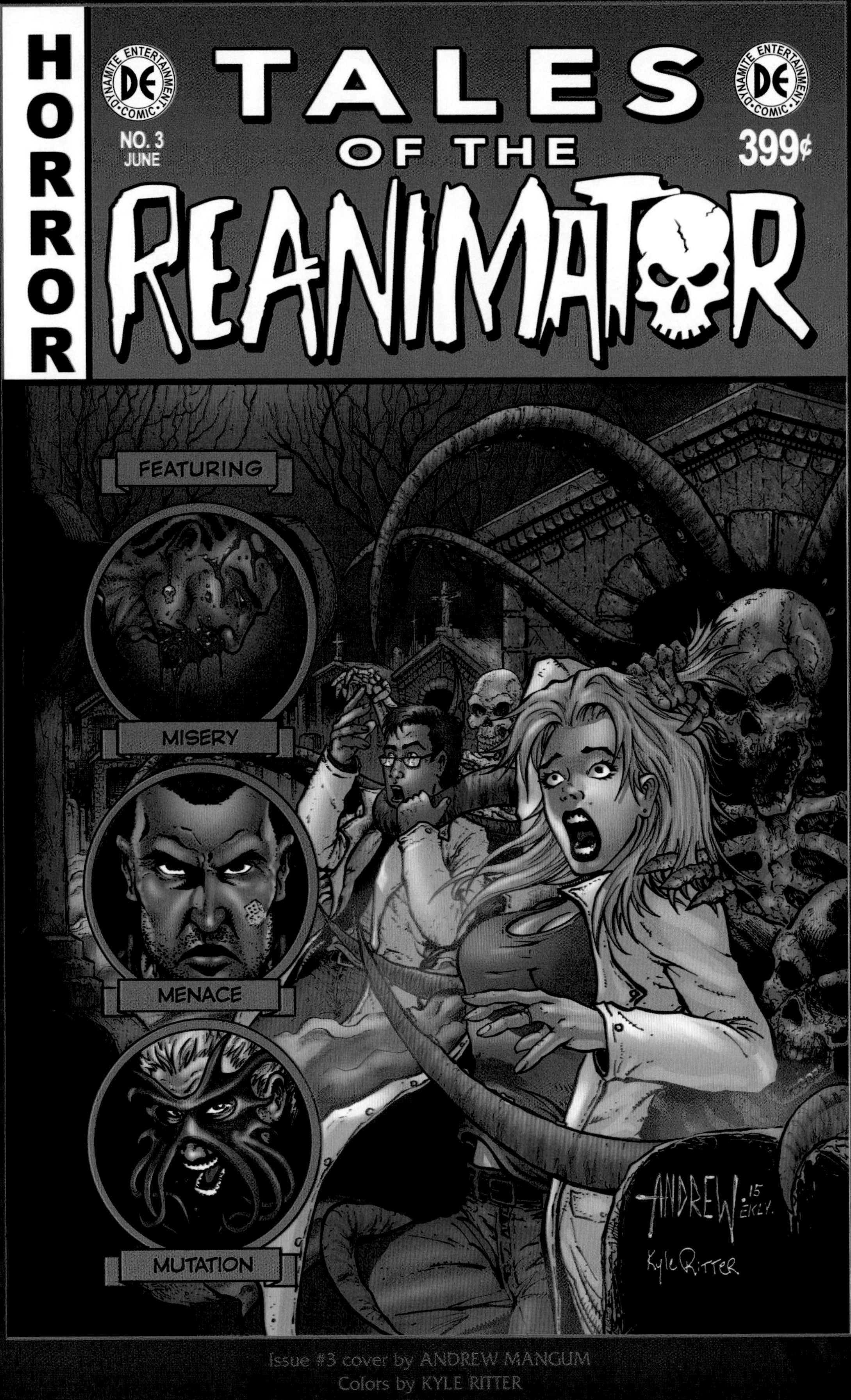
HORROR
DYNAMITE ENTERTAINMENT DE COMIC
TALES OF THE REANIMATOR
DYNAMITE ENTERTAINMENT DE COMIC
NO. 3
JUNE
399¢
FEATURING
MISERY
MENACE
MUTATION
ANDREW 15 EKLY.
Kyle Ritter

Issue #3 cover by ANDREW MANGUM
Colors by KYLE RITTER

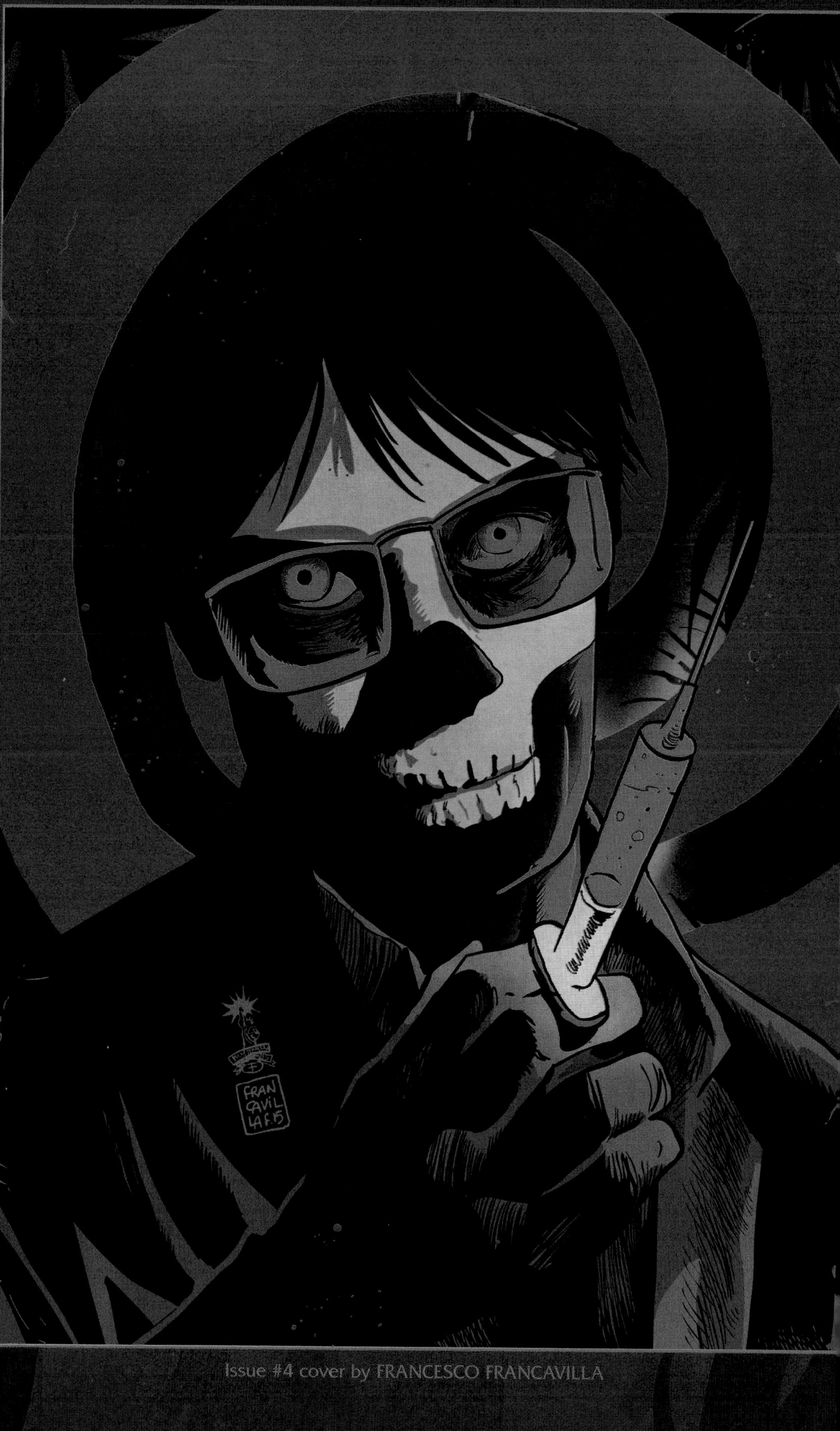

Issue #4 cover by FRANCESCO FRANCAVILLA

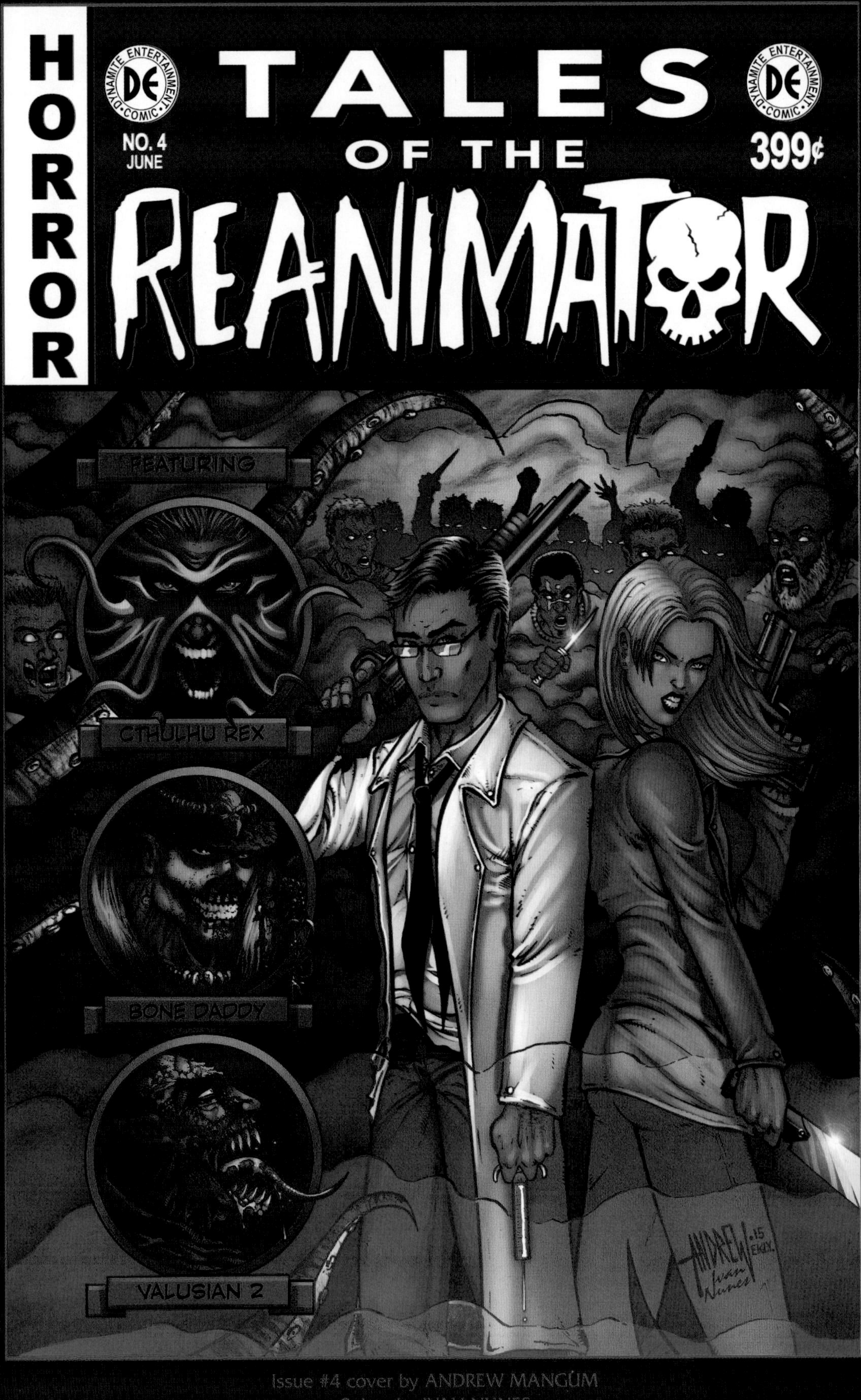
HORROR
DYNAMITE ENTERTAINMENT DE COMIC
NO. 4
JUNE
TALES
OF THE
REANIMATOR
DYNAMITE ENTERTAINMENT DE COMIC
399¢
FEATURING
CTHULHU REX
BONE DADDY
VALUSIAN 2

Issue #4 cover by ANDREW MANGÚM
Colors by IVAN NUNES

try these other great collections featuring

HERBERT WEST, THE REANIMATOR

only from Dynamite!

Army of Darkness Omnibus Volume 1
Trade Paperback
ISBN: 9781606901007

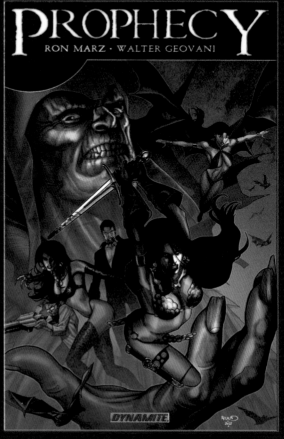

Prophecy
Trade Paperback
ISBN: 9781606903995

REANIMATOR